Profitable Sarbanes-Oxley Compliance

Attain Improved Shareholder Value
and Bottom-Line Results

BY C. Lynn Northrup CPA, CPIM

Copyright ©2006 by J. Ross Publishing, Inc.

ISBN 1-932159-35-5

Printed and bound in the U.S.A. Printed on acid-free paper
10 9 8 7 6 5 4 3 2 1

Library of Congress Cataloging-in-Publication Data

Northrup, C. Lynn, 1939-
    Profitable Sarbanes-Oxley compliance : attain improved shareholder value
and bottom-line results / by C. Lynn Northrup.
        p. cm.
    Includes index.
    ISBN 1-932159-35-5 (hardback : alk. paper)
    1. Disclosure in accounting—United States. 2. Corporate
governance—United States. 3. Auditing, Internal—United States. 4.
Managerial accounting—United States. 5. Financial statements—United
States. 6. United States. Sarbanes-Oxley Act of 2002. I. Title.

HF5658.N67 2005
657′.3—dc22   2005022253

Phone: (954) 727-9333
Fax: (561) 892-0700
Web: www.jrosspub.com

DEDICATION

This book is dedicated to my wife, Jessica, who tirelessly edited, provided suggestions, made improvements, and enhanced the diagrams. Thank you for all your help, support, and guidance.

DEDICATION

TABLE OF CONTENTS

THE AUTHOR

C. Lynn Northrup is the principal of C. Lynn Northrup, CPA, based in Wilmington, North Carolina. In addition to his CPA and consulting practice, he develops and teaches continuing professional education programs and is the author of *Dynamics of Profit-Focused Accounting,* published by J. Ross Publishing in 2004. Lynn was previously with McGladrey & Pullen's national manufacturing consulting practice, where his specialty was conducting operational and workflow assessments focused on business process improvement and performance measurement. He also worked on the application of strategic cost management and analysis concepts.

After starting his career in public accounting with Arthur Young and PriceWaterhouseCoopers, he was the controller at Schlegel Corporation in Rochester, New York. Schlegel, a complex multinational manufacturing company, grew rapidly from $10 million in sales to $300 million from 1965 to 1984. Lynn developed and implemented the cost accounting, financial, and budget forecasting systems for this company on a worldwide basis, which included over 35 profit centers located in 17 different countries.

In addition to creating his own CPA and advisory practice, Lynn has held various management and executive positions in industry, including controller and vice president of finance. His experience includes working with a wide variety of manufacturing companies in diverse industries, construction, and service industries, including CPA firms, mail order, hospitality, real estate, and nonprofit organizations.

Lynn received a B.B.A. from Clarkson University in 1960 and was certified in production and inventory management (CPIM) with APICS in 1999. He is licensed as a Certified Public Accountant in New York, North Carolina, and Oregon and is member of the American Institute of Certified Public Accountants and the North Carolina Association of CPAs. He is also an active member of APICS. Lynn can be reached at cln@northrupcpa.com.

*Free value-added materials available from
the Download Resource Center at www.jrosspub.com*

At J. Ross Publishing we are committed to providing today's professional with practical, hands-on tools that enhance the learning experience and give readers an opportunity to apply what they have learned. That is why we offer free ancillary materials available for download on this book and all participating Web Added Value™ publications. These online resources may include interactive versions of material that appears in the book or supplemental templates, worksheets, models, plans, case studies, proposals, spreadsheets and assessment tools, among other things. Whenever you see the WAV™ symbol in any of our publications, it means bonus materials accompany the book and are available from the Web Added Value Download Resource Center at www.jrosspub.com.

Downloads available for *Profitable Sarbanes-Oxley Compliance: Attain Improved Shareholder Value and Bottom-Line Results* consist of the following: The *performance measurement scorecard* is a baseline assessment scorecard for conducting self-assessments that contain both financial and nonfinancial metrics. It is in Excel template format. The *self-assessment checklist and scoring template* is a guide and checklist to assist internal auditors and management when performing a self-assessment of the control environment. It provides a weighted scoring of answers and is in Excel template format. The *Sarbanes-Oxley compliance management checklist* provides key questions for management relative to Sarbanes-Oxley compliance in checklist format. The *business process management checklist* provides critical questions for management relative to the effectiveness of business processes in checklist format. The *compliance and internal control resources and tools* provide key resources to compliance questions, together with hyperlinks that will assist in accessing critical information and data, including authoritative information as well as useful web sites that reference software and other tools.

A CALL FOR GOVERNANCE

The world changed in 2001. Terrorists attacked the U.S. homeland, the economy plunged into recession, and corporate fraud destroyed the pensions and retirement plans of millions of people. The competitive landscape in the 21st century has become brutal with global outsourcing of jobs. The speed of innovation accelerated, with the customer becoming the focus of attention. Corporations are learning that knowledge management and intellectual capital have become a strategic and competitive necessity. These issues have challenged corporate leadership and created pressure that produced fraudulent and illegal activities at the highest corporate levels, which continue to capture newspaper and television headlines. CEOs and CFOs were being judged by how effectively they managed their quarterly earnings and not on the value created by the corporation. Likewise, audit firms became focused on cross-selling nonaudit services, not on the quality of audits being conducted. These corporate scandals involving fraudulent accounting not only rocked investor confidence, but also exposed the weaknesses in business processes and internal controls that have eroded corporate competitiveness.

It has become the trend to mix black and white with varying shades of grey. Financial statements within the guidelines of generally accepted accounting principles (GAAP) have become the tools to drive stock prices and increase executive compensation by making one plus one equal three. The average CEO's paycheck was more than 500 times that of the average production worker's by the year 2000. Stock options or other performance-based pay have become almost 80% of CEO compensation. It is little wonder that top corporate management bent the rules in favor of its own interests. In essence, greed overcame ethics and corporate governance.

GREED, NOT GOVERNANCE

Governance relies on individuals to make ethical decisions based on determining what is morally right within the context of corporate culture and policies. The impact of the dot.com bust and the soft economy left managers and executives in uncharted waters. The lack of a compass and a map combined with greed and the feeling that they could get away with cooking the books without repercussion was a sure-fire recipe for fraud and deceit. Acts of misconduct by employees, according to the 2003 National Business Ethics Survey, included abusive behavior, misreporting of data, lying, and withholding of needed information.

Clearly, the continuing stream of misrepresented financial results and corporate fraud stems from a lack of governance at the top that permeates all levels of the organization. The 2003 survey indicated a tendency for younger employees with low tenure to avoid reporting misconduct. We have seen younger managers caught in the cross-fire of fraud because they were ambitious to a fault and did not have effective guidelines. There was a failure of organizations to provide ethics programs and education and training that would help managers through the defining moments of choosing right from wrong. These failures combined with a lack of accountability for improper actions have led far too many executives in trusted positions to take the wrong turn when facing a fork in the road.

A key finding that emerged from the 2003 survey was that actions at the top of the organization counted. It was apparent that misconduct and fraudulent financial acts are strongly related to the actions of top management and supervisors. When employees see top management acting ethically and doing the right thing rather than bending to pressure, there is a greater likelihood that fraud and inappropriate actions will be avoided. Greed now has its penalties, as many high-ranking executives who placed themselves beyond governance have discovered.

ETHICS WITHOUT HONOR

Ethical dilemmas represent a constant challenge for individuals and corporations in addition to society. Business is a component of multiple social systems including economic, legal, and political institutions. Our capitalistic system includes a balance of ethical rightness or wrongness governed by laws, policies, and regulations. What has occurred in the recent past is that ethics for many executives and organizations clearly failed to provide the necessary guidance between moral right and wrong. We need to fix what was broken by creating linkages between moral right and wrong, codes of professional conduct, and societal laws. The result is legislated ethics.

Ethics is a system or code of conduct based on moral duties and obligations that provide guidelines on individual behavior. The American Institute of Certified Public Accountants has a code of conduct to guide accountants in carrying out their responsibilities. The code states that "in carrying out their responsibilities as professionals, members should exercise sensitive professional and moral judgments in all their activities. CPAs should accept the obligation to act in a way that will serve the public interest, honor the public trust, and demonstrate commitment to professionalism." While not all the accounting officers guilty of fraud and misrepresentation were CPAs, the accountants conducting the audits were certified and bound by the code of conduct. Ethics is a system or code of conduct that is based on moral duties and obligations that direct how we behave and deal with the ability to distinguish between right and wrong. Essentially, ethics represents the commitment to do what is right. Along with commitment is the necessity to act on what is right. What action would other prudent and ethical people take irrespective of the consequences? In other words, if we cannot affirm that everyone would act in the fashion we have acted, we know our action is wrong.

Society has agreed on rules for ethical behavior and actions. People are expected to be honest and have the integrity to keep their promises. In addition, society places a premium on fidelity, fairness, and caring. Citizens are expected to be responsible and have respect for others. No less is demanded of corporate citizens, especially the leaders who are responsible to employees and shareholders. What we have witnessed in recent days and months is trusted executives and auditors who have not lived up to ethical standards. Many of these people felt that they were beyond ethics and the law. They committed fraudulent and unethical acts because they were tempted by the opportunity to twist the truth, because of greed and the lack of will and fortitude to do what was right.

MANAGEMENT WITHOUT RESPONSIBILITY

We have witnessed increased occurrences of fraudulent acts, the most publicized of which was financial reporting fraud by corporations. KPMG conducted a survey of executives from 459 public companies in 2003 regarding incidences of fraudulent activities. The survey revealed that 75% of the companies surveyed experienced some type of fraud in their organization, representing an increase of 13% compared to the 1994 and 1998 surveys. The incidents of financial reporting fraud doubled compared to the earlier surveys. The costs of fraud incurred by companies are staggering, particularly financial reporting fraud. The average annual cost of financial fraud is $25.8 million according to the survey.

The pressure of preserving high-paying positions and living a life on the edge offer temptations that some managers and executives are unable to resist. This is especially true in public companies, but also has implications in smaller privately held businesses. In addition to meeting Wall Street's expectations, the temptation can be just as real when complying with bank loan covenants or governmental laws and regulations. The tendency for financial misrepresentation falls into four primary categories:

- Asset revenue misstatement
- Concealed liabilities and expenses
- Improper revenue recognition
- Inadequate omissions or inappropriate disclosures

The temptation to buy time until the situation can be fixed is more than some executives can resist. Based on recent events, it was clear that ethical codes of conduct were not enough to deter some managers from lying and cheating.

The line between fraud and ethics becomes very thin when management rationalizes its actions as being beyond reproach, creating a slippery slope. One of the issues is management compensation and its relationship to share price valuation. William J. McDonough, chairman of the Public Company Accounting Oversight Board stated that "the recent increases in executive pay are terribly bad social policies and perhaps even bad morals." Chief executive officer pay increased 535% from 1990 to 2000, while corporate profits increased 116%. The greed factor associated with compensation combined with the complexity and speed of business has clearly been a contributing factor in the breakdown of controls associated with accounting fraud. A key component of the compensation issue is the linkage to employee stock options that has provided the temptation to "cook the books." When the incentive is outrageous wealth created by stock options, executives began to engage in a variety of accounting sleight-of-hand maneuvers to keep stock prices rising. Jim Collins, author of *Good to Great,* indicated that "we've looked at 75 years of company data and never found the slightest correlation between executive compensation and company performance."

In addition to a system that is clearly broken, the pace of global competition and the information age speed of business transactions have created intense pressure for executives to perform. Not only is there more work and less time, but employees also face the threat of losing their jobs to outsourcing and drastic cutbacks to preserve profit margins. It is little wonder that accountants reporting to top management cave in to pressure from the top. This is a dramatic contrast to the "tone at the top" mandate now issued by the Securities and Exchange Commission (SEC) as a result of the Sarbanes-Oxley Act of 2002.

ENRON'S HOUSE OF CARDS

The collapse of Enron was the motivation for the Sarbanes-Oxley Act that was signed into law in July 2002. Enron's chronology was the first of a continuing list of financial and accounting fraud stories to hit the headlines. The *Wall Street Journal* now has a special section entitled "Executives on Trial" that monitors the regular procession of executives who are facing charges for fraudulent actions.

Enron Corporation had more than $49 billion in total assets for 2001 and was listed as the seventh largest U.S. corporation, as ranked by *Fortune* magazine. The sudden filing for bankruptcy protection on December 2, 2001 rocked the capital markets and shook investors' confidence. The scandal created intense media and congressional interest surrounding the operation of financial markets, practices of corporate management, and how accounting and auditing standards are applied. Legal proceedings against Enron and its executives continue as this is being written. The life savings of thousands of people were wiped out with the collapse, in addition to loss of jobs and careers and the effect on lives that will never again be the same.

Understanding Enron's house of cards provides the foundation for the passage of the Sarbanes-Oxley Act and the changes it brings to how publicly traded corporations will be held accountable. The reality is ethics by legislation. Enron executives operated in a culture based on greed and deception. These executives held themselves above Enron's Code of Conduct. The culture was one of corruption in which money meant everything. The house of cards was built using creative accounting and misleading financial statements combined with off-balance-sheet partnership entities that enabled Andrew Fastow, Enron's CFO, to operate on both sides of every transaction in order to manipulate the financial statements for the purpose of inflating profits. Enron's stock traded for $84 a share on December 28, 2000, and 11 months later was trading at less than a dollar. Today, the stock is worthless, and the New York Stock Exchange suspended trading on January 15, 2002. In the midst of this chaotic mess, Arthur Andersen, Enron's external auditor, launched a destruction of documents in October 23, 2001, leading to the implosion of the firm.

Going beyond the collapse of Enron is the ongoing saga of criminal investigations and federal prosecutions that have transpired and continue today. Kenneth Lay, the former chairman of Enron's board of directors, has been formally charged. Andrew Fastow was charged with 98 counts of conspiracy, fraud, insider trading, money laundering, obstruction of justice, and other felonies. The end result was that Fastow entered a plea to two counts of wire and securities fraud and was sentenced to 10 years in prison without parole. In exchange, Fastow agreed to cooperate with prosecutors in the conviction of other former Enron executives. Fastow's wife, Lea, originally charged with conspiracy to commit wire fraud, money laundering, conspiracy, and filing false tax returns, ended up pleading guilty to filing a false tax return and was sentenced to a year in prison. Fastow's cooperation will be instrumental in the conviction of Lay, Jeffrey Skilling, and other former Enron executives. A component of Fastow's plea bargain was the forfeiture of almost $24 million remaining from the off-the-book partnership deals that Enron used to hide debt and inflate profitability. According to *CNN Money*, authorities say that the Fastows diverted approximately $45 million to their accounts from these smoke-and-mirrors deals.

In the aftermath of the Enron collapse, more than 12 executives and employees have been indicted, seven of whom have pleaded guilty. Jeffrey Skilling, the ex-Enron CEO, was indicted on February 19, 2004 on 36 charges, together with new charges against Richard Causey, the former chief accounting officer. Causey was a former Andersen accountant who was on the Enron audit prior to joining the company. Skilling was indicted five weeks after Fastow pleaded guilty to wire and securities fraud in exchange for agreeing to help with the ongoing investigation of the fraud. Skilling faces a long prison sentence and huge fines if convicted. Skilling and Causey proclaim their innocence. Skilling resigned abruptly in August 2001, just four months prior to the company's bankruptcy, and has never wavered from his claims that his departure was in no way related to the collapse. Andrew Fastow was Skilling's protégé who started creating special-purpose entities that were designed to shift Enron's debt outside the company, but without giving up control over the assets that supported the debt. Skilling has a keen intellect, which makes it hard to believe that he did not comprehend Enron's fiscal situation. Congressional investigations revealed that Skilling cashed in and profited greatly from disposal of Enron stock from 1999 to the collapse of the company. What must be underscored is the ethical deficit in corporate culture and the complete lack of morality that the scandal has revealed, where a select greedy few benefited at the expense of thousands of employees and shareholders.

ARTHUR ANDERSEN'S IMPLOSION

The firm of Arthur Andersen LLP was the external auditor convicted of obstruction of justice for launching the destruction of Enron-related documents on

October 23, 2001. Andersen was one of the "Big Five" accounting and auditing firms and Enron was one of its largest clients. On October 16, 2001, Enron reported a loss totaling $618 million and announced to analysts that it would reduce shareholder equity by $1.2 billion, resulting in the collapse of Enron's share price. Andersen had been notified by Sherron Watkins, an Enron employee, that the off-balance-sheet "special-purpose" entities had been used to cover up the company's true financial condition. When Andersen learned of the warning and of possible SEC inquiries, its employees were instructed by partners and others to destroy documents that could be used by Enron and the SEC. The order to destroy Enron records was also given to Andersen personnel working in Portland, Oregon; Chicago, Illinois; and London, England. These illegal actions resulted in David B. Duncan, former Andersen partner, pleading guilty to obstruction of justice charges in April 2002.

After a 6-week trial and 10 days of deliberation, a jury found Arthur Andersen guilty of obstructing justice when it destroyed documents relating to Enron in advance of a pending SEC investigation. Andersen's defense that the documents were part of its housekeeping duties and not a cover-up in advance of the probe into questionable Enron accounting practices. Andersen received the maximum fine of $500,000 and five years probation. This verdict essentially destroyed the firm, with the resulting loss of 35,000 jobs worldwide. Duncan was fired by Andersen in January based on a probe that revealed he shredded documents and deleted electronic data. Duncan testified that Enron was one of Andersen's top five clients, responsible for $58 million in revenue.

The impact of the Andersen audit relationship with Enron reverberated into legislation with amazing speed as the Sarbanes-Oxley Act was signed into law on July 30, 2002. Corporate ethics and how we do business became a matter of law. Auditors are now forced back to auditing and independence as a result of the dishonesty and greed exhibited by corporate America and the accountants who did the auditing. The shift of audit firms into becoming providers of other services under the guise of trusted advisors was a clear target of the legislation. This shift clearly damaged the independence of audit firms as evidenced by the Andersen example relative to Enron's collapse.

ASLEEP AT THE WHEEL

Enron and Andersen represent only the tip of the iceberg. Tyco International, which operates in over 80 countries with revenues in the range of $36 billion, faced questions on its accounting for numerous acquisitions. Dennis Kozlowski, Tyco's former CEO, was forced to resign, as were former CFO Mark Swartz and former Chief Corporate Counsel Mark Belnick. Investigations revealed that

Tyco overreported its 2002 results by nearly $400 million. Tyco executives are accused of stealing approximately $600 million through loans, bonuses, and illegal stock sales.

WorldCom was the target of a $7 billion accounting fraud led by its former CFO Scott Sullivan, who plead guilty and agreed to cooperate with prosecutors in the indictment of former CEO Bernie Ebbers. Also indicted was David Myers, WorldCom's former controller. David Myers said that he was directed to make entries on WorldCom's books that had no justification and that were not in accordance with GAAP. The huge fraud also involved other accounting executives who pleaded guilty to securities fraud and conspiracy.

The fraud investigation revealed instances of operating expenses that were improperly classified as capital investments. WorldCom also created a big slush fund by recording large reserves to cover uncollected payments from customers, judgments in lawsuits, and other potential losses. These reserves were used to lift operating profits in quarters when there appeared to be a risk that numbers might not meet Wall Street's expectations. In effect, these reserves were used to manage earnings and smooth out fluctuations. Former chairman of the SEC Arthur Levitt called these "rainy day reserves," which distorted financial reporting. These instances of flagrant fraudulent accounting beg asking where the auditors and oversight boards of directors have been.

The list of fraudulent accounting incidents is long and continues to grow. HealthSouth, Quest, Adelphia Communications Corp., and Global Crossing experienced accounting fraud and efforts to cover it up. The Parmalat Dairy scandal resulted in the collapse of one of the world's largest dairy product producers in December 2003 when the Italian company reported that a $4.9 billion bank account in the United States did not exist. CEO Tanzi admitted cooking the books for over 10 years and skimming off as much as $640 million to cover losses in family businesses. The scandal involved $13 billion in missing assets, a forged letter to auditors, and fake invoices for hundreds of millions in bogus sales. Banks that were impacted included Citigroup and Bank of America. Auditors included Deloitte and Grant Thornton.

Xerox was fined $10 million in a civil action for violating antifraud, reporting, and record-keeping provisions of the federal securities laws. In addition, six former Xerox executives agreed to pay over $22 million in penalties, disgorgement, and interest. The action resulted from the acceleration of equipment revenues by approximately $3 billion and increasing pretax earnings by $1.4 billion in Xerox's 1997–2004 financial results. What is critical here is evidenced by Stephen M. Cutler, the SEC's director of enforcement, as he indicated that "a public company's stock price should reflect economic reality, not a distortion of that reality. As alleged in the complaint, Xerox's senior management substituted accounting devices for the company's true operational performance. The investing public pays an enormous price for such fraudulent conduct." These comments were based on the fact that the executives used accounting actions not disclosed to investors to improve Xerox's earnings in nearly every reporting period between 1997 and 1999. Two of the executives charged were members of Xerox's board of directors during the period of accounting manipulation and set a "tone at the top" for the company according to the SEC's federal court complaint in a release dated June 5, 2003. In conjunction with this action, the SEC charged KPMG and four partners with fraud for allowing Xerox to close a $3 billion gap between actual values and results reported to the investing public during the period from 1997 to 2000.

The dialogue could continue with inclusion of the gory details of how Adelphia maintained two sets of books and the 35-day month at Computer Associates. The continuing theme supports the argument that auditors have done a poor job of auditing and that boards of directors have been asleep at the wheel. Investors are now demanding that corporations overhaul their boards of directors and put an end to the "good old boy" syndrome by appointing independent members to their boards of directors. Sarbanes-Oxley is a wake-up call to corporations and auditors to fix a broken system.

BUSINESS PROCESS MANAGEMENT

In setting the stage for exploring and understanding the impact and implications of the Sarbanes-Oxley Act, it is critical to provide a discussion on how corporations measure and report strategic and operating results. From the earlier discussions, we have witnessed the increase in pressure being placed on corporations and management to produce. This is an issue that transcends ethics and governance and addresses the system itself. The information age has placed growing demands on real-time reporting and on how performance is measured. Strategy has become a critical necessity in managing risk and for corporate management to more effectively execute strategy in a competitive environment. One of the reasons why corporate executives are feeling such intense pressures is due to the huge gap that exists between strategy and execution.

Business process management (BPM) will become a component in communicating strategy and expectations to both employees as well as boards of directors and shareholders. The real-time reporting requirement combined with the impact of the scandals described is creating new focus on the accuracy, in addition to timeliness, of financial forecasts and financial reports. The Sarbanes-Oxley Act will force public corporations to improve their utilization of BPM to maximize value and minimize risk. The objective will be to minimize the risk of noncompliance as well as business risk and increase value to the shareholder using BPM components.

Compliance with Sarbanes-Oxley will drive fundamentally sound business management practices and internal controls. Section 404 will require management to assess its internal controls which drives all the business processes both operationally as well as commercially. The assessment process will likely become a continuous process of collaboration, communication, and coordination to effectively maintain a reliable financial reporting and management system in an increasingly competitive business environment.

CHALLENGES OF CORPORATE PERFORMANCE MANAGEMENT

Financial managers are under the gun of Sarbanes-Oxley and are facing increased pressure to produce reliable financial data. This is a growing challenge because of increasingly complex organizations and an expanded number of product and service offerings. The job is made even tougher because of the requirements for innovation in the age of information and technology. This has placed increasing importance on knowledge assets, intangibles, and intellectual capital. Measuring and managing in this challenging environment is called corporate performance management (CPM). The measurement methodologies available to companies are diverse, with no single tool capable of representing the ultimate solution. All of the methodologies were described in my book, *Dynamics of Profit-Focused Accounting*.

Traditional cost management and cost accounting under GAAP have lost relevance, and that is the primary reason why CFOs and controllers have adopted other tools to help fill the gap. The needs include monitoring strategy, operational excellence, forecasting, and value creation. The decision-making process within organizations requires much more than historical financial results that are clouded by traditional accounting principles and disclosure formats. Understandability and speed are other hurdles that must be overcome. Today's global economy has created an acceleration of outsourcing to a variety of contract suppliers or to subsidiaries established in multiple locations to take advantage of lower costs. This makes simplicity and understandability critical issues. Reporting formats need to be capable of being understood by line managers at the source of the information. Alignment and execution of strategy is a top priority. Therefore, simpler formats make top to bottom buy-in and linking to operational results much more effective.

The Sarbanes-Oxley Act has far-reaching implications that impact CPM. The act makes it mandatory for companies registered with the SEC to assess the capability of their internal controls to produce reliable financial reports. The assessment of internal controls is a process that companies will need to perform on a continuing basis. The complexity of the supply chain combined with the requirement to ensure that data are reliable represents an ongoing challenge for organizations. These requirements will push companies to solidify their business processes and simplify reporting. Real-time reporting and continuous forecasting of future data will make it critical for front-line managers to be involved. High-level corporate financial managers who are not linked and aligned to operations cannot orchestrate the process. Financial managers need to understand operations, and vice versa, operating managers will need to comprehend the final reporting concepts and the CPM model being employed.

This trend will create greater emphasis on financial reporting. It is apparent that firms will continue to employ a wide range of CPM methodologies. Therefore, it is critical that education on CPM and the best use of enabling tools become a high priority.

Business intelligence analytics can be applied to incorporate profit-focused accounting to take advantage of the simplified direct costing approach that embodies the emphasis of the Theory of Constraints on throughput. Profit-focused accounting includes economic value added and value-based management, as well as balanced scorecard and activity-based management. The balanced scorecard approach of mapping strategy linked to the perspective of knowledge management and using nonfinancial metrics makes a great deal of sense. Sarbanes-Oxley recognizes the significance of nonfinancial measurements because of the emphasis investors place on brands, technology, innovations, and other knowledge-related assets, especially the workforce. The legislation may well represent a blessing that will not be appreciated right away. CPM will evolve as companies search for the combination of tools that are best suited for them.

TONE AT THE TOP

The continuing list of corporate accounting scandals represents strong support for legislated business ethics and morals. Governance for many executives and accountants did not appear to exist in their tool kits. The Sarbanes-Oxley Act of 2002 is putting "tone at the top" as a key component of compliance. Section 302 requires the CEO and CFO to certify the accuracy of financial statements submitted to the SEC. Section 404 mandates that management include in its annual report certification that it has assessed established internal controls capable of providing reliable financial reporting. Outside auditors are required to issue an "attestation" to management's assessment so that shareholders and investors have a basis to rely on management's description of the company's internal controls over financial reporting. Essentially, the legislation is requiring management and external auditors to provide adherence to reliable and responsible business and professional standards.

We have seen repeated examples of corporate leaders who did not follow their company's code of conduct. We have seen not only where GAAP has lost relevance, but also where crooked executives have taken advantage of the gaps to enrich their own coffers. There have been vociferous complaints about the cost of compliance with the new legislation and the effort required to ensure that deficiencies in internal control do not create material weaknesses. In reality, many of the problems stem from having to do work that should have been done in the first place.

The impact and reality of Sarbanes-Oxley extend well beyond the common perception of internal control. The issue is not just reliable financial reports; it is the effectiveness and efficiency of operations. Technology and software can check to ensure that all the linkages are connected, but they cannot train employees so they effectively utilize all the tools. Examples will be provided in later chapters showing where failed enterprise resource planning implementations have required companies to report extraordinary charges on their financial statements. We have to develop assurance that the overall structure of the system and its components minimize the risk of surprises.

Internal control needs to embrace the risk of uncertainty and provide managers with the ability to minimize operational surprises and losses. Many companies implemented systems in anticipation of Y2K and in many instances rushed past the fundamental basics. Typical examples include inaccurate inventory balances that cause employees to lose trust in the system and adopt process steps that leave the door open for surprises. Inaccurate bills of material and routing steps lead to errors in shipping, poor quality, and excessive investment in inventory. The manufacturing process suddenly is showing more scrap and poor yield in contrast to management's expectation. Poor process control can also lead to warranty claims and unexpected losses.

Many companies have simply not achieved control over their production and commercial processes, leaving the door open for potential problems and financial statement surprises. Sarbanes-Oxley requires that executives address the problem by taking the approach of evaluating the infrastructure of the organization and fixing the broken components. This means a new focus on implementing and maintaining the basic processes and the transaction disciplines to ensure that the related internal controls are reliable.

Compliance with Sarbanes-Oxley can be either a hassle or viewed as an opportunity. There are many issues and complexities that organizations will face in the months ahead. Smaller companies registered with the SEC will not have to comply until 2007. Larger companies are just starting to meet the compliance deadlines. There are many approaches to dealing with the compliance issues. Compliance is not just an information technology fix that requires real-time reporting and alignment of technologies to comply with the guidelines—it is an organization-wide issue that extends to operational effectiveness and efficiency. The self-assessment approach will ultimately represent the only real solution, as it will become a standard for others to follow.

Sarbanes-Oxley will become more than a requirement for publicly traded companies; it will become a standard that all organizations will seek to attain. Not all companies tried to win the Baldrige Award, but those that did lifted their organizations to a higher level of performance excellence. The Baldrige Award is based on conducting a self-assessment, as is the framework for the European Foundation for Quality Management. Self-assessment will become a real-time event for many companies as a standard for how business is conducted. Those that adopt it will benefit, and those that do not self-assess will struggle. It will be an ongoing process of learning about the realities of operational effectiveness and corporate performance management.

Senior leadership will be required to act in a manner that sets the tone for the rest of the organization to demonstrate by their actions and not just by their words. The initial thrust of compliance is not going to make everything "okay" so that life goes on as it was in the good old days. A new standard of accountability and measurement will emerge as management teams realize that traditional silos must be dismantled to create an environment for competitive effectiveness in the 21st century.

SARBANES-OXLEY RESPONSE

It is appropriate to follow the call for governance by an action plan presented by President George W. Bush and issued on March 7, 2002. The action plan was a "*10-Point Plan to Improve Corporate Responsibility and Protect America's Shareholder.*" Three core principles upon which the action plan was predicated included:

- Information accuracy
- Information accessibility
- Auditor independence

The President's 10-point plan became the foundation for the most extensive reform of business practices in decades. The legislation was called the Sarbanes-Oxley Act of 2002 and was signed into law on July 30, 2002. The act was spearheaded by Paul Sarbanes, a senator from Maryland, and Michael Oxley, a congressman from Ohio. The legislation was passed on July 26, 2002, with a House vote of 423–3 and a Senate vote of 99–0. The act became the launching pad for the Corporate Fraud Task Force and the creation of a new accounting oversight board to police the practices of the accounting profession. It also focused on enhancing the accountability of corporate officers and directors and the quality of financial reporting. The tone for corporate and accounting governance was etched into law, setting a new standard for the future. It provided a foundation for companies to secure a new competitive advantage.

LEGISLATIVE RESPONSE

The Sarbanes-Oxley Act of 2002 provides a clear and definitive response to the President's 10-point plan and set in place new accounting oversight rules for corporate America. The 10-point plan spells out the following objectives:

1. Each investor should have quarterly access to the information needed to judge a firm's financial performance, condition, and risks.
2. Each investor should have prompt access to critical information.
3. CEOs should personally vouch for the veracity, timeliness, and fairness of their companies' public disclosures, including their financial statements.
4. CEOs or other officers should not be allowed to profit from erroneous financial statements.
5. CEOs or other officers who clearly abuse their power should lose their right to serve in any corporate leadership position.
6. Corporate leaders should be required to tell the public promptly whenever they buy or sell company stock for personal gain.
7. Investors should have complete confidence in the independence and integrity of companies' auditors.
8. An independent regulatory board should ensure that the accounting profession is held to the highest ethical standards.
9. The authors of accounting standards must be representative of the needs of investors.
10. Firms' accounting systems should be compared with best practices, not simply against minimum standards.

The legislation now known as the Sarbanes-Oxley Act of 2002 answered each of the 10 points enumerated in the plan to curb corporate and executive abuse of power and accounting rules.

The new rules apply to any company that lists its stock on a U.S.-based stock exchange regardless of where the company's headquarters is located. The legislation requires management to certify to the accuracy of the company's financial reports on a quarterly basis. The law will have a major impact on CPAs. CPAs auditing public companies will be monitored by an accounting oversight board that will be responsible for setting the rules and evaluating audit quality and compliance. In addition to calling for real-time reporting, Sarbanes-Oxley requires management to assess the internal controls and the external auditor to attest to and report on management's assessment. The Sarbanes-Oxley legislation also spelled out new rules regarding types of services auditors can provide to firms in order to avoid conflicts of interest.

Creation of the Public Company Accounting Oversight Board (PCAOB) provided for administration and monitoring of auditing firms and accounting rules. The Securities and Exchange Commission (SEC) administers the PCAOB, which sets forth the guidelines for internal control. This chapter includes discussion of the key components of the Sarbanes-Oxley legislation and their ramifications.

COST OF ETHICS

Since Sarbanes-Oxley was enacted, the reality and cost of compliance have started to settle in on corporate America. It could be argued that auditors and corporations brought on the cost as dictated by legislation because they failed to take appropriate steps to avoid the corporate collapses and acts of accounting fraud through ethical and moral self-policing actions. Higher levels of professional performance could have averted these disasters. For some corporations, the cost will simply be compliance with no residual benefits. In other instances, organizations will view the mandate as an opportunity to achieve a competitive advantage by using it as a tool to improve efficiency and productivity.

According to a Gartner Research report, large public companies might expect to spend in the neighborhood of $2 million to meet the compliance requirements of Sarbanes-Oxley. That estimate comes very close to the costs reported in a Financial Executives Institute survey conducted in January 2004. Obviously, compliance costs will vary depending on the size and complexity of the company. The quality and effectiveness of a company's business systems and processes will also impact the compliance effort.

Compliance costs fall into a range of different categories. Most notable will be an increase in audit fees, as external auditors will be required to audit not only the financial statements but also management's assessment of internal controls. Internal process documentation or implementation of process improvements to fill deficiency gaps will be an eye-opener for many corporations that have never documented and mapped their business processes. This segment may represent the true opportunity emerging from compliance since it represents a critical first step to business process improvement that can lead to strategic and competitive advantage. Too many businesses have limped along and never faced up to continuous self-improvement. Sarbanes-Oxley compliance now provides the opportunity. The cost of additional personnel to cope with compliance in addition to training existing personnel also represents additional layers of cost for many corporations. Also, organizations will definitely see increased insurance premiums for board of director liability because of the new increase in risks.

The size difference in companies will have a telling impact on the relative cost of Sarbanes-Oxley compliance. According to a PriceWaterhouseCoopers survey, larger companies typically have in place a more defined infrastructure of systems, processes, and documentation than smaller companies. There appear to be differences of opinion regarding the expected ongoing cost of compliance. Some continued increase in costs is anticipated as companies move past the initial year of compliance, particularly with respect to Section 404. A Foley & Lardner survey released in May 2004 cited that increased cost of compliance was not a one-time event and that these significant costs were becoming increasingly unpredictable. The survey reflected a double-digit increase in fees paid to auditors correlated with a decline in the feedback of advice due to auditor independence concerns. This correlates to input received from participants attending my workshops regarding auditor adversity to taking any risk.

There were several interesting executive responses targeted at the new legislation in a *USA Today* article dated October 19, 2003. Scott McNealy from Sun Microsystems indicated frustration with Sarbanes-Oxley, saying that it was like throwing "buckets of sand into the gears of the market economy." Ciena CEO Gary Smith called it post-Enron "chemotherapy" that was better than the alternative. Interestingly, Jim Schneider, CFO of Dell, stated that "nothing can be all bad when it creates a greater awareness of what is going on inside the company." I think Schneider's point embodies the true spirit of the legislation.

OVERSIGHT BOARD

In response to the accounting failures and corporate scandals, the passage of the Sarbanes-Oxley legislation created the PCAOB. It is a private sector, nonprofit corporation. The primary purpose of the PCAOB, which operates under the oversight of the SEC, is overseeing the audits of public companies and protecting investors by helping restore trust in a culture of greed and arrogance. The critical mission is providing oversight in the preparation of reliable and informative independent audit reports. The board was created on October 25, 2002 and consists of five members, of which only two can be CPAs. Anyone who holds the chair may not have practiced in the last five years. A seat on the board is a full-time position, with members serving a five-year term with a maximum of two terms. Oversight and governance has its price as the PCAOB is funded primarily by fees allocated to public companies in proportion to their market capitalization to cover a 2003 budget that totaled $68 million. Most of the fees are paid by the largest 1000 companies with the largest average monthly equity market capitalization.

The PCAOB is charged with establishing auditing and attestation standards for the accounting profession. The board also sets the quality, ethical, and independence standards for CPA firms and accountants. It is the new rule-setting body that regulates audits of public companies. In this regard, the PCAOB has four major responsibilities:

1. Registering accounting firms
2. Inspecting registered firms
3. Conducting investigations and disciplinary proceedings
4. Establishing audit standards

One of the major areas of impact is corporate governance. The standards developed and issued by the PCAOB were not intended to be a checklist for compliance, but for accountability. Improved corporate governance and the tone at the top are meant to relate to appropriate actions and accountability from the top to the bottom and across organizations. Understanding the PCAOB is important because it provides the spirit of compliance and beyond, which is the focus of this book. The PCAOB has raised the bar for new standards and rules for professional and corporate accountability, together with how they are applied and followed.

OFFICER CERTIFICATION

Corporate executives can no longer shirk responsibility for the reliability of financial data, as did many who were involved in the rash of corporate scandals. Provisions of the new legislation now require CEOs and CFOs to personally certify financial results. Furthermore, the Sarbanes-Oxley Act backs up the requirement with fines and imprisonment of up to 10 years for violations. The spirit of these certifications has experienced a cascade effect, with lower ranking executives taking part in the certification process. It is an "if I'm on the hook, so are you" type of response.

Section 302 of Sarbanes-Oxley is linked with Section 906 in addressing the issue of officer certification, with the addition of criminal penalties. CEOs and CFOs are required to certify that the financial report fully complies with requirements of Section 13(a) or 15(d) of the Exchange Act and that the information contained in the report fairly presents, in all material respects, the financial condition and results of operation of the issuing company. Any officer who knowingly or willfully provides a false certification is subject to the new criminal penalties provided by Section 906. The HealthSouth scandal was a direct result of violations of these provisions.

There are additional requirements beyond the absence of material misrepresentations or omissions and a fairly stated financial position. CEOs and CFOs also need to certify responsibility for establishing internal controls designed to ensure that material information concerning the company and subsidiaries is made known to them during the time in which the annual or quarterly report is being prepared. They also have to certify that they have evaluated the effectiveness of their company's internal controls and their conclusions regarding the effectiveness of those controls. There is also a requirement to certify the communication regarding material internal control weaknesses to the external auditor and the audit committee.

"Falling asleep at the wheel" is no longer an option for corporate executives. Now that certification is a legal requirement, it places the onus on executives to understand what is really going on in their organization. The importance of business process management and true operational effectiveness will now drive the need for more effective and reliable financial reporting. Another benefit is the cascade certification process, which will start providing a basis for more effective communication within organizations. Combined with an improved awareness of internal controls, this will be helpful in achieving cross-functional continuous improvement.

FINANCIAL REPORTING DISCLOSURES

Reliable financial reporting was clearly an objective of the new legislation. In addition to outright fraudulent accounting, the scandals revealed the necessity to overcome the "smoke and mirrors" pursued prior to 2002. Financial reporting includes disclosures in footnotes and management comments in releases and annual reports. Section 401 provides the regulations relative to financial reporting and disclosures. The PCAOB and SEC further elaborate on the details of what is expected, and these will be clarified in greater detail in later chapters. One thing that is very clear, as evidenced by remarks made by SEC Chairman William J. McDonough in a presentation to the New York Society of CPAs on September 9, 2003, is that the SEC and the PCAOB mean business. McDonough stated: "I expect that you, as members of a regulated profession, know what the rules are. I expect that you are following those rules, both in their letter and their spirit. If you depart from those expectations—that is, if you break the rules, if you ignore the spirit of the law even while meeting the letter—woe be unto you. There will be consequences, and they will be grave." Xerox is a clear example: a $10 million fine was levied on the corporation and heavy penalties, both monetary and loss of privilege to serve in an executive capacity, were assessed against former executives.

Accuracy of financial reports is a target because of the rash of financial restatements due to accounting errors. The Huron Consulting Group indicated that there were 323 restatements in 2003 compared to 330 in 2002. These restatements cost investors billions of dollars because of the fluctuation in value resulting from reaction to the changed information. The majority of financial restatements resulted from improper recognition of revenue and timing of expenses and through the application of fuzzy reserves and contingency accounts. In response to Enron's accounting practices, the SEC adopted tougher rules with respect to off-balance-sheet transactions and the use of special-purpose entities. Financial Interpretations No. 45 and 46 specifically address these issues.

Another financial reporting issue addressed by Sarbanes-Oxley is the use of pro-forma statements. Companies were releasing pro-forma earnings that reported the good news but concealed the impact of factors such as:

- Research and development costs
- Amortization of intangible assets
- Impairment of goodwill
- Costs of restructuring
- Write-off of obsolete and slow-moving inventory
- Costs of business realignment
- Adjustments in the allowance for doubtful accounts receivable
- Unrealized gains and losses

Flagrant examples include Whirlpool, which reported a net loss of $394 million in 2002 compared to a $420 million pro-forma profit. The differences occurred from a change in accounting impairment for goodwill, an after-tax restructuring charge, and a write-off of aircraft lease assets. Another illustration of the gap is Cisco Systems, which reported a pro-forma net income of $3.09 billion contrasted against a generally accepted accounting principles (GAAP) basis loss of $1.01 billion. Some of the exclusions from the pro-forma numbers included acquisition charges, payroll taxes on exercising stock options, restructuring costs, excess inventory charges, and net gains on minority investments. Nokia reported a 2001 net profit of $676.2 million on a pro-forma basis compared to a GAAP net income of $165.5 million, with the difference resulting from the exclusion of amortization of goodwill and other nonrecurring items.

The Section 401 regulations issued by the SEC provides for avoiding misleading or untrue statements and requires the reconciliation of pro-forma financial information to results of operation as presented under GAAP. Non-GAAP financial measures are defined as a numerical measure of a company's financial performance. These measures are compared to comparable measures included in the company's GAAP statements. The critical component of the pro-forma presentations is the avoidance of misleading presentations, which would be subject to antifraud provisions. The first evidence of the SEC's response to misleading statements was Trump Hotels & Casino Resorts for attempting to put its 1999 numbers in a more positive light by including a one-time gain and excluding a one-time charge, causing the share price to rise 7.8% on the day of the earnings release.

In a nutshell, the SEC approved Regulation G, which applies whenever a company publicly discloses or releases material information that includes a non-GAAP measurement. Information containing non-GAAP financial measurements, which could be misleading, will require a quantitative reconciliation using a schedule or other method that is readily understood. The SEC wants to avoid having self-serving measurements that attempt to deceive or might mislead investors. These situations could become the object of enforcement actions and penalties depending on the severity of the violation.

MANAGEMENT'S ASSESSMENT OF INTERNAL CONTROL

The reality of Sarbanes-Oxley is brought to focus with Section 404, which requires that management have responsibility for establishing and maintaining adequate internal controls for financial reporting. This is historically an area where management fell down on the job and auditors failed to live up to professional standards. The examples provided in Chapter 1 provide lots of support for the need to improve performance on both sides of the financial statement. The investing public and the American capital markets badly needed to restore trust and confidence in financial reporting, auditing, and management.

A critical component of the legislation is that management is responsible for assessing its internal controls and reporting on their effectiveness as of the end of the fiscal year. The PCAOB has set a standard for auditors to use in determining if managements of public companies have accurately reported on their assessment of internal control over financial reporting. Congress was especially mindful of the failures that occurred in internal control as it drafted the Sarbanes-Oxley legislation. The legislative reality is that management is now accountable for internal control and auditors are responsible for making sure the job is being done as a component of their audits. The new audit is now conducted on both internal controls and the fairness of the financial statement. The standards require that the audits be performed together and not be separated from one another.

I want to set the tone for compliance with Section 404 here because it offers opportunities extending beyond checklist compliance. Internal controls need to be established based on an acceptable framework, and the SEC has approved the COSO Framework as being suitable. This model framework was created by the Committee of Sponsoring Organizations of the Treadway Commission in September 1992. The original title is *Internal Control—Integrated Framework* and it was created based on extensive study and input from participating organizations. The framework is based on best practices methodology and having a control system in place. The three objectives of the COSO Framework and its five components will be explained and documented in subsequent chapters as the foundation for using Sarbanes-Oxley as an opportunity for continuous improvement and building a competitive advantage. Other frameworks have been created and they will be described and included in the discussion where appropriate. One of these frameworks is the COBiT Framework issued by the IT Governance Institute (ITGI) and supported by the Information Systems Audit and Control Association (ISACA). Another new framework developed by COSO is the Enterprise Risk Management Framework, which was issued in draft form in 2003 and finalized in 2004. This builds on and enhances the Integrated Framework. Discussion of both these and other frameworks will be included in subsequent chapters.

Management is faced with developing an approach to meeting the internal control assessment requirements. Some of the critical issues include developing a plan for conducting the assessment and documenting the management assertions. Other issues include the techniques for conducting and managing the self-assessment. Management needs to provide for effective communication and training, including a review of best practices. The assessment will involve documentation of the key business processes, including all of the information technology components of the system.

Since the internal control assessment under Section 404 will drastically change the way audits are conducted, it is important for management to communicate with the external auditor. An internal auditor from General Electric attended one of my Sarbanes-Oxley training programs. GE uses an approach very similar to its Six Sigma program for its assessment, and a key was early communication with its external auditor. GE opted for early compliance, representing a good step toward eliminating and avoiding surprises during the assessment process.

After reading the new PCAOB Audit Standard No. 2, it was very clear that the PCAOB expects management to be actively involved in the assessment process. A management self-assessment represents new unplowed ground for many management teams and organizations. The concepts offered by the Malcolm Baldrige National Quality Award for performance excellence provide guidelines for benchmarking best practices, as does Fundamental Concepts of Excellence provided by the European Foundation for Quality Management. It is clear that management will have to get in the game and not sit in the stands in order to effectively comply with Sarbanes-Oxley.

CODE OF ETHICS

Ethics relates to the code of conduct or a code of morals about how people act, live, and work. It relates to people, organizations, professions, and religions. Ethical behavior might be what is good for the individual and society. A code of ethics is a moral code or standard that provides guidelines on standards for personal behavior. We have witnessed corporate scandals where corporate executives failed to live up to their own corporation's code of ethics and conduct. Likewise, auditors and CPAs failed to comply with the codes for professional conduct.

The Sarbanes-Oxley Act addressed this issue and adopted a code of ethics as a legal requirement and mandated that corporations disclose whether or not they have adopted a code of ethics for their senior financial officers and principal executive officer. Section 406 mandates the disclosure. If a company has not adopted a code of ethics, it must disclose why it has not done so.

Section 406 of the Sarbanes-Oxley of 2002 was adopted and became effective in its final form on March 3, 2003. A look at the SEC's definition of the term "code of ethics" is appropriate. The definition is broken into five components to deter wrongdoing and promote:

1. Honest and ethical conduct
2. Full, fair, accurate, timely, and understandable disclosure in financial reports
3. Compliance with applicable governmental laws and regulations
4. Prompt reporting of violations of the code
5. Accountability for adherence to the code

Originally, the SEC included avoidance of conflicts of interest in the preliminary regulations, but removed it since honest and ethical conduct was presumed to have addressed this component. The rules obviously do not address every detail that a company must include in its code of ethics and fall short of prescribing specific language that should be used. It is noteworthy that if companies choose not to live by their own code of ethics as stated and reported to investors, they will have to face consequences mandated by law.

It is interesting that we have come to the point where it is necessary to legislate ethics. Tom Morris authored a book entitled *If Aristotle Ran General Motors*. In it, he talks about the "new soul of business." The book was published in 1997, four years before the Enron scandal and market collapse. Morris describes ethics as all about "spiritually healthy people in social harmonious relationships." In contrast, his feeling is that too many people were just trying to stay out of trouble. Morris states that "there are two ways to stay out of trouble. One is to do the right thing. The other is to do what ever you want but camouflage it to make it look like you're doing the right thing." It is going to take more than a legislative act of Congress to teach corporate America the reality of ethics and morality.

The narrowness of thinking that exists in the executive suites will need to be broadened and executives educated to overcome Oscar Wilde's definition of a cynic as applied by Morris to executives: "A person who knows the price of everything and the value of nothing." The Sarbanes-Oxley Act is making it a mandate for corporations to state the ethical rules and then requiring management to conduct self-assessments to make sure that there is a system of internal control to keep everybody driving between the lines.

NEW RULES OF THE ROAD

Revised maps are continuously being printed as directions and rules are being created for publicly traded corporations and their auditors, with ongoing clarification of the new rules of the road. One of the new rules that represent a major change in how companies manage and report is the requirement to provide real-time disclosure of material events that could impact the business. Specifically, Section 409 calls for disclosure on a rapid and current basis of material changes in financial conditions or operations. This means that it is now a requirement to report material changes in the business literally as soon as they happen.

In addition to internal control assessments, companies now need to be capable of disclosing material events almost immediately, together with some indication as to how these events will impact the business, both qualitatively and quantitatively. The SEC provided some guidance on the types of events that would trigger a reporting disclosure for 8-K filings; these events include:

- Entry into or termination of a material definitive agreement
- Bankruptcy or receivership
- Material acquisition or disposal of assets
- Results from operations and financial condition
- Creation of a direct financial obligation or arrangement of an off-balance-sheet arrangement
- Triggering events that accelerate or increase a direct financial obligation under an off-balance-sheet arrangement

- Costs associated with exit or disposal activities
- Material impairments

Companies now have only four business days to report events that might materially affect their financial statements under the "rapid and current basis" requirements of Section 409. This new requirement drives the necessity for real-time information and exposes the unvarnished reality that many companies do not have either the organizational structure or discipline matched with necessary technology to effectively comply. This represents a real challenge and an incentive for companies to achieve the necessary business process management and measurement capabilities for effective compliance.

Many companies have used their CPA firms to assist with a variety of specialized services that are no longer allowed by the Sarbanes-Oxley Act. Services that are prohibited include:

- Bookkeeping and related services
- Design and implementation of financial information systems
- Appraisal or valuation services
- Actuarial services
- Management or human resources services
- Investment or broker/dealer services
- Legal and "expert services unrelated to the audit"

These new rules were implemented in an effort to make audit firms truly independent and curb the growing tendency to continuously cross-sell more profitable consulting services rather than provide high-quality audits. The new rules have teeth, as evidenced by Ernest & Young being banned from accepting new audit clients for six months. The violations occurred because of the firm's failure to disclose independence issued in audits of PeopleSoft from 1994 through 2000. The SEC charged Ernest & Young with violating auditor independence rules because it jointly developed and marketed a software product and earned millions of dollars in consulting revenues through an "implementation partnership agreement" with PeopleSoft.

Other new rules include the requirement for concurring or second partner reviews on audits. There is also a ban on firms auditing any SEC-registered client whose CEO, CFO, or controller was on the audit team of the firm within the past year, in addition to requirements associated with the length of time audit partners can be on an audit before they must be rotated. In light of the shredding of Enron documents, audit firms are now required to retain audit work papers for a period of seven years from the end of the fiscal year in which the audit was concluded. Audit firms will also be accountable to the new oversight board, which is the focus of Chapter 3. Management can no longer select its audit firm. Independent audit committees now take on a new meaning and responsibility as they have to select and supervise the independent auditor.

THE AUDIT COMMITTEE WATCHDOG

Publicly traded companies are now required to have independent audit committees with new and strengthened responsibilities. This change was highlighted by the need to have strong audit committees with independence from management and charged with the authority to supervise the audit process. The rules give new meaning and responsibilities to audit committees. This means that all members of the audit committee will need to be independent and at least one audit committee member must meet the requirements of an "audit committee financial expert" as set forth in Section 407. The penalty for noncompliance is delisting.

The new rules reflect the seriousness of the legislation's intent to develop strong independent audit committees as a critical component of the corporate governance system. After the wholesale failure of corporate governance, audit committees were charged with responsibility to provide independent oversight as the watchdog over a company's financial reporting processes, internal controls, and independent auditors.

New rules were created whereby "whistle-blower" provisions were established, requiring audit committees to implement procedures for the reporting of complaints by employees regarding concerns about questionable accounting or auditing issues. In complying with their new responsibilities, audit committees have the authority to engage advisors, experts, and independent counsel as necessary. The committees also have responsibility for monitoring and directing internal audit activities including selecting the chief audit executive. Corporate boards will be facing new scrutiny and challenges as they cope with the new responsibilities. Both the NYSE and NASD, among others, revised their listing standards relating to audit committees. The implications of the new watchdog role for audit committees are discussed in depth in Chapter 12.

THE NEW EXECUTIVE LOOK

The pinstripes that executives wear to work could easily be exchanged for prison stripes by failing to comply with the new mandate. Clothing budgets will drop because selection will be simple and the daily commute to the office will be much easier. Stiff penalties have been created for corporate and criminal fraud committed by company insiders. It is now a crime to destroy, alter, or falsify records in a federal investigation or a bankruptcy proceeding. The guilty parties will be subject to stiff fines and as much as 20 years in prison, or both. The fines can be up to $5 million in addition to forfeiture of bonuses and profits resulting from the execution of fraudulent schemes.

The behaviors that attract these stiff penalties include failure to maintain audit work papers for seven years, reckless violation of the certification of company financial statements, mail and wire fraud, and alteration of documents. In the case of the Xerox executives, they lost the privilege to serve in an executive capacity in addition to payment of fines and disgorgement of bonuses. In response to the Tyco abuses, among others, it is no longer legal to extend personal loans to executives in most instances, and in the permitted circumstances, the loans cannot be more favorable than those offered to the public.

Sarbanes-Oxley is the most wide-sweeping legislation to have been enacted in over half a century. The White House's 10-point program has changed the landscape for corporate governance and management. Those who think that Sarbanes-Oxley is another Y2K are sadly mistaken. Beyond governance, the legislation, clearly, will impact how companies measure performance and how the data will be gathered. Real meaning has been given to internal controls, and "tone at the top" will now have the attention of all corporate executives. The penalties for "falling asleep at the wheel" are too severe to ignore.

SETTING THE TONE

Corporate governance and leadership have new rules and guidelines as the result of the creation of the Public Company Accounting Oversight Board (PCAOB) under Section 103 of the Sarbanes-Oxley Act. This is making corporations play by new rules. Auditors are finding out that accounting and auditing standards can no longer be self-directed. When the founding members of the PCAOB were appointed on October 25, 2002, it marked the end of self-regulation and compulsory oversight. These changes have had a sweeping and profound impact on businesses and the accounting profession. Even more changes are expected as the impact of the legislation filters down to privately held companies and their auditors. Right now, we have big generally accepted accounting principles (GAAP) and little GAAP. One wonders how long it will be before we have just GAAP.

Investors' confidence could not have been restored without the aid of the new legislation. Too many executives and accounting professionals were shading the black-and-white rules with their own self-interested interpretations. In many ways, the new Sarbanes-Oxley rules and standards will create better managed companies because they force executives and accountants to start focusing on the basics and the details. In addition to creating a framework for better business processes, higher standards for leadership ethics and morality have been returned to the business society. Both executives and accounting professionals have now been brought back to what they should have been doing in the first place.

THE NEW REALITY

While the PCAOB is an accounting oversight board, its real impact extends to corporate governance. Sarbanes-Oxley has taken dead aim on the effectiveness of corporate boards of directors and how well they perform their jobs. Audit committees are required to be independent and have been given added responsibilities that formerly were performed by management. Under the new audit standards that will be discussed in Chapter 14, an ineffective audit committee is a significant control deficiency and a clear signal of a material weakness in financial reporting and internal controls. Accordingly, effective audit committees will be a factor that external auditors will be required to assess as a component of the new audit standards.

Corporate boards are expected to set the "tone at the top" of the corporate structure that sets the standard for the rest of the organization. The events leading up to Sarbanes-Oxley have placed increased emphasis on corporate ethics. Because of the newness of the regulations, it is still too early to determine the true impact on governance. In most instances, change does not really kick in until people feel the heat. Awareness is now beginning to gain focus based on surveys that have been conducted. A survey conducted by Deloitte and Touche and *Corporate Board Magazine* indicates that most companies have formal codes of conduct, but only about three-quarters of those surveyed are actually checking to make sure that their code is being followed. Less than 70% of those companies surveyed provide training to their employees on the requirements and responsibilities contained in the code of ethics. This trend should improve as auditors begin applying the new audit standards and audit committees start to assume their new responsibilities.

The continuing theme of "tone at the top" is a song the PCAOB hopes that everyone impacted by Sarbanes-Oxley learns to sing and takes to heart. The reality of the far-reaching impact extends to the very essence of how the accounting profession operated and was governed. All public accounting firms that audit publicly traded companies are required to be registered with the PCAOB. This amounts to more than a thousand accounting firms at the time this is being written. Firms that audit more than 100 public companies will be inspected annually and other firms will be inspected at least once every three years.

A focus of the PCAOB is the "professionalism" of auditors. Some of the factors considered in evaluating professionalism include "tone at the top," partner evaluation and compensation, and the standards used by firms to accept or reject audit clients. The PCAOB is very focused on the character of firms conducting audits, including the attitudes and philosophy of their leaders. The statement that "organizations tend to adopt the culture of their leadership" is directed to audit firms with the realization that they will represent standard bearers of professionalism. If the firms conducting audits of public companies fail to exhibit "tone at the top," then it is unlikely that standards will carry forward to audit committees and corporate executives.

Prior to the new oversight board, the American Institute of Certified Public Accountants set auditing standards through the Auditing Standards Board. The PCAOB now has this responsibility. The new landscape created by the Sarbanes-Oxley Act has provided auditors with new requirements for maintaining work papers and on the types of service they can provide to audit clients. Accounting rules are established by the Financial Accounting Standards Board (FASB) and are officially recognized by the Securities and Exchange Commission (SEC) as the authoritative source for standards on accounting and reporting. Although the FASB operates as an independent entity, it is dependent upon the PCAOB for its funding. The direction of accounting standards is moving toward an objective that reports the economic substance of transactions and events more in line with today's faster pace of change. This will also facilitate the convergence of U.S. GAAP and international accounting standards. While the AICPA still provides standards for nonpublic companies, it appears that direction will be established by the PCAOB.

RESPONSIBILITIES OF LEADERSHIP

Execution of responsible leadership by corporate leaders and the accounting profession is fundamental to secure the continued stability of our capital markets. When so many corporate leaders and auditors acted in their own interests rather than in the public interest, the result was chaotic waste and loss. The corporate mandate of meeting the quarterly numbers at any cost will be difficult to overcome. The upward path of progress is almost never a straight line. Tom Morris makes an excellent point when he states that "corporate spirit is a dynamic thing, and is created day by day by the actions of everyone in the organization, from the front lines to the executive suites. Nothing is irrelevant. Everything matters." There are many companies that live the example envisioned by the PCAOB, but there are many that fall short, just as there are auditors who know how to audit and others who just want to follow a checklist. The new responsibilities will carry more than just a price, because all the little things that make a difference will produce the value.

The responsibilities of leading the changes that have been legislated will take time and a great deal of effort. The flywheel effect described by Jim Collins is a good illustration of what it will take to achieve "tone at the top." The flywheel is a huge iron wheel that takes a great deal of time and effort to get moving. However, once the wheel begins to turn, it starts to gain momentum and accelerate. A legislative jump-start was needed to achieve momentum and acceleration. The PCAOB realized the intent of Congress and then focused its attention on the people and components of organizations that would need to change to make a difference. The first step was changing the composition of boards of directors and the role of directors to take a stronger position in providing guidance and governance. Before directors can provide leadership, they first need to understand what they are leading. The reality is that corporate directors and audit committee members are going back to school to achieve some level of financial literacy. The *Wall Street Journal* reported that several corporations are holding workshops just to get their directors and senior managers up to a minimal level of financial savvy. It appears that a great deal of work needs to done before board members will be ready to fill their role as spelled out by the new rules.

Next below the board level are the CEO and financial officers who will be guided by the tone set by the board of directors. Examples will be set by senior executives, not just by what they say but also by backing up their statements with actions. When governance is created based on execution, employees will follow the lead. We see too many companies comprised of people who tend to avoid reality. There is a human tendency to ignore problems and attempt to buy time, hoping that luck will improve the situation. Corporate culture starts at the top.

Legislation of culture change is perhaps the medicine that a greedy and arrogant corporate America needed to fix its problems. The National Association of Corporate Directors is holding regularly scheduled workshops and seminars that are geared to provide much needed training for board members. For some corporations, the transition to Sarbanes-Oxley will not represent a major challenge. However, for others the transition will not be so easy. When realism is injected into the fiber of decision making and measurement, then a framework for corporate governance and competitive advantage can be established. This is the responsibility of corporate boards and management as they attempt to improve the effectiveness of their culture. This can only be accomplished through effective execution. Corporate boards will need to begin asking the right questions of management, and this process will begin cascading throughout the organization as responsible actions begin to take hold. One of the steps is for board members to start getting into the trenches and asking questions. Many companies, such as General Electric and Home Depot, require their directors to visit operating units unaccompanied by management. This is likely to become a growing trend, together with increased education workshops for directors.

Responsibilities of leadership extend beyond doing a better job of financial reporting and accounting. Auditors will be required to exhibit higher levels of professionalism and judgment as the call comes for more credible and understandable financial information. The buck does not stop there as investors, creditors, and other users of financial information will need to accept the consequences associated with increased volatility that are associated with financial statements that reflect economic reality. It is critical to understand that reality results in effectiveness, which can translate into a competitive edge for those willing to shoulder responsibility and accept the challenge. The Sarbanes-Oxley Act had the objective to improve our system of financial reporting and this includes the questions surrounding the approach by which accounting standards are established. The PCAOB has addressed this matter.

PRINCIPLES-BASED ACCOUNTING STANDARDS

One of the directions taken by the FASB is the process to adopt a principles-based approach to U.S. accounting standards similar to the approach used in developing international accounting standards that are used in other developed countries. The International Accounting Standards Board (IASB) establishes the international standards. A proposal titled *Principles-Based Approach to U.S. Standard Setting*, dated January 3, 2003, was issued by the FASB. This proposal outlined the steps and challenges associated with making a principles-based transition. Sir David Tweedie, chairman of the IASB, testified to the U.S. Senate Committee on Banking and Urban Affairs that International Financial Reporting Standards are similar to U.S. GAAP. He commented that U.S. GAAP, however, "tends to be more specific and includes much more detailed implementation guidance." The international approach requires auditors and companies "to take a step back and consider whether the accounting suggested is consistent with the underlying principle." This approach requires the exercise of more professional judgment in the public interest and a strong commitment to resist client pressures. The process does not work without the commitment. This enables companies and auditors to move more responsively as a result of avoiding detailed rules.

The SEC submitted a study on the adoption of a principles-based accounting system that was prepared by the Office of the Chief Accountant and the Office of Economic Analysis. This was in response to the provisions of Section 108(d) of the Sarbanes-Oxley Act and indicated that standards should contain the following characteristics:

- They should be based on an improved and consistently applied framework.
- They should clearly state the accounting objective of the standard.
- They should provide sufficient detail and structure so that the standard can be operational, effective, and applied on a consistent basis.
- They should minimize exceptions from the standard.

- They should avoid the use of percentage tests, known as "bright-lines," that permit the engineering of technical compliance with the standard while evading the intent of the standard.

This principles-based approach is designed to head off Enron-type situations—use of special-interest entities and off-balance-sheet partnerships to inflate earnings—since both management and auditors would be held accountable for the substance of the transactions in the financial statements. This approach is expected to lead to more meaningful and informative financial reporting.

Among the benefits of a principles- or objective-based approach is more responsiveness to today's pace of business. Accounting standards should be capable of addressing emerging issues and provide real-time guidance. Adoption of this approach is expected to produce financial reporting that comes closer to reflecting economic reality. A trade-off is greater volatility in reported earnings. Robert T. Sprouse, a former FASB board member, made a case that "to the extent volatile economic events actually occur, the results should be reflected in the financial statements." If financial reports cannot reflect reality, how can they be expected to be effective? Companies and investors need to face the unvarnished truth, and providing simpler, more understandable financial reports in a more timely fashion cuts to the heart of the issue. The FASB and the IASB still have work to do to narrow the distance between the two standards, but with the advent of the PCAOB assuming the responsibilities of leadership to serve the public interest, we appear to be heading in the right direction.

One of the evolving issues is the distinction between big GAAP and little GAAP. This difference has emerged because of the complexity of new accounting pronouncements that developed from large company abuses by Enron, WorldCom, Tyco, and others. Pronouncements dealing with equity-based compensation, business combinations, and other complicated topics have been the target of criticism due to the complexity and expense of implementation for smaller companies. The FASB formed a Small Business Advisory Committee as a response to develop appropriate solutions that would mitigate the problem. The trend is toward a principles-based approach, and a major concern was the ability to understand the standards. It seems that the FASB is listening, and forming the committee represents taking a step forward. By taking time to allow for implementation and effective education, the FASB will accomplish a great deal. This is not just an issue for smaller companies; board directors and senior management need to understand the impact and meaning of accounting standards and financial statements. The simplicity of a principles approach grounded in a foundation of understanding represents a significant advance in progress.

RELEVANT MEASUREMENT

While much has been said regarding board independence and "tone at the top," a shift is rapidly occurring in the role of financial and accounting leadership. Principles-based accounting systems call for financial reports that capture the economic substance of transactions and events. Public interests in capital markets want greater assurance regarding future risks. Historical financial statements driven by accounting systems produce lagging indicators about what happened last quarter and last year but not much guidance about the future. Dynamic real-time reporting is now placing new demands on the financial function to contribute strategically and operationally to help optimize the strategic and operational elements of the business. This new challenge is not limited to corporate financial functions. External and internal auditors face greater pressures to exercise professional judgment in an objective-based environment. Strategic and operational measurement will utilize predictive measurements in an "on-demand" environment. These changes will make additional training mandatory as process management and strategic alignment and execution take the forefront. Together with these new requirements will be the issue of selecting and implementing relevant leading measurements that drive the business.

The role of the financial function will need to move past initial compliance and continuing compliance due to the strategic and operational complexities associated with the increased pace of business. Traditional silo management structures will lose their competitive advantage to more agile management teams that apply cross-functional concepts. This means that operational and sales personnel will need to have a better understanding of performance measurements, including the ability to respond to them. In order for key performance metrics (key performance indicators) to be effective, it is necessary to empower organizations to take the necessary action to identify root causes and solve problems. Effective use of dynamic real-time measurement tools will require understanding of the business so that the proper measurement systems and metrics are effectively utilized. This means that CFOs and controllers will need to become more knowledgeable about strategy, operations, and how financial systems should be aligned to create a bottom-line impact.

Competitive advantages from Sarbanes-Oxley result from the requirements for having reliable internal controls supporting financial reporting. Based on a solid foundation utilizing the available frameworks, financial functions will start

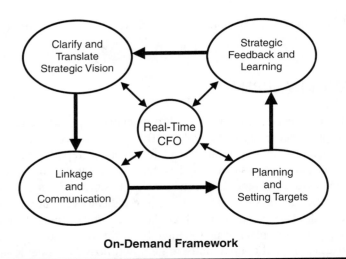

On-Demand Framework

Figure 3.1.   Real-time CFO.

taking a more active role in selecting and monitoring relevant measurements from a sound base that will consist of information technology and personnel trained to make the most effective use of these tools. This transformation will unfold over the next few years as businesses begin to better understand the compliance issues and organizations begin to apply the appropriate levels of training. Making better decisions faster will require financial people to move away from their traditional bean-counting role and get closer to the action on the front lines. The real-time CFO will emerge as a central component, as depicted in Figure 3.1. These concepts will be explored more thoroughly in Chapters 15 and 16.

Relevant metrics will emerge from the clarification and translation of the strategic vision. Process-based accounting and feedback systems will allow CFOs to effectively monitor the results of operations to determine if any Section 409 disclosures have occurred or if there is a risk of them occurring. Through the use of customer relations management systems that are integrated into the organization's business intelligence network, CFOs will be capable of tracking customer satisfaction and then linking this data to customer profitability metrics. Other nonfinancial leading indicators can be used in predictive ways to provide feedback on strategic targets. Key measurements of quality, employee satisfaction, supplier performance, and knowledge management will also be components of the system. Measurements will include feedback mechanisms on societal, governmental, environmental, and geopolitical issues. The PCAOB has clearly made the call for boards, management, and auditors to get in the game and get back to the basics.

SELF-ASSESSMENT

Management is required to assess the effectiveness of the company's internal control over financial reporting as of the end of the company's most recent fiscal year, including a statement identifying the framework used in the assessment. In addition to this assessment and disclosure, the company's external auditor, in conjunction with an audit of the company's financial statements, is required to issue an attestation report on management's assessment of internal controls. While this is an annual requirement, management is required to evaluate any change in the company's internal control that occurred during a fiscal quarter that has or could materially affect the company's internal control over financial reporting. This is in essence the requirement as directed by Section 404 of the Sarbanes-Oxley Act. Basically, if management and external accountants are going to set the tone, they better understand the control system in place to provide reliable financial reports and be sure that it is capable of getting the job done.

The requirements for Section 404 become effective for larger companies with a market capitalization greater than $75 million for fiscal years ending after November 15, 2004 and July 15, 2007 for smaller companies. Over 200 comment letters were received in response to the proposed release. The tone is being set as a new era of legislated ethics and accounting reform begins to take hold.

Since Section 404 relates to internal control, it is critical to understand what it means. Section 404 was meant to provide a focus on financial reporting. The SEC in its interpretation settled on the COSO Integrated Framework as satisfying its criteria as an evaluation framework for management's annual internal control evaluation and disclosure requirements. Having said that, it is important to review how the SEC's final rules define internal control over financial reporting. The final rules state that internal control is "a process designed by and implemented by, or under the supervision of, the company's principal executive and financial officers, and approved by the company's board of directors." In other words, management and the board of directors are clearly responsible for designing and maintaining the system of internal control. Internal control, as defined in the final rules, indicates that they should provide reasonable assurance regarding the reliability of financial reporting and the preparation of financial statements for external purposes in accordance with GAAP.

It was clearly intended in the final rules that internal control contain policies and procedures about maintaining records in reasonable detail and that would accurately reflect transactions. Internal control policies and procedures also need to provide reasonable assurance that transactions are recorded in accordance with GAAP and made based on authorization of management and the board of directors. Another requirement is the prevention of unauthorized acquisition, use, or disposition of assets that would have a material effect on the financial statements. The COSO Framework defined internal control as providing reasonable assurance regarding three categories:

1. Effectiveness and efficiency of operations
2. Reliability of financial reporting
3. Compliance with applicable laws and regulations

The definition contained in the SEC's final ruling does not encompass the elements of the COSO Report relating to the effectiveness and efficiency of operations and compliance with applicable laws and regulations except for preparation of financial statements under the SEC's requirements. However, it is apparent that internal controls that did not provide for the effectiveness and efficiency of operations could ultimately have an adverse impact on financial results and unreliability in financial reporting since the safeguarding of assets could be impaired.

Management is required to provide an internal control report based on its assessment of the effectiveness of internal control over financial reporting. This report is to cover the assessment "as of" the end of the company's fiscal year. The assessment must include disclosure over any "material weaknesses" in the company's internal controls. What the regulations make clear is that management teams and their boards of directors are bound by law not only to design reliable internal controls and implement them but to regularly assess their effectiveness. The compliance requirements extend well past assessment. The controls need to be documented, with solid evidence supporting them and management's assessments. This will represent a significant initial undertaking and then additional ongoing effort to stay in compliance. While these requirements may seem overwhelming and a waste of time, one does not have to go far to witness the billions of dollars that went down the drain because companies did not or would not do what they should have done from the beginning.

Some companies will not have difficulty with compliance. Others have a good deal of work ahead of them. A good portion of my career was spent auditing and conducting assessments of countless companies. Based on personal experience working with companies, frequently management has some idea of problems but no clue about where they are or how to deal with them. Frequently, employees close to the action could have told management the answer if the questions had been asked. Often, employees have not been properly trained to do their jobs or taught how to utilize the company's information systems. Now, by legislative decree, those in management are going to be forced to roll up their sleeves and find out what is really going on and then provide detailed documentation of their assessment.

Section 404 is going to require some new thinking about "tone at the top" and involvement in the controls and systems used to compile and report financial data. A glaring illustration is Goodyear Tire & Rubber Company. After an intense effort to reconcile certain general accounts, the company was advised that there were material weaknesses in internal controls that caused a cumulative decrease in net income totaling $89.2 million through June 30, 2003. Based on work done by PriceWaterhouseCoopers LLP, the company learned that material weakness in internal control spanning several years had occurred. The failure to properly monitor these procedures represented the root cause of the restatement adjustment. A significant portion of the adjustments arose from the integration of a new enterprise resource planning system (ERP) into the company's accounting system. Based on my experience, the Goodyear situation is not an isolated one and illustrates the need for regular recurring evaluation of internal controls.

AUDIT CHALLENGES

Auditors have new standards for conducting audits of public companies with the advent of Sarbanes-Oxley. Audits are no longer just on the fair presentation of financial statements in accordance with GAAP, but also must include the attestation of management's assessment of internal control (Figure 3.2). Auditors will have to significantly revise their approach to audits as they used to know them. The new audit standards, discussed in Chapter 14, will require utilization of more senior people due to the necessity of testing and understanding internal controls and transactions. It will also be necessary to make sure that controls are truly effective and not just because of outstanding employee effort to overcome weaknesses. Increased testing of transactions will be required by auditors in lieu of accepting the work of others. The PCAOB has made it clear that an audit approach of accepting that management is honest and therefore does a good job is no longer acceptable.

Training takes on new dimensions for auditors as they scramble to learn the new requirements. We have seen the transition toward principles-based accounting standards, requiring a shift in thinking and demanding higher levels of professionalism from auditors. Consistent with the movement back to auditing and away from providing services that are no longer permitted, auditors will need to learn more about operational concepts in an effort to effectively interview employees and understand the internal control systems they will be testing. Effective attestation of management's assessment of internal control will put auditors much closer to the action, and this will place an additional premium on business savvy and professionalism.

PURPOSE — COMMITMENT — CAPABILITY

- Setting Business Objectives
- Assessing Risks
- Adequacy of Internal Controls

Product Innovation

Employee Empowerment

Management Self-Assessment

- Facilitated Workshops
- Interviews
- Questionnaires
- Surveys

Knowledge Management

Strategic Execution

Customer Satisfaction

Business Performance Management

Figure 3.2. The new audit challenge: building competitive advantage with self-assessment.

One of the big changes introduced with Sarbanes-Oxley is that auditors are selected by and take direction from the audit committee. This move is to ensure greater independence from management. Not only does this change move to accomplish independence, but it also places responsibility on the auditor to evaluate the effectiveness of the audit committee. The tone of the audit, its challenges, and its responsibilities clearly have been given new significance by Sarbanes-Oxley and the PCAOB.

BOARDS CAN MAKE A DIFFERENCE

A new reality is facing corporate boards of directors as their roles have received increased scrutiny since July 2002. The new rules look to boards, and specifically audit committees, to help put new focus into audits and auditors. Audit committees need to be comprised of independent members, and this is creating a churn at many companies as they move toward compliance. Further, at least one member of the audit committee must be a "financial expert" because of new responsibilities for selecting auditors and guiding the audit. The movement is spreading to the composition of nonaudit committees of boards as shareholders are making their voices heard by requesting more independent board members.

Internal audit functions also receive their direction from the audit committee. This responsibility includes selecting and supervising the chief audit executive and monitoring internal audit projects. Beyond the linkage of the external and internal audit activities, the committee must also coordinate with the financial management function. This is a big step beyond attending regularly scheduled board and committee meetings. It is little wonder that the oversight board insisted that at least one audit committee member be a financial expert. The issues and complexities of the audit committee and the audit are discussed in Chapter 14.

Much of the focus of the new rules and the oversight board was directed at the audit committee. Another objective concentrated on the overall intent of setting "tone at the top" for both the board of directors and top management. By strengthening boards of directors through tighter rules and requiring greater independence, the oversight board meant to create more ethics and responsibility that would better serve the public interest. These changes have created some concern over liability issues at the board level, but after witnessing the breakdown and failures in recent years, perhaps some stress is a step in the right direction. Boards of directors, like management, are going to be forced to get closer to the action. Board meetings will end up being more than just a "show-and-tell" rubber stamp of management decisions. Boards will now need to become more knowledgeable about the business and the managers who run it. Balancing a fine line of letting management run the business will require careful effort and thought, but the end result will produce a better "tone at the top."

We have seen several examples where management has broken or stretched the rules to achieve objectives. Prior to Sarbanes-Oxley, those in management frequently got away with such actions because there were not many good tools for boards of directors to reel them back into the boat. A good illustration of how the system is supposed to work is the story of controller Daniel Thobe of DPL, Inc. When he came on board as a newly hired controller, Thobe had concerns regarding internal control and corporate governance whereby people in the trenches were given the message not to ask questions. Thobe took his concerns to the chairman of DPL's audit committee, W. August Hillenbrand, under the provisions of the new Sarbanes-Oxley rules. An independent inquiry resulted, and while there was no evidence of any material inaccuracies in the financial statements, the report supported the most serious concerns reported by

Thobe in his allegations. The board chairman, the CEO, and the CFO resigned prior to the board meeting when the report was presented. Daniel Thobe went back to his controller job, something that would not have happened prior to Sarbanes-Oxley. The system does work, but it takes an employee with courage to step forward and an independent director who takes governance and leadership to heart.

Improved "tone at the top" is what the architects of Sarbanes-Oxley had in mind when responding to the 10-point presidential plan. The oversight board kept all these objectives in mind when setting the final rules. It seems that management and boards of directors of most companies recognize that the new rules represent an approach that makes good sense and best business practice. "Tone at the top" means demonstrating tone through actions and doing the right thing in defining moments rather that just talking about what to do and what should be done.

RELEVANCE OF RISK

Risk has real relevance in a business environment, especially when the pace of change is continuous acceleration. Corporate leadership and boards of directors are facing new challenges as they design and evaluate internal controls under the new Section 404 rules. These rules require the use of an appropriate control framework when designing and evaluating internal controls. The Securities and Exchange Commission (SEC) and the oversight board have clearly stated that the COSO Integrated Framework meets their criteria. The Committee of Sponsoring Organizations of the Treadway Commission issued its report in 1992. The committee created a follow-up study in 2001 called the Enterprise Risk Management (ERM) Framework and released it in draft form on July 15, 2003 and the final version in September 2004. A basic understanding of the two frameworks is important, together with insight into how the tools can have impact extending past Sarbanes-Oxley compliance.

The ERM Framework pushes past the original COSO Framework, which has become the model for a strong system of internal control. ERM provides a model for evaluating an organization's risk management activities. Strategic formulation is added to the three business objectives of operational effectiveness, reliable financial reporting, and compliance with laws and regulations. The intent was to provide a framework that would enhance governance judgment with the flexibility of a principles-based approach to evaluating and responding to business risk. The oversight board did not specifically require operational effectiveness or mention the ERM Framework in its final rules. However, these concepts offer organizations best practice insight that will aid and enhance the Sarbanes-Oxley efforts of management to achieve a competitive advantage from compliance initiatives.

RELIABLE RISK

Risk is a reality; the goal for all organizations is to more effectively manage it. ERM is a process that is comparable to internal control since it involves people. Internal controls operate to provide reasonable assurance regarding the achievement of objectives. ERM helps to determine the level of risk an organization can or wants to accept in pursuing the objective of creating increased shareholder value. The COSO Integrated Framework is contained within the ERM Framework that addresses the process of identifying and analyzing risk on a company-wide basis. The framework considers the strategic implications of risk together with operational, financial, and other components of the business environment. Because of management's requirement to assess and evaluate the effectiveness of internal control, management is now provided with tools that can bring a strategic focus to the process. This brings more cross-functional involvement, which helps to break down the functional silos that inhibit organizational effectiveness.

The ERM approach strives to align a company's appetite for risk with its strategy. Involvement of the entire organization, from top to bottom, is required to link growth objectives and return with the associated risk of achieving organization-wide goals. Section 404 assessments provide an excellent opportunity to bring the entire organization closer to the action in an effort to make risk decisions more reliable. Overall communication can be enhanced, allowing companies to respond operationally to minimize downside risk and improve the chances for successful execution of strategies.

Since the audit committee of the board now has a greater role in risk management, it makes sense to utilize the internal audit function in a risk evaluation monitoring role. Since the internal audit function reports to the audit committee, linkage of the audit function with other components of the organization can be achieved. In a 2002 study, the Institute of Internal Auditors learned that a large number of boards of directors were not even aware if their organizations had a risk management program. The framework approach combined with the Sarbanes-Oxley Act now puts boards in a position to understand the effectiveness of how management teams are managing risk. Alignment of the audit and internal audit functions combined with effective governance from the board, especially independent boards, should begin to start showing a significant improvement in the effectiveness of risk management.

Achieving a level of reliable risk needs to be a function of an integrated management process that encompasses an internal control structure designed and maintained under the core COSO Framework enhanced by application of the ERM Framework. The process of board oversight and management assessment represents a unique opportunity to involve all levels of the organization in a strategic-focused risk evaluation and execution process. Before exploring the components of the two frameworks, it is important to realize that strategy and risk go hand in hand. The Sarbanes-Oxley response to failure of Enron and other scandals will push corporate management and directors into details that have not been properly addressed in the past. Too many executives have talked the talk but not made the walk and fail to realize that the devil is in the details. Better alignment of strategy and risk combined with effective execution utilizing reliable control systems will improve the competitive capacity of corporations in our global business landscape.

The need for a framework to assist management and boards to evaluate and measure risk is partially driven by problems evolving from the accounting and corporate scandals. Another driver is the increasing complexity and pace of global business combined with the extended enterprise. Risk is no longer something that can be monitored in isolation without considering the broad scope of the entire organization and the environment in which it operates. Clearly, a model and an approach for corporations to identify and manage risk across the enterprise from a portfolio perspective are needed to help guide corporate boards and management. The ERM model combines the three objectives of the Integrated Framework used for internal control with a strategic focus. Accordingly, enterprises are in a position to better cope with uncertainties of their environments and make better decisions linked with integrity-driven value. Risks are inevitable. However, more reliable and effective decisions can be made when companies utilize enablers that help to navigate the unknown and mitigate the dangers.

COSO FRAMEWORK

The COSO Framework was developed by the Committee of Sponsoring Organizations of the Treadway Commission, otherwise known as COSO. The commission was formed in 1985 to sponsor a national commission on fraudulent financial reporting and was named after James C. Treadway, a former chairman of the SEC. The sponsoring organizations were the five independent financial professional associations in the United States:

- American Institute of Certified Public Accountants
- American Accounting Association
- Institute of Internal Auditors
- Institute of Management Accountants
- Financial Executives Institute

Representatives included independent advisors from industry, public accounting firms, education, and investment firms. The purpose of the commission was to improve financial reporting, internal controls, and corporate governance.

The commission issued the Integrated Framework in 1992; it provided a model for internal control and how it can be used by organizations to improve and maintain profitability by providing management with a set of standards for assessing and improving its control standards. Since the COSO Integrated Framework was designated as acceptable for companies to use in assessing their internal control under Section 404 of the Sarbanes-Oxley Act, it is very important to understand the framework. In addition to providing the foundation for reliable financial reporting and compliance, the internal control framework enables the promotion of efficiency and management of risk. We have noted a considerable number of instances where poor internal control or circumventing controls created serious financial losses that could have been avoided.

The key components of the framework will be discussed in specific chapters throughout the book. The COSO Framework consists of the following three objectives:

1. Effectiveness and efficiency of operations
2. Reliability of financial reporting
3. Compliance with applicable laws and regulations

Internal control is a process that is driven and created by people. The framework was developed to provide a standard of best practices that businesses and organizations could follow to provide reasonable assurance of achieving their objectives.

The Integrated Framework also included five components that are integrated with management's process for running the business. These five components central to management's assessment of internal control required by Section 404 are:

- Control Environment: People and their attributes, including culture
- Risk Assessment: Awareness and evaluation of risk
- Control Activities: Control policies and procedures
- Information and Communication: Capturing and exchanging information
- Monitoring: Monitoring the process

The three objectives and the five components are all interrelated, and how a company manages them will determine success in achievement of the objectives. Figure 4.1 shows the interaction and relationship of the objectives and components. It is important to note that only reasonable assurance can be

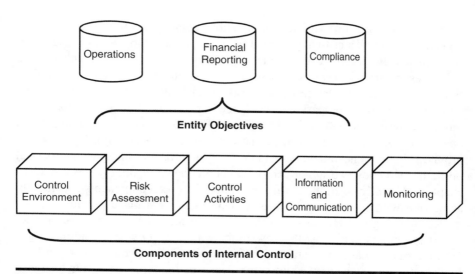

Figure 4.1.   COSO Framework.

expected from internal control. Also, when focusing on reliable financial reporting, the data can relate to nonfinancial as well as financial data. This information will be gathered from both internal and external sources to determine if an organization is producing reliable financial statements and complying with laws and regulations. The core components of the Integrated Framework will also be a critical part of the ERM Framework.

ERM FRAMEWORK

Evolution of the extended corporate enterprise entering the 21st century provides expanded challenges for management and boards. In a risk-prone environment that includes spreading global competition and geopolitical threats, a reliable model for managing risks is badly needed. COSO, in recognition of the void, formed a new task group that produced the ERM Framework in draft format and distributed it for comment in July 2003. The final version is now available. The new structure builds on the Integrated Framework that guides Section 404 internal control compliance and goes beyond by offering a "best practices" model for identifying and analyzing enterprise risk.

Again, the ERM Framework must be integrated into an organization, in contrast to attaching a component that identifies and manages risk in a vacuum. The model developed by COSO includes four objectives and eight components, using the original framework as a foundation. Strategy has been included as an objective, which is a critically needed focus for most companies. The eight key components are internal environment, objective setting, event identification, risk assessment, risk response, control activities, information and communication, and monitoring. These components again build on the original internal control model to encompass the challenges of linking strategy and risk to an internal control foundation that will foster effective execution of strategic and operational activities. The ERM Framework model is depicted in Figure 4.2 to provide a better conceptual understanding of the process. Since we are focused on Sarbanes-Oxley, we will touch on the components separately in subsequent chapters. The discussion here will be limited to those components specifically associated with risk management and business process management.

Recognizing the state of board awareness, or lack of it, regarding corporate risk management activities, the new framework will provide a common basis for understanding and evaluation. COSO's objective as stated by Chairman John J. Flaherty, retired general auditor for PepsiCo, Inc., was to "offer boards a commonly accepted model for discussing and evaluating an organization's risk management efforts." Companies can use the model to design and create an

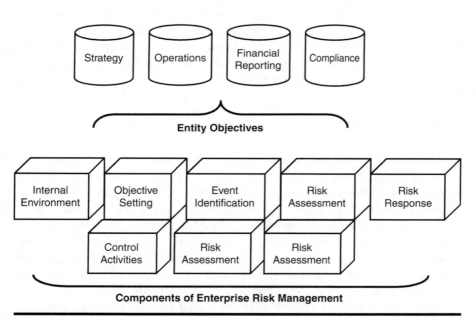

Figure 4.2. ERM Framework.

effective system of internal control and utilize the structure to identify, measure, prioritize, and respond to risk. What is likely to evolve is the creation of integrated models that corporations will use to coordinate governance, strategic risk management, and compliance with laws and regulations. Such approaches will involve business process management concepts that will include performance measurement and value creation through the utilization of business intelligence and real-time reporting. This will follow the COSO model and Public Company Accounting Oversight Board's emphasis on "tone at the top" that requires effective communication and execution of strategy and operational initiatives on an organization-wide basis.

Defining risk includes the chance or opportunity for loss as well as future possibilities for profit. Clearly, these offsetting factors need to be balanced so that the pendulum does not become predominantly one-sided. Because of the complexity of extended enterprises, the risk evaluation process needs to encompass not only senior leadership and the board, but also unit managers and others who can provide information and measurement across the entity. The ERM Framework takes the view that risk needs to consider the possibility that an event will occur and adversely impact the achievement of objectives. This allows for management to consider potentially negative outcomes and their impact.

The framework defines ERM as a process that is created by an organization's board of directors and management in a strategy setting and applied across the enterprise. ERM is designed to identify potential events that might affect the firm and to manage risks within the company's risk appetite and provide reasonable assurance regarding the achievement of entity objectives. The critical concepts of ERM spelled out by COSO are as follows:

- It is a process
- It is effected by people
- It is applied in strategy setting
- It is applied across the enterprise
- It is designed to identify events and manage risk within its appetite
- It provides reasonable assurance to management
- It is geared to the achievement of entity objectives

The linkage of strategy with identification of risks and managing them for the purpose of achieving objectives is where the Integrated Framework stops and the ERM Framework takes hold. In this context, let's move forward to clarify the unique add-ons that will help to guide corporations in the creation of risk management in a new age of governance and compliance.

STRATEGIC AND OTHER OBJECTIVES

For risk management to be effective, an entity needs to have a vision of its direction and intent. This is frequently called mission or the purpose of the organization. It is management's job to articulate and craft the vision, together with oversight from the board of directors. From this foundation, strategic objectives are formulated and strategic actions are initiated operationally to create shareholder value. This becomes the strategy-setting process that cascades throughout the enterprise. Figure 4.3 portrays the concept of strategic foundation. Creating a strategic foundation that is articulated and understood across the company and which is effectively linked and aligned with the core business processes represents one of today's greatest challenges facing corporations. This is a dynamic process that requires corporations to assess enterprise-wide risks in achieving and executing their strategies. Embedded within the strategic vision are the governance values of the organization that will help drive risk assessment and build a more effective management process.

Linked to the strategic objectives of the organization are its operational objectives relative to enterprise activities, which are critical to success. Operational objectives enable the identification of the factors that drive success. These are called critical success factors and represent the things that must happen in

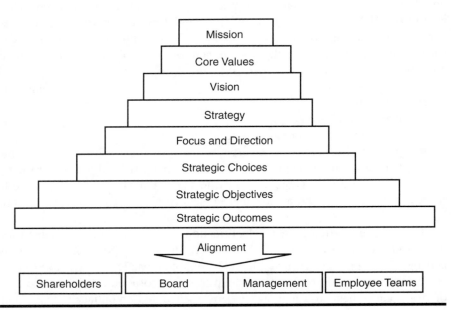

Figure 4.3.   Strategic foundation.

order for the organization to achieve its goals at all levels of the entity. The critical success factors not only will be used to identify and manage risks, but will largely determine the key performance metrics used to monitor results. These performance metrics will be both financial and nonfinancial.

From the development of strategic objectives, entities will formulate the other three objectives of the ERM Framework that include operational effectiveness, reliable financial reporting, and compliance with laws and regulations. The COSO frameworks provide management and boards with a model and foundation that guide the risk identification and management process. Linkage of strategy and operational objectives is frequently a step that is ignored or minimized due to a failure of understanding and training at all levels of the enterprise. The framework will help to provide clarity on how to do a better job of pulling together the range of enterprise objectives.

Operational objectives will vary from company to company because of the many variables that play into their development depending on the type of business and industry environment. Some of the considerations will include competition, customer-related concerns, quality, technology, product development, knowledge management, and a host of other factors. One of the operational issues will be how efficient the entity is at executing its efforts and directing its resources. While operational effectiveness was not spelled out by the SEC in its final rules, failure to achieve operational effectiveness can result in financial impairment of assets through inappropriate direction of resources and management of risk. Operational objectives will drive the entity's selection of performance measurements that becomes a focal point in effectively directing and applying resources. Internal control design and execution will also impact the effectiveness of operations and the establishment of critical success factors.

Achieving strategic and operational objectives requires a foundation of internal controls to provide management with reliable financial reporting. Reliable financial reporting extends beyond external financial statements and disclosures. Examples of internal financial reports might include daily real-time flash reports of sales and productivity. My book *Dynamics of Profit-Focused Accounting* provides examples of internal financial reports, including templates and financial and nonfinancial measurements that provide direction and insight to a full range of options for establishing reporting objectives. The new Sarbanes-Oxley rules demand accuracy in external reporting and disclosures that hinge on sound internal reporting, which enables reasonable assurance to management and board understanding on an ongoing basis. Supportive reporting objectives combined with the internal control infrastructure make strategic and operational objective setting and monitoring more effective when properly designed and executed.

The fourth ERM Framework objective is compliance with relevant laws and regulations. Today's business environment is complex, requiring entities to be cognizant of a wide range of issues. In addition to SEC rules and regulations, there are accounting principles and taxes, as well as environmental and employee welfare regulations that must be considered. In the global competitive arena, it is important to consider international trade regulations. Packaging and labeling must be in compliance, as infractions here can cause irreparable damage to a company's name and image in the market and in the eyes of the investing public.

There are many areas where the four objectives can and will merge and overlap. It is very important for management and boards to realize how the failure of achievement of objectives can lead to losses on the financial statements. Objective setting is a component of risk management that carries with it varying levels of significance depending on the objectives and the business. Aligned with objective setting is monitoring through reliable financial reporting using properly designed and operationally effective internal controls. The timely detection of trends associated with the use or disposition of assets allows entities to do a better job of managing the associated risks of strategic and operational objectives. This correlates directly to reporting and compliance risks leading to discussion of control environment and activities. By identifying four key objectives, the ERM Framework provides management and the board with a process for enabling alignment of enterprise-wide strategic missions with appropriate objectives that are consistent with the appetite for risk. Figure 4.4 presents the key elements for setting and establishing objectives. From this foundation, a balance between risk and return can be developed to create shareholder value and measure progress toward the attainment of the entity's objectives.

CONTROL ENVIRONMENT AND ACTIVITIES

Enterprise environment consists of a complexity of factors driven by company history and culture and the philosophies of management and the board of directors. An enterprise's historical tradition of integrity, ethical values, and management style shapes the "tone" of the organization, extending from top to bottom. Control environment is a component of the COSO Integrated Framework and internal environment in the ERM Framework. It shapes the development of strategies and objectives together with control activities and the identification and assessment of risk. How an enterprise operates depends on a variety of components including ethical and moral values, competence, personnel, assignment of responsibility, and the organization's style for making decisions. The ERM Framework builds on the COSO Integrated Framework by including risk management philosophy, risk appetite, risk culture, board of

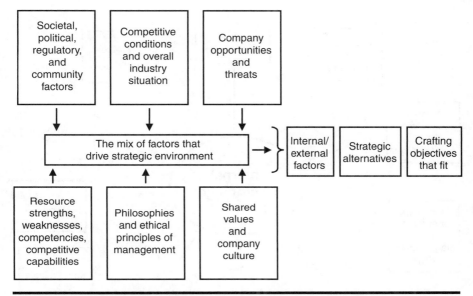

Figure 4.4. Key elements of setting objectives.

directors and management integrity, and other factors that are presented in Figure 4.5, which represents the 11 components of the internal environment.

Risk management philosophy represents how the organization's management and employees recognize and manage risk. The underlying driver of risk management is how management and organizational teams apply their knowledge, attitude, perceptions, and techniques to preserve and create value. Perception of shareholder value will vary from company to company, but the key is contained in the actions demonstrated on a consistent basis over time and under the pressure of day-to-day decision making. This demonstrated application of risk evaluation determines the risk culture of the entity based on attitudes, values, and practices. ERM deals with risk appetite, which is the level or amount of risk an entity is willing to assume in the pursuit of value creation. In many organizations, the culture for taking risks evolved on an ad hoc basis without any formalized framework. Now, a model is available to guide management teams to become more effective in identifying and coping with the realities of risks facing their organization.

The board of directors is a critical component of the internal environment of an organization and in the new age of Sarbanes-Oxley exercises greater impact on the "tone at the top" and risk management culture. Board independence from management will prompt more questions and involvement in both

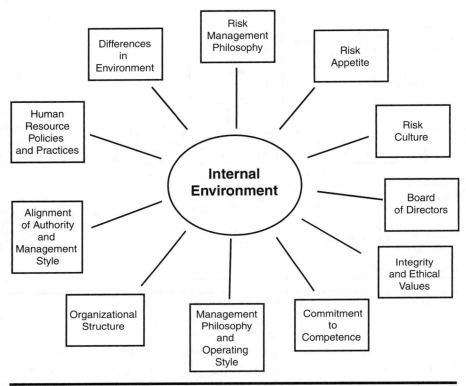

Figure 4.5.   Composition of internal environment.

strategic and operational objective setting. The oversight role of the board is strengthened with the new rules relative to vigilance for wrongdoing and in providing a check and balance on management. The ERM Framework now gives boards a model for understanding and evaluating the management of risk. This model represents a new and effective tool for governance. Board independence offers more opportunities for elevating the level of corporate ethics and moral behavior. Boards will not supplant management, but they can provide examples of behavior and management styles that have been missing from the culture of a great many corporations. This will help to inject more of an economic long-term vision in corporations, in contrast to the recent emphasis on short-term quarter-to-quarter profitability.

Competence and knowledge represent a competitive advantage, and this is one of the potential benefits from Sarbanes-Oxley. Codes of conduct are mandatory, and enterprise-wide training will be necessary for employees to fully comprehend and understand them. Beyond knowledge of the code, it is important for employees to see firsthand that the CEO and board have "done the right thing." Training the workforce to achieve higher levels of competence will start a trend that will enhance the capability of not only managers but employees at all levels of the organization. Empowerment of the workforce can mean surrendering control, with the associated elevation of risk. Elevating the level of employee competence will mitigate risks associated with expanded empowerment. Aligned with employee training is improved communication—particularly strategy and strategy execution—through utilization of balanced scorecards to elevate understanding and buy-in. Since structural change will occur, it is critical to utilize enabler tools along with the framework to accomplish a smoother transition to a more effective internal environment structure.

Control activities are actions of people to implement policies and procedures that represent management's response to risk. These actions occur throughout the organization and at all levels impacting processes and functions. Typically, management will strive to integrate control activities directly into the management process so that there is a smooth seamless flow of execution. The idea is to institute control activities that serve as mechanisms for managing achievement of objectives. Control activities can be grouped into categories as shown in Figure 4.6.

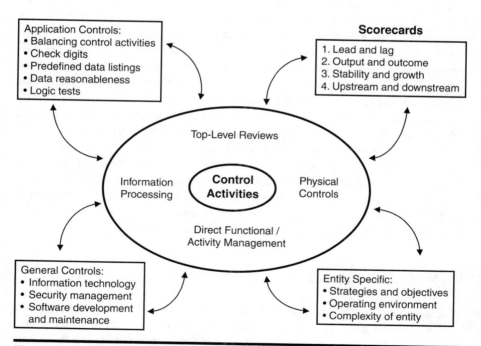

Figure 4.6.   Components of control activities.

Risk response provides attention on control activities that ensure appropriate and timely response in the pursuit of strategic and operational objectives. Control activities provide a mechanism for managing objective initiatives and are frequently embedded in the business processes. Companies will utilize a range of control activities throughout their business processes to accomplish a variety of tasks ranging from manual to management controls. Manual or human controls are called functional or activity management to perform compliance, reconciliations, analysis of trends, and other tasks to keep the organization on course. These activities include preventive, detective, manual, computer, and management controls. Transaction accuracy, completeness, and authorization are frequently accomplished through information processing. Control activities also employ physical controls to secure equipment, inventories, cash, and other assets and are reconciled with control records. Performance dashboards and indicators are utilized by management to analyze and monitor business trends and help trigger corrective action to keep the organization on course toward the achievement of the four categories of objectives.

Application and use of policies and procedures vary depending on the size and complexity of the organization. Policies and procedures are frequently written and documented in larger organizations and unwritten in smaller entities. While layers of management and infrastructure will vary, it is important to have a foundation of communication and understanding to ensure that the policies and procedures are consistently applied and provide effective control relative to organizational objectives. Controls over information systems will range from general controls to application controls. In other instances, these controls may be entity specific due to the unique complexity of an entity that impacts the nature and scope of its activities. General controls extend to information technology, infrastructure, security management, and software. Controls relating to software include acquisition and development together with requirements for maintenance. Software controls also include testing in addition to access to source code. These issues will be explored in greater depth in Chapters 8 and 9 as we dig into the complexities and challenges associated with governance of information security. The control environment and its activities drive to the heart of risk management because it sets the tone and provides the framework for evaluating and responding to risk across the enterprise.

IDENTIFYING EVENTS

Risk management centers around identifying the potential positive and negative events that can have an impact on the organization both from internal and external perspectives. It is important to realize that events can be offsetting and estimate the likelihood that an event will occur and to what degree of severity. From a platform of strategic vision extending to all four categories of objective setting, the risk management process then needs to include the critical internal and external factors that could potentially occur. Each organization should develop its own matrix of event categories to include internal and external factors. Internal factors should include consideration of the following:

- Infrastructure issues relating to facilities and equipment
- Personnel activities such as human error or fraud
- Process occurrences or events in both the productive and commercial areas
- Technology issues that could create either a positive or negative impact

Identifying external factors is also important to the risk management process. External factors can include:

- Economic and business events that impact the market or competitive landscape
- Natural environmental issues such as natural disasters such as floods, hurricanes, earthquakes, or similar events
- Geopolitical events such as changes in government, political agendas, and legislation
- Societal factors such as changing demographics, work/life priorities, and other trends
- Technological factors such as evolving capability that impact data or infrastructure costs

Once the internal and external factors are identified, it is possible for management and boards to consider the materiality and significance of an event or combination of events and the potential impact it might have on the company.

There are a number of different options relative to methodologies and techniques that can be employed to identify and evaluate potential risk-producing events. One of the obvious methods is to maintain detailed listings of potential events that are common to certain industries which can be drawn on by management to monitor various possibilities for occurrence. Another technique is internal analysis utilizing information obtained from customers, vendors, or intelligence input from personnel within the organization. These sources might be internal or external content experts utilizing both tacit and explicit sources of information. Members of the internal audit team are also frequently a source of information based on work they perform throughout the organization. Because of its independence and objectivity, the internal audit function represents a very effective filter for the evaluation of risks. Business process management offers a wide range of business intelligence that provides another effective source for identifying events. The performance measurement process also generates clues to potential events through the utilization of leading nonfinancial indicators that allow predictive forecasting.

A tool utilized by many internal audit teams is the control self-assessment, employing a combination of facilitated workshops, one-to-one interviews, and surveys which typically produce an overwhelming amount of critical data. These tools, when combined with process flow analysis, will allow the management team access to an even wider range of data. These tools are usually reserved for consultants in performing business process improvement and conducting operational assessments. I have used all of these techniques and recommend their use. Management teams can and should use these tools in conducting its assessment of internal control required by Section 404.

Managements and boards can utilize the ERM Framework together with these event identification tools and techniques to facilitate more effective management of risk and build competitive advantage. Figure 4.7 summarizes the structure of event identification. Once the events are identified, they can then be categorized and one can distinguish between risks and opportunities. From this platform, risk assessment can be launched with greater effectiveness and efficiency.

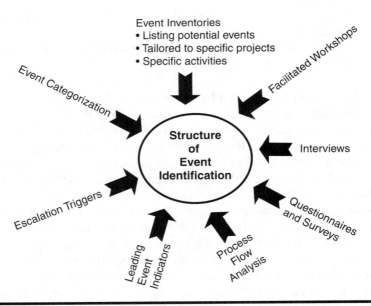

Figure 4.7.   Structure of event identification.

ASSESSING RISK

Risk assessment cannot start until potential events have been identified based on internal and external factors. These factors will vary between organizations based on their history and objective setting, and some factors will be common within an industry. The mix of relevant potential events will shift based on an entity's activities and will also be influenced by its size, complexity, and regulatory factors.

Management's risk assessment process must consider inherent and residual risks. Some risks are inherent regardless of any risk management activities that are taken by an entity. Risk management activities are those steps taken to alter either the likelihood of an event or minimize its impact. Residual risk is the remaining risk after preventive steps and action have been taken in response to the risk. Management's response to risk will be geared to minimize the impact that unexpected events will have on the execution of strategy and achievement of operational objectives. A component of the risk assessment process will be to provide for mitigating the unexpected occurrence that might have a material effect on the four objectives contained in the ERM Framework. After management develops responses to inherent risks, it then applies risk assessment techniques to the determination of residual risk. A model of risk assessment is presented in Figure 4.8.

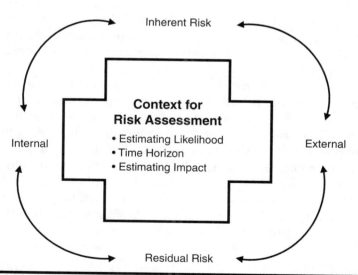

Figure 4.8.   Model of risk assessment.

Risk assessment looks at uncertainty in terms of potential impact and the chances of occurrence. Management's first step is to assess the likelihood that the event will occur and the varying degrees of likelihood. Management assessment approaches to quantify "likelihood" will vary but will ultimately boil down to exercising best judgment based on the best data and facts available. Another component of assessment is the degree of impact that could be created by an event. I find good examples close to home, having lived through 9 hurricanes in 10 years. Based on the severity of storms and their historical frequency, a variety and range of events produce reaction responses that are geared to an entity's strategic and operational situation. More than likely, contingency plans are put into place that allow the organization to effectively deal with events and the varying level of severity. The risk management process will utilize feedback from its business process management and measurement systems to gauge and plan for risk response. Issues such as customer service and response or interruption of production will be closely monitored and measured.

Development of reliable data based on historical patterns represents an effective tool for evaluating the likelihood of occurrence and providing preventive measures that will disable or minimize the impact of a material event. Other techniques include both analytic and qualitative methodologies and will depend on the sophistication and competency of an organization to apply them. Benchmarking using collaborative approaches can provide an abundance of information and data. Simulations and models that will yield critical information to support the risk assessment process can be developed and employed. These tools can be employed across the enterprise and directed to specific areas of potential concern relative to risk. It is a process of evaluating the relationship of risk likelihood and impact that management needs to consider and employ where appropriate.

Whatever methods and techniques are chosen to identify and assess events, they need to be used to reduce the impact an event can have on the entity's business. Businesses need to inventory all the possible events that could have either a positive or negative impact on their objectives, together with the potential for occurrence of a sequence of events. Consideration of organizational complexity is another factor, along with likelihood. What are the chances that an event or sequence of events could affect multiple business units? For example, changes in commodity prices such as oil would have an impact on a company utilizing petroleum-based products in its manufacturing process, in addition to transportation costs. There are wide ranges of risk possibilities and impact. Risk assessment needs to consider all of the interrelationships and their potential impact.

RESPONDING TO RISK

How an entity responds to risk can be grouped into four categories: avoidance, minimizing or reducing it, sharing it, and accepting the risk. By avoiding risks, management has to consider the costs of alternative responses relative to the benefit derived from the alternative actions that might be taken. Risk reduction can consist of any number of options that the management team will face in its decision-making process. This goes to the heart of a solid and reliable internal control system that provides the best and most accurate data available for making these critical decisions. It also underscores knowledge management and employee competence. Sharing risks represent other options and include insurance, hedging, and outsourcing. Accepting a risk is taking no action to minimize the potential impact of the occurrence of an event because the off-setting cost of other responses is not justified versus the cost of the event occurring.

Responding to risks requires evaluation of the four response options. This is a process that management needs to engage in to determine the impact from inherent risks and the potential responses that could produce a residual risk level that the entity can tolerate. The key is to determine how individual responses as well as combinations of responses will mitigate the level of the risk. Another component of the assessment analysis is consideration of not only the impact but also the likelihood of occurrence. The analysis should consider trends and past history together with scenarios of the best and worst cases for the future.

Risk management ultimately boils down to a cost versus benefits analysis that requires consideration of a wide range of factors. Usually, management teams start with cost, which is much easier to quantify than benefits. However, it depends on the risk being evaluated. The direct or variable costs can be fairly easy to compile, but when it comes to putting a figure on management time and effort, the clarity begins to blur. Activity-based analysis is one tool that is utilized to quantify costs. Also, it is difficult to put a hard number on market intelligence and customer data. New analytical tools such as business intelligence and customer relationship management have emerged, but they still fall short of producing definitive answers. The benefit side of the ledger will resist quantification, so qualitative judgments and calculated estimates tend to prevail. When considering opportunity costs, an effective tool is the weighted average cost of capital in evaluating alternative resources.

Responding to risks emanates from risk identification and the inclusion of positive as well as negative factors. The process of risk management offers unique challenges to those in management to develop responses that require pushing the limits of what they imagined to be possible. From cost-benefit analysis effort activities, management is required to consider not only individual risk responses but also combinations that can produce more tolerable levels of risk. The evaluation process is iterative and requires careful consideration of all the options to produce the best result. This leads to taking an enterprise-wide or portfolio view of risk and matching it with the organization's overall appetite for risk based on its strategic objectives. Evaluating risk from a portfolio basis can change management's response to individual risk after considering the possible assortment of responses. In those situations where an individual event occurs in isolation without correlation to other events, management might group that event together with other events to obtain a portfolio view when assessing potential impact and likelihood of occurrence on an overall basis.

EFFECTIVE BUSINESS PROCESSES

While the ERM Framework provides a blueprint for management and boards to follow, it does not offer a surefire solution to eliminating and mitigating risk. Aside from leadership and governance, one of the most important considerations is the reliability of the organization's business processes. Weak business processes represent a risk event that many companies fail to recognize, mainly because they lack the understanding of how significant a role they play in the accomplishment of objectives. The ERM Framework is built on the COSO Framework that serves as management's internal control model in complying with Section 404. Business processes and systems are a critical component of that model.

Effective and efficient business processes make the entire business more reliable. Many businesses have never mapped their business processes, and this is a key step to making them more effective and reliable. From a foundation of reliable predictive business processes, companies are better equipped to identify internal events that pose a risk. Also, effective and reliable processes enable risk response and facilitate cost-benefit analysis.

Entities are better equipped to manage external events and provide for more meaningful risk responses when they have effective business processes in place. One of the critical outputs of solid business systems is generation of reliable data, financial and nonfinancial, for risk management and decision making. Evaluation of possible risk responses is challenging enough, but is less so when management knows that it has created a solid foundation of business processes. Some risk responses will demand innovative solutions that are enabled by a continuous process of improvement and identification of root causes. Enhanced business process management required for real-time reporting and decision making starts with effective business processes. You have to walk before you can run. Business process management is a method to help maximize business value through improved communication, collaboration, control, and coordination while using the ERM Framework to minimize risk.

INTEGRATING RISK GOVERNANCE

With the emergence of a framework on ERM, it is incumbent on senior management and boards to overlay it with a vision and philosophy based on high ethical and moral standards. There is widespread disconnection of process management silos operating in many organizations, which inhibits effective risk management. These disconnections will not self-correct. Risk management is driven based on reliable processes and information, and this needs to be a focus for governance based on actions and not just words.

Governance is a critical component of ERM since it is the cornerstone of value creation. Value is created by management decisions and board oversight. If these activities are not grounded based on the highest standards of governance, then value can quickly be eroded or fall short of shareholder expectations. Governance at the top of the organization is what drives the creation of strategic objectives and their implementation. This means that communication needs to be effective from the top down, bottom up, and across the enterprise. Effective integration of ERM will fail if appropriate risk culture is not nurtured throughout the organization and supported by deeds and not just words.

5

A DYNAMIC PROCESS

Internal control is the system and process that companies utilize to manage and run their operations and generate financial reports for internal and external purposes. People are an integral component in the design and operation of the control system that functions to manage and minimize risk, provide for effective and efficient operations, and ensure compliance with laws and regulations. Section 404 of the Sarbanes-Oxley Act focuses on internal control, and requires that management annually conduct an assessment of its controls as of the end of each fiscal year. The legislation put a spotlight on internal control, and the oversight board sanctioned the COSO Integrated Framework as being an acceptable framework for companies to follow in the design and evaluation of their control systems.

In Chapter 4, the COSO Enterprise Risk Management (ERM) Framework, which is the new enterprise risk management model that has been under study and recently released, was described. The discussion of the ERM Framework included only those objectives and components that dealt with managing and mitigating enterprise risk. The purpose in this chapter is to provide an overview of the original COSO Integrated Framework and set the stage for drilling into the components that relate to effective design and operation of internal control systems under the compliance legislation.

INTERNAL CONTROL DEFINED

Internal control is a people-driven process that consists of processes and sub-processes that contain tasks and activities which provide the foundation for enterprise-wide value creation and containment of risk. Supporting the process is an evolution of policies, procedures, and activities that serve to document and support the system. Internal control requires good judgment since it can be expected to provide only reasonable assurance and not absolute certainty of control and risk containment. This means that even excellent internal control systems cannot be relied on to eliminate poor decision making, human error, and circumvention of control processes, management override, and other unforeseeable events.

The COSO definition elaborates that internal control is a process designed to provide reasonable assurance of the achievement of the following three objectives:

- Effectiveness and efficiency of operations
- Reliability of financial reporting
- Compliance with applicable laws and regulations

Internal control goes beyond just a system of checks and balances; it is something that is embedded into the operations of the company and a component of its culture relative to how the business is managed. Because of the multiplicity of interpretations of what internal control is and what it does, it is critical to follow a framework, such as COSO, that provides consistency of understanding. The people-based process needs to be capable of responding quickly to evolving risks arising from internal factors, as well as to changes in the external environment in which the business operates. In a broad business sense, internal control needs to safeguard assets and prevent business losses, in addition to providing reliable internal and external financial reports and helping to ensure compliance with laws and regulations. The reality of internal control is that it boils down to people and how they work and communicate. Tools and technology will not supplant people, because they alone are responsible for creating and using reliable business processes.

PROCESS BASED

It is important to understand that internal control is process based. This means that the system of controls needs to be embedded into the infrastructure of the business. A common perception among business leaders and managers is that internal control is another burden to add cost without a corresponding benefit. Sarbanes-Oxley compliance is costly, but so were Enron, HealthSouth, Xerox, WorldCom, and the other occurrences of fraud and poor controls. A look at the definition of process will clarify what we are talking about.

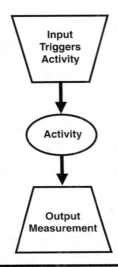

Figure 5.1.   Process inputs and outputs.

A process is an activity or group of activities requiring an input and adds value to it as it provides an output to either an internal or external customer. Figure 5.1 illustrates the input and output relationship. Processes utilize the entity's resources to provide results and add value. Processes consist of production processes and business processes, which are service related, that support the productive activity. The business processes utilize logically related tasks that consume resources of the entity to provide defined results in support of the entity-wide objectives. It does not take much imagination to conceive that there will be hundreds of processes in operation within a complex organization that need to be controlled. Interestingly, most businesses are organized vertically, while the flow of most processes is horizontal, as illustrated in Figure 5.2. Process control and improving the effectiveness of how processes operate offer the potential of billions of dollars in savings, in addition to providing reasonable assurance of the accomplishment of the entity's objectives and management of risk. Effective process control lies at the heart of enabling an organization to compete and also prevents errors from occurring and provides a solid basis for the business measurement system. Processes left unregulated without a framework for control will change for the convenience of the people operating the processes rather than for the focused achievement of enterprise-wide objectives. The practice of building the internal control processes into the infrastructure of the entity allows organizations to be more responsive in meeting competitive threats and enhancing both quality and profitability.

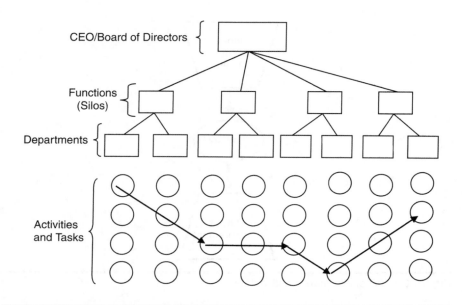

Figure 5.2. Process flow.

PEOPLE DRIVEN

Processes are used by people to achieve their objectives and control results. Organizations are created by people and structured into functions and departments that drive production and services, supported by the underlying infrastructure, to fulfill the vision of the organizers. Figure 5.3 provides an illustration of how these pieces fit together. Internal control provides the processes needed to monitor, measure, and control the production and business that represent the existence and purpose of the organization. The COSO Integrated Framework states that "internal control is affected by the board of directors, management, and other personnel." Internal control inherently takes its own direction if processes are not monitored and controlled. This is a critical factor to understand when evaluating and assessing the effectiveness of internal control.

Everything an organization does is created by processes, and its economic survival relies on effective processes. For an organization to build value for shareholders, it is imperative for its people to focus on the processes that will create this value. A near-term profit focus without consideration of process building supported by knowledgeable and ethical people will ultimately risk failure. Building effective processes requires change based on a considerable

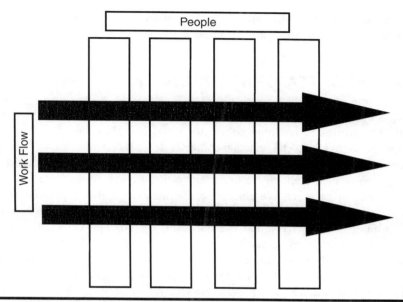

Figure 5.3. A people-driven framework.

amount of enterprise-wide effort and, most of all, clear and steady leadership from top to bottom. The reputation of a company is built on what people do and say. People who comprise the enterprise build the objectives for the firm and put control mechanisms in place.

Dependency on people and the processes they utilize requires a mechanism to help keep activities and actions on track. This framework provides the enterprise-wide guidance for responsibilities, conduct, authority, and job performance. In other words, internal controls tell people what they can do, how to do it, and when it needs to be completed. This is not only a top-down process, but transcends across the organization and also feeds information back up to management and the board. Internal control allows processes to produce the right results, helps minimize resources, and enables the entity to adapt to changing conditions. When an effective system of internal control is in place, companies are able to more effectively manage and mitigate risks, which produces better business decisions.

The people aspect of internal control needs to include the board of directors in addition to management and other employees. Directors are responsible for more than just oversight. They provide input on management decisions and strategic direction, plus authorize certain transactions. Boards also enact policies that guide the decisions and set a tone throughout the entire entity. Therefore, the internal control that frames the processes used to achieve organization-wide objectives is process driven, created by people.

CONCEPT OF REASONABLE ASSURANCE

Today's business operates in an environment where the only certainty is uncertainty. Enterprises face global competition and a rapid pace of technological change and innovation. The financial collapses that have proliferated have brought about increased regulation and complexity. Combined with customer-driven markets that spawn competitive uncertainty, these issues underscore more than ever the need for responsive enterprise risk management and reliable internal controls that can provide a competitive difference for companies operating in today's environment. Given that internal controls are people driven and process based, it is important to realize that a system of controls will never be perfect. Controls will shift and change based on the many forces that impact their structure. Accordingly, the best we can expect from an internal control system is reasonable assurance of achieving an entity's objectives.

Reasonable assurance needs to be understood relative to assessing control effectiveness. Assessment of internal controls focuses on identifying significant control deficiencies and material weakness that could prevent failure to achieve an organization's objectives. A control deficiency occurs when the design or operation of a control fails to allow or alert management to prevent or detect misstatements or events on a timely basis. A deficiency exists when a control step is missing or is poorly designed, allowing the control to operate without detecting an event or missing an objective. A deficiency in operations occurs when a properly designed control fails to operate as intended or a person performing the control lacks the authority or skill to execute the control properly.

A significant deficiency occurs when a control deficiency or a combination of deficiencies puts the company into a situation where there is more than a remote likelihood that an objective will not be met or will create a misstatement of the financial statements. In order to understand what *more than a remote likelihood* is, the suggested guidance is Financial Accounting Standards Board Statement No. 5: Accounting for Contingencies. The standard defines *probable* as a future event or events that are likely to occur. *Reasonably possible* is defined as the chance of the future event or events occurring is more than remote but less than likely. *Remote* is defined as the chance of the future event or events occurring is slight. Using these guidelines produces a situation that is either reasonably possible or probable when the likelihood of an event is *more than remote*. A *material weakness* is a *significant deficiency*, or *combination of significant deficiencies,* that results in *more than* a remote likelihood that a material misstatement or event will *not be prevented or detected.*

Internal control will be expected to provide reasonable assurance that there is a remote likelihood that material misstatements will not be prevented or detected on a timely basis. This means that the controls will not provide absolute assurance, but still provide a very high level of assurance. The Sarbanes-Oxley Act and the Securities and Exchange Commission (SEC) have stated that management's assessment of internal control under Section 404 should be based on and expressed at the level of *reasonable assurance.*

It is important to have an understanding of reasonable assurance because it is such a critical factor in the new focus of management assessment of internal control. This concept will need to be clear to management, boards, and auditors. The best assurance that can be attained is reasonable assurance, regardless of how the internal control system is designed and operated. Human judgment will never be perfect and failures are bound to occur. Recognizing this factor, it is important to make sure that the cost of a control does not exceed the benefits that will be derived from it. Reasonable assurance should be based on good business judgment.

FRAMEWORK COMPOSITION

Since the COSO Framework has been sanctioned by the SEC as being an acceptable internal control model, it will be described here to provide a foundation for compliance. Control environment is the base on which the framework is constructed. Since the control environment foundations set the tone and culture in which people conduct their activities and apply their control responsibilities, this represents a logical starting point for the framework. Risk assessment was described in the ERM Framework discussion in the last chapter and is the component whereby the organization evaluates and manages the variety of risks faced in pursuing objectives. Management initiatives and directives implemented to achieve the entity's activities include control policies and procedures and represent the next layer on top of risk assessment. This layer is called "control activities" and represents a component in both COSO frameworks. Surrounding the two layers of risk assessment and control activities is the infrastructure of information and communication necessary for the organization's personnel to conduct, manage, and control its operations. On top of the pyramid lies the component of how the processes are monitored and modified to adjust as needed to changes in the internal and external operating environment. These five components are:

1. Control environment
2. Risk assessment
3. Control activities
4. Information and communication
5. Monitoring

Figure 5.4 presents a visual illustration of the relationship of internal control components.

In addition to the five components of internal control, the framework consists of three objectives that are supported by the framework. Effective and efficient use of resources together with reliable internal and external financial statements plus compliance with laws and regulations are the three objectives supported by the five interrelated components. Corporate culture is driven by the control environment setting the "tone at the top" and providing the ethical and moral foundation for the people who are responsible for the internal control processes. An entity's control environment provides the discipline needed for a sound system of internal control. Also, the control environment sets the tone for how risk is managed relative to objectives. It will influence how events are identified, how risk is assessed and analyzed, and how the entity will likely respond to these risks.

Control activities represent the actions carried out in response to risk and for conducting business. Policies and procedures are instituted to govern how the activities are applied and may be either written or implied depending on the organization. The accounting system is an element of the information and

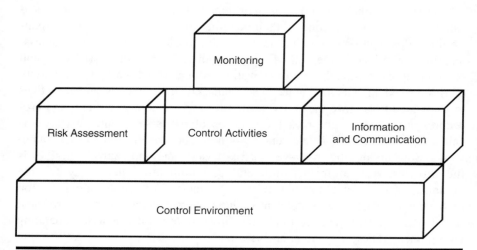

Figure 5.4. Components of internal control.

communication component. Also, the information technology which provides the structure for how information is captured and shared throughout the entity is crucial to business operations and management. The final COSO component deals with how the control process is monitored. Monitoring will determine how the entity responds and reacts to the flow and tone of the other four components. Evaluating the effectiveness of how the five components function and interrelate is the key to Section 404 compliance. It is also the means for applying the framework to accomplish continuous improvement and in maintaining the entity's competitive edge.

OVERSIGHT MODEL FOR COMPLIANCE

By specifying the COSO Framework as the guide or model for use in Section 404 compliance, the SEC modified the requirements and limited the objectives specifically to external financial reporting and compliance with laws and regulations. Those looking for a detailed step-by-step checklist approach to compliance on how to use the COSO Framework will be disappointed. The framework is not a cookie-cutter approach. It is a framework and a set of guidelines that will require judgment and application of principles in contrast to a specific set of rules. Information technology and software have been used by many companies to address the complexities of compliance. Since this text is being written after compliance efforts began and after issuance of the final regulations, we have the advantage of observing what has been done and suggesting what should be done. The COSO Framework is introduced here as a foundation for understanding, and we will drill into specifics in later chapters.

Let's go back to the 10-point presidential plan to understand the intent of the Sarbanes-Oxley legislation. There was a clear intention to create a tone of corporate governance whereby management is responsible for designing and maintaining a reliable system of internal control. The "Kenny-boy" (Kenneth Lay) syndrome of pleading ignorance to what went on and then blaming someone else (Andy Fastow) for all wrongdoing is not the scenario envisioned by the oversight board. Management and boards are expected to be engaged and provide governance, and "sleeping at the wheel" is not an intelligent alternative. While the COSO Framework was developed in 1992, it represents an extremely thoughtful approach to internal control for organizations, both large and small. It was not intended to be a rule-based information technology checklist, but rather a framework for managing risk. The oversight model omitted the objective relating to operational effectiveness, but included the balance of the framework as representing a sound platform for reliable financial reporting and compliance with laws and regulations. The Treadway Commission used the same foundation components developed 15 years ago for its updated ERM Framework and enhanced it with strategy and risk management components to provide management and boards with a model for competitive effectiveness in the 21st century.

FRAMEWORK LIMITATIONS

Some management teams and boards view internal control as "controls" rather than being responsible and "in control." This is a "bolt-on" versus a "built-in" approach. The CPA of a firm that provides "outsourced" internal audit and Section 404 compliance support stated in a discussion that "our clients just don't have time to monitor and provide input on internal control, so they have en-gaged us to provide this service." It is clear to me that the accounting profession continues to view audits and internal control through a set of eyeglasses that are not seeing the clear picture of a new way of business management and operations. New independence rules require internal audit functions to be in-dependent of management and responsible to the audit committee. Management cannot abrogate its responsibility to an internal audit function, let alone an outsourced function provided by a third-party consultant. Management and boards need to wake up and smell the coffee of reality. Perceived limitations of the COSO Framework may result because it is not a rules-based checklist that yields a yes or no approach to compliance. The oversight board along with COSO recognizes that internal control is an ever-changing process being driven and affected by people and is process based. The accounting profession together with management will need to develop a new understanding of business pro-cesses in addition to learning new auditing standards.

Reasonable assurance is not ironclad. This concept associated with internal controls as spelled out by the COSO Framework is hard for some to accept into their operating style. We have been explicit about the people-driven process foundation. This means that all employees must take internal control respon-sibility seriously and understand their individual roles. This implies a level of cross-functional involvement that many U.S. corporations have struggled to adopt. One does not have to go further than the Toyota Production System to comprehend the difficulty many companies have incurred with implementing its concepts. A few companies like Danaher and Dell have flourished and their bottom-line results speak for themselves. Other companies have been unsuc-cessful in adopting a continuous improvement approach, which helps to explain the emphasis they place on quarter-to-quarter results without building long-term shareholder value. One of the primary benefits from the legislated ethics of

Sarbanes-Oxley is continuous improvement and identification of root causes resulting from management self-assessment of internal control processes.

Another limitation of the framework is the lack of clarity associated with information technology relative to Section 404. Information security governance is also an issue that is all too frequently handed down from the boardroom to the CIO with no ownership at the top. A detailed discussion of the COBiT Framework is provided in Chapter 8, along with tips, techniques, and ideas for blending the COBiT concepts with the COSO Framework. Information technology is a tool which is an enabler to the people-driven process approach, which is the reality of the COSO Framework. Governance lies at the heart of the Sarbanes-Oxley Act. The control environment which is the foundation of the framework calls for "tone at the top" and demonstrated responsibility grounded in action and not words. We explore the legal obligation of CEOs and boards of directors to step up to the challenges of information security. In an age of information, handing off information security with the hope that it will be addressed is not an option. It is hard to believe that any internal control system would be complete without considering the full safeguards for securing information and a secure backup recovery plan that is in place in case of a disaster. The framework may not provide detailed instructions in these areas, but the tone of the message and discussions on integrating its components to secure objectives is clear both in the Integrated Framework and the ERM Framework.

EXTERNAL FINANCIAL REPORTING

External financial reporting under the Sarbanes-Oxley Act takes on new dimensions. No longer does financial reporting encompass just the annual and quarterly results; it now includes internal control and real-time reporting of events that can have a material effect on the business. The game has changed for management and directors, who will need to assess the design and effectiveness of internal control and report on their assessment. Auditors can no longer just issue an opinion on the numbers; they must attest to management's assessment of internal control. They must also be careful to maintain their independence by avoiding the prohibited services under the new legislation. As a result of the sweeping new changes, the COSO Framework needs to be understood because of the guidance it provides as businesses and auditors enter uncharted waters.

Included in *Internal Control—Integrated Framework* is an addendum dealing with reporting to external parties. The Treadway Commission report recommended that management should report on the effectiveness of the company's internal controls. This report stated that the investing public had a right to understand the extent of management's responsibilities for internal control in addition to how management discharged its responsibilities. While a great many large companies did include reports on some elements of internal control, it has now been legislated and documented in the SEC's final regulations. Section 404 compliance and reporting relative to internal control, including deficiencies and material weaknesses, will be explored in depth in later chapters. However, there are other legislated issues relating to ethics and real-time reporting that are touched on by the COSO Framework.

Ethics is the subject of Section 406 and requires the formal disclosure of the entity's code of conduct. The COSO Framework is emphatic that formal codes of conduct should be an important element of the control environment. Not only should the code be included in management's external disclosure, it must be an important consideration in management's self-assessment of the design and effectiveness of internal controls. The framework suggests that periodic meetings of management with employees and other efforts to communicate and set the tone would represent an element in an assessment that would reduce the risk of material errors or irregularities in the entity's financial statements. Also, the lack of integrity on the part of management could be considered to be a material weakness. The framework offers examples of how the lack of ethical behavior and integrity can be avoided and detected through the application of control environment activities and a strong code of conduct, which is demonstrated by management action versus just words.

Real-time reporting, required by Section 409, is an issue that will ultimately require the COSO Framework's guidance. Without a solid system of internal control processes in place, timely reporting is not going to be possible or reliable. Effective and efficient processes represent the key to providing the necessary communication and feedback monitoring tools that will enable companies to comply with Section 409. This new requirement provides companies with just four business days to issue 8-K reports for events and occurrences that have a material effect on financial results. A reporting and control infrastructure must be in place in order to monitor events across complex business environments. COSO provides the initial direction on how to build continuous effective processes that will be capable of achieving the needed level of risk management effectiveness. It must be a process-based reporting concept that utilizes the COSO fundamentals. It is important to realize that we need to walk before we run, so building on fundamentals is the place to start. This approach will create real-time reporting processes that are built in and not bolted on. Management and boards, and auditors, need to realize that silver bullet solutions and quick fixes will not get the job done. I believe the oversight board has provided good advice by suggesting that companies utilize the COSO model for reliable financial reporting and risk management.

6

DESIGN
EFFECTIVENESS

Internal control is a process designed by, or under the supervision of, an entity's principal executive and financial officers. The Securities and Exchange Commission (SEC) rules went beyond COSO by placing responsibility for internal control squarely on the certifying officers. Section 404 requires management to assess the effectiveness of internal controls, which management has responsibility for designing and maintaining. Now, more than ever, management will need to understand processes and how to document them.

Management's assessment must evaluate not only the design of internal control over financial reporting, but also its operating effectiveness. This goes beyond the common level of thinking about Section 404 that a team of people can gather with clipboards and check off the list of key processes and then proclaim that the company is in compliance. Management and boards will now have to get in the trenches and understand the processes that allow the company to operate. Those who immerse themselves in the details will benefit from planning that will build processes and prevent poor performance. The rewards can extend beyond just compliance and provide a foundation for creating a strong competitive advantage through continuous business process improvement. Extending beyond understanding the evaluation and improvement of processes, we will examine the opportunities for building an infrastructure of business process management and business intelligence.

DOCUMENT CONTROLS

Documentation of controls cannot occur until controls relevant to financial reporting and disclosure have been identified. This step entails assessing the process risks and determining what could go wrong and correspondingly matching up the controls in place that could mitigate any potential damage. The assessment and documentation step requires that all the processes be prioritized relative to the significance of the control and the level of risk of financial misstatement. This is a top-down approach to documenting and identifying processes associated with financial reporting and disclosure. Companies need to provide for mapping and documenting their business and operational processes. This is a step where the SEC requires external auditors to examine and document evidential matter relating to the design and testing of controls. The documentation should provide reasonable support for management's assessment. Management needs to realize that the documentation expected may be extensive.

Documentation should address all significant controls that are designed to prevent or detect significant financial misstatements. Minimum documentation should include financial statement accounts, classes of transactions, disclosures, all relevant financial statement assertions and each of the five COSO components of internal control. Documentation can be done manually or by using a computerized tool to help automate the approach. Some companies have used a combination of the two methods. Some of the tools being used are discussed in Chapter 8.

Identification of critical processes begins with determining the significant financial reporting processes and having management summarize the transaction flows by types of transactions and related systems. Identification of significant areas should include the following steps:

- Prioritize the financial reporting elements
- Identify individual accounts or groups of related accounts
- Assess the risk of material misstatement for individual accounts and on a combined basis
- Identify areas that have the greatest risk for material misstatement or untimely disclosure
- Obtain input from management
- Obtain input from the audit committee
- Validate the significant areas with the external auditor

Transaction types include revenue, purchasing, conversion, treasury, and financial reporting.

Greater benefit can be achieved from compliance by segmenting the organization into its critical business processes. Typically, complex business processes flow horizontally and include subprocesses which are called cross-functional business processes. Organizations can have hundreds of business processes and thousands of subprocesses. Ideally, a business has previously identified and documented those processes that will provide a starting point for documenting the critical processes affecting financial reporting. This documentation is based on identifying the significance of each process associated with financial reporting and where there is a higher risk or likelihood of a control weakness. These processes are then linked to the priority accounts or groups of accounts and disclosures and their relevance to financial reporting. Many companies do not have good documentation of their business processes. This will be an eye-opening experience for those who have not mapped or who have incomplete documentation. From this starting point, companies can move from compliance to business process improvement.

Some documentation considerations need to include the financial reporting requirements, entity-level controls, and relevant processes. This is done by assessing the "as is" or current state of controls and business processes and identifying those that are relevant. Another element of documentation is identifying all of the business units. In this regard, many complex organizations utilize shared services and systems for managing key functions, such as information technology, payroll, accounts payable, and other common services. Process documentation needs to start with high-level flow and then include interfunctional analysis together with procedural and process narratives for additional support for relevant critical areas. Control units will vary in different organizations and can be a business unit or a profit center, a division, subsidiary, or a common operational area that is autonomous in terms of setting business objectives. It is important to understand the extent of common processes and the degree of centralization versus decentralization in evaluating the internal control system.

Documentation will vary depending on the size and complexity of the company. Larger organizations will typically utilize written policy manuals, formal organization charts, written job descriptions, operating instructions, and information flowcharts. Smaller companies will have considerably less documentation. This does not mean that controls are not in place, but the informality of operations allows fewer layers of management and a better flow of communication. It is still necessary for documentation to support management's assessment and evaluation of internal control.

Many controls can be informal and undocumented, but this does not render them ineffective. However, some level of documentation should be done, as this makes the evaluation more efficient. It also facilitates understanding by employees relative to how the systems work and their individual role within the system. When system or control modifications are necessary, documentation makes the change easier. Under Section 404, documentation will need to be more substantive since assertions are being made to the investing public and others. Management will need to develop and retain documentation of the internal controls, which also needs to include the evaluation process.

Documentation methods include many tools, among which are checklists and questionnaires. Process mapping may be done using flowcharting with computer software such as Microsoft Visio or other similar products. Documentation may also include quantitative analysis and techniques together with internal and external benchmarking. Other considerations include utilization of management consultants or industry peer review functions. Nevertheless, it is always necessary to realize that differences will vary based on objectives, facts, and circumstances.

EVALUATE DESIGN

A key element of the new audit standard issued by the Public Company Accounting Oversight Board (PCAOB) is that internal controls must be designed properly so that appropriately qualified people can perform and operate the processes to provide reasonable assurance as to the fairness of the financial statements. This is known as design effectiveness. Auditors are required to make a decision on the effectiveness of the controls as originally designed. The purpose of this audit test is to ensure that the controls are functioning as designed. If personnel operating these controls are overcoming design weaknesses just to avoid deficiencies, then the control is not designed effectively. This reveals that there is a deficiency in the design of the control.

Auditors will be required to test and evaluate design effectiveness by interviewing company personnel, observing the controls in operation, and conducting walkthroughs of the business processes. This requirement places new demands and higher standards on both management and the auditors to make sure that the controls can provide reasonable assurance in preventing and detecting financial misstatements. A higher level of professional judgment is required from auditors in applying knowledge and experience relative to internal control over financial reporting.

Design effectiveness focuses on determining if a control is properly designed to prevent or detect material misstatements relative to specific financial statement assertions. These assertions deal with financial statement objectives that the control is expected to achieve based on the COSO Framework. When referring to the COSO Framework, it entails objectives that deal with each of the five components as they relate to reasonable assurance of fair financial reporting and compliance with laws and regulations. Simply stated, hundreds of processes and thousands of subprocesses need to be effectively designed with objectives in mind and aligning all the inputs and tasks throughout the entity and at all activity levels. The process documentation techniques will help with the design in order to achieve process effectiveness.

Design effectiveness needs to begin with organization by identifying processes and linking them with the COSO Framework objectives. This allows the entire organization from top to bottom to understand each process. From this platform, measurement and evaluation can occur for the purpose of documentation and assessing if the process is effectively designed. By creating a baseline for each process, it is then possible to develop plans to correct any deficiencies in design. Appropriate measurement and feedback mechanisms need to be installed, allowing for process monitoring that will set the stage for continuous improvement efforts to fill deficiency gaps and implement process enhancements as needed. Figure 6.1 illustrates the five levels of maintaining design effectiveness for all critical processes.

Documentation of design effectiveness is a critical step and must be done properly. Failure to include process flow maps could result in a failure for an independent accountant to issue an audit report. Process mapping can be at a high level and then drill down into a more detailed process-level flowchart. I like to begin at a high level to gain understanding to create a framework for building segmented detail maps. All critical processes should be mapped in detail. There is one additional level of process mapping that relates to cross-functional process flow. Most complex processes will flow horizontally across functional silos of responsibility. This is illustrated in Figure 6.2. The financial

Considerations for Evaluating Design Effectiveness

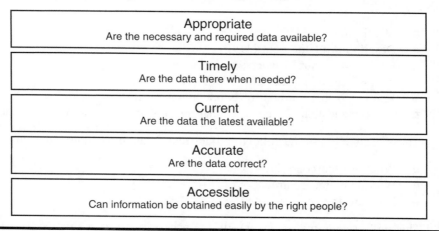

| **Appropriate** |
| Are the necessary and required data available? |

| **Timely** |
| Are the data there when needed? |

| **Current** |
| Are the data the latest available? |

| **Accurate** |
| Are the data correct? |

| **Accessible** |
| Can information be obtained easily by the right people? |

Figure 6.1. Five levels of design effectiveness.

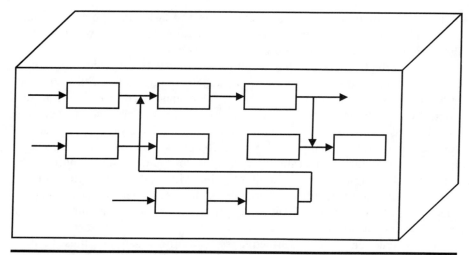

Figure 6.2.   Cross-functional process flow.

closing process falls into this category and should be mapped and documented. Cross-functional process analysis offers opportunities for cost reduction and eliminating nonvalue activities.

The SEC indicated in its final rules that "...a company must maintain evidential matter, including documentation, to provide reasonable support for management's assessment of the effectiveness of the company's internal control over financial reporting. Developing and maintaining such evidential matter is an inherent element of effective internal control." Documentation should include:

- Identifying specific risks
- Description of the controls
- Process or control ownership
- Assessment of the design effectiveness
- Validation that the control is operating effectively
- Recommendations for control enhancements or correction of deficiencies

These steps address the following questions relative to control design:

- What are the controls?
- Who owns the controls?
- How are the controls rated?

This will provide management with the necessary answers relative to risk, controls, and analysis of gaps. When combined with the various levels of process maps, it not only offers documentation but also provides a critical foundation for continuous improvement of the business processes.

Design effectiveness of processes and related controls and documentation should include the results of the following considerations:

- Assessment of entity-level controls
- Assessment of pervasive information technology controls
- Identified financial reporting risks and assertions
- Effectiveness of all five COSO Framework components
- Identification of the nature and types of errors that could occur and how the controls will mitigate the risks of those errors
- Defined state of control capability
- Impact of potential changes in the business on internal controls

Effective design of internal controls should be based on the operation of the controls by reasonably competent people. Controls that require overly qualified personnel to operate are not effectively designed and should be redesigned.

OPERATING EFFECTIVENESS

Operating effectiveness means that internal controls are functioning as designed for all significant accounts and disclosures in the financial statements. Both management and external auditors need to thoroughly understand the concept of operational effectiveness in conducting assessments and audits of internal control. Audit Standard No. 2 expects that management's assessment will be an extensive and detailed process to ensure that controls are designed to operate effectively and then verify their operating effectiveness with sufficient documentation and evidence. Auditors will not be allowed to just take management's word regarding these assertions. They are required to perform tests and obtain evidence that will support the operating effectiveness of the controls. Given its significance, operating effectiveness needs to have a high priority in Section 404 compliance.

Evaluation of internal controls by management must include demonstration that management has knowledge of the organization's underlying processes and that they are operating effectively. Documentation and design effectiveness, discussed earlier, go a long way toward management demonstration of knowledge. However, this is not going to be good enough. Management needs to get in the game and assess the effectiveness of how the controls are operating. After assessing control design and effectiveness, management needs to validate the operational effectiveness of controls to be sure they are functioning as designed. The assessment techniques indicated here will be elaborated on in Chapter 11.

Controls can be validated by having the process owners monitor and test them. Entity-level controls can be tested by management, operating unit management, or the internal audit function. Testing might be some combination of management and internal audit using a variety of control self-assessment techniques, interviews, and surveys. There are a variety of techniques and tools that include web-based and other software-related tools. Application of the assessment tool kit will be driven by the nature of controls in place and level of reliability. There are four types of controls:

1. System-based preventive controls
2. System-based detective controls
3. People-based preventive controls
4. People-based detective controls

Controls placed at the source of the risk are preventive; detective controls are downstream from the source of control within a process. System controls tend to be more reliable than people controls. This is especially true when they are designed and maintained for use in e-commerce environments and are applied and secured. System controls are better suited to high-velocity and high-transaction volumes. They are less prone to error than the find-it-and-fix approach utilized in detective controls. Properly designed controls prevent errors and omissions at the source and free up people for critical tasks.

The COSO Framework should be applied to all applications of process controls. The framework provides Evaluation Tools that offer suggested questions and checkpoints to help assess operational effectiveness for each of the five components. The tools can be applied for operational effectiveness, financial reporting, and compliance with laws and regulations. Figure 6.3 itemizes component steps for pervasive process controls, information process controls, operational process controls, and compliance process controls.

Audit Standard No. 2 will be discussed in Chapter 14; however, it is important to note the relevance of operating effectiveness in audit tests when applying the standard. Auditors must have a high level of competence and a high level of objectivity in performing their work. They will be required to perform their own independent tests and interview personnel operating the control to ensure that it is operating effectively and as designed. The tests need to include inspection of relevant documentation and reperformance of the application of the control as appropriate. These steps are in addition to attesting management's assessment of operating effectiveness.

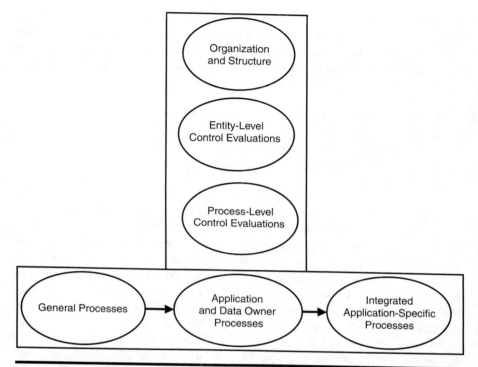

Figure 6.3.   Applying internal control at the process level.

COSO EVALUATION CRITERIA

Internal control is deemed to be effective when it provides reasonable assurance to management and the board of directors regarding the achievement of objectives. The three COSO objectives requiring reasonable assurance are:

1. The entity's operational objectives are being achieved
2. External financial statements are reliable
3. The entity is in compliance with laws and regulations

The determination as to the "effectiveness" of an internal control system results from an assessment that the five components are operative and functioning as they were designed. All five criteria need to be fulfilled; however, this does not mean that each of the components will function in the same fashion because of the trade-off that can and will exist between the components. Also, there will be differences between entities as to how and where the components will be applied. Risks will be different, so there will be variations in how components may be applied. The evaluation issues for the following management activities will be reviewed:

- Establishment of control environment factors
- Risk identification and analysis
- Conducting control activities
- Information identification, capture, and communication
- Monitoring

There are other management activities that occur but do not directly relate to internal control. These activities include strategic planning and establishing an entity-wide vision. The management process will also consist of setting activity-level objectives, risk management, and taking corrective actions as necessary and appropriate. Each COSO internal control component can have multiple factors that should be considered in evaluating effectiveness. A summary of typical factors for each component will be presented and in some instances will be discussed in greater depth later in the book.

Control environment will be explored in the next chapter; however, this discussion will be prefaced by quickly touching on some of the factors that should be considered in evaluating effectiveness. The "tone at the top" is built on the foundation of culture created within the control environment. Organizational integrity and ethical values can be correlated to the existence and implementation of a code of conduct. Effectiveness should consider the independence of the board and audit committee together with management's commitment to excellence as documented by job descriptions and maintenance of high levels of knowledge and skill necessary for effective execution.

Additional factors for evaluating entity-level effectiveness include management philosophy and operating style. These attitudes will translate into an effective organizational structure and how responsibilities are assigned. Another critical control environment factor is the extent to which human resources and policies are established and followed. These are only a few of the many control environment issues that drive effectiveness. Assessment of the control environment will require an extensive amount of professional judgment from both management and auditors. Testing the control environment is not a transaction-oriented process. Judgment comes into play when considering the variety of evaluation factors and determining if the entity is in fact talking the talk or walking the walk.

Evaluating effectiveness of the control environment needs to consider how management is assessing risk. This process should include, as a minimum, how management is establishing entity-wide objectives and their linkage to strategies, business plans, and budgets. Additional factors that need to be considered in the assessment are the linkage of activity-level objectives with entity-wide objectives. A component of the evaluation should include assessing how all levels of the management team participate in objective setting and their level of commitment. Additional thought should be given to activity-level objectives in light of their relevance to significant business processes and the adequacy of available resources.

Enterprise risk analysis should have a mechanism for identifying both internal and external sources of risk. A determination must be made relative to the likelihood of an event occurring and the range of response actions available to mitigate losses. Finally, an assessment by management and auditors has to consider the ability to cope with, react to, and manage changes that might impact entity- and activity-level activities and objectives.

Evaluation of control activities needs to consider the relationship to the risk assessment process and their appropriateness relative to achieving management's objectives. Management's assessment needs to determine if the control activities are relevant not only to the assessment of risk, but also to their proper application. From an internal control perspective, information deals with getting the right information to the right people in a timely fashion. Effectiveness of information requires properly designed systems that are linked to both strategy as well as entity-wide and activity-level objectives. Communication is important not only within the organization but even more so with customers, suppliers, and other external parties. The structure of information and communication evolves from strategic design and continues throughout the extended supply chain. Successful application of business process management and measurement applications together with business intelligence can have a huge impact on how companies cope with a real-time world.

STRATEGIC DESIGN

Success in today's real-time world requires effective execution of business strategy. Effective strategic execution is dependent on the optimization of processes and applications capable of supporting the entity's vision and mission. The ad hoc evolvement of business processes has hindered financial reporting and business intelligence needed to sustain a strategic and competitive advantage. Effective design of internal control is the key to supporting the speed necessary to achieve real-time reporting to gain competitive advantage. Organizations need to first develop appropriate strategies to establish the foundation for designing processes and systems. Strategy is also the basis for effective risk management.

Typically, there is no shortage of strategy. Breakdowns occur when strategic steps are implemented throughout the organization. Business process management is needed to ensure communication of the strategy to the levels of managers required to execute it. Management needs tools to monitor progress toward meeting goals and objectives, using the output from an effectively designed system capable of supporting the overall strategic direction. Once the strategic foundation is established, it is then possible to select and implement technology and software suitable for supporting the metrics and management tools required to monitor progress and make corrections needed to keep the organization on track.

Traditional concepts based on planning and budgeting cycles are no longer valid in a world of real-time reporting and continuous forecasting. Rolling forecasts combined with web-based planning solutions are now replacing the spreadsheet-based foundation that has been the norm. The key with these new approaches is to determine the performance measurement structure that best fits the organizational strategy. This entails assessing systems currently in place within the organization to determine the current state platform and measurements. This will provide a launching platform for developing a future state design to match the needs of the strategic direction and future of the company.

Elements of the business performance management system will need to consider all the sources of information and requirements for disseminating it. Figure 6.4 illustrates the composition of this foundational platform. This graphic shows the architectural relationship of enterprise resource planning systems with customer relations management and the extended supply chain. Understanding these basic components is critical in the strategic design of the processes and information flow. Governing the structure of this foundation will be the composition of the organizational structure.

ORGANIZATIONAL DESIGN

Once the strategic vision and direction of the organization have been established, the next logical step is to evaluate the organization and its needs. This, again, is a process of documenting how the organization is structured and evaluating its ability to optimize and execute the strategic vision and objectives of the company. Considerations must include people, processes, and technol-

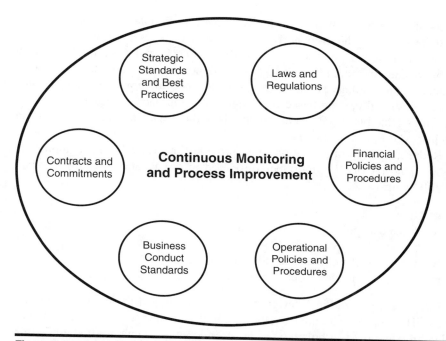

Figure 6.4. Strategic sources of information: real-time governance—risk architecture.

ogy. Customer requirements and the need for future innovation will influence and impact the design of the organization and its ability to compete.

Organization design represents a unique opportunity to make improvement and enhancement components of the compliance effort. This effort will, or should, include assessment of all existing systems and their adequacy for meeting the needs of the company's performance management. Many companies have systems that are either inadequate or poorly implemented, or both. Spreadsheet mentality still proliferates in many companies when the need for integrated business intelligence represents the real issue.

Many companies focus on technology and software, believing that they represent a silver-bullet solution for the future. This is a scenario that I have seen repeated all too many times. Management fails to really understand the challenge of training and proper installation of systems and software and fails to realize that people hold the key. Effective processes are conceived and developed by people, who then use technology and software as enabling tools.

Organizational design begins with management. Management needs to blend the strategic vision of the organization with a careful assessment of human assets and capability. Based on the assessment of people skills, consideration must be given to the competitive landscape and needs of customers. These factors must be evaluated to determine the organizational design that will best accommodate the strengths, weaknesses, opportunities, and threats prior to considering technology solutions. It is critical to decide how the organizational processes should operate based on design. This approach emphasizes the integration of effective processes based on where the organization needs to go and not just where it exists today.

Redesign of the organization must provide for oversight and compliance. Some of the factors that must be considered in organizational design include the following issues:

- Laws and regulations
- Financial policies and procedures
- Standards for conducting business
- Operational policies and procedures
- Strategic vision and best practices

Effective organizational design will build and embed these factors into the design. This approach assures that they are built into the organizational structure and culture and not just bolted on as an afterthought. Companies that apply this thinking to their Sarbanes-Oxley compliance will create a foundation for building integrated competitive advantage.

SUPPLY CHAIN IMPLICATIONS

Today's supply chains are complex. They extend beyond the enterprise to encompass a wider array of suppliers, partners, and customers. Process design needs to consider the multitude of complex relationships and logistic challenges facing the organization. This complexity is challenged by the speed of communication required to attain operational effectiveness.

Supply chain complexity is illustrated in Figure 6.5. We can see where manufacturers are subcontracting to a wider variety of partners and selling direct to customers. The flow is not linear, and the value chain must now consider an increasing number of points of focus that require information and communication. Technology enables and enhances these requirements and provides for new and better solutions. Although we now have a growing number of sophisticated solutions, it is important to remember that the processes supporting the infrastructure are still people driven and operated.

Supply chain strategies will require the tools and methodologies introduced in *Dynamics of Profit-Focused Accounting*, such as lean, Six Sigma, balanced

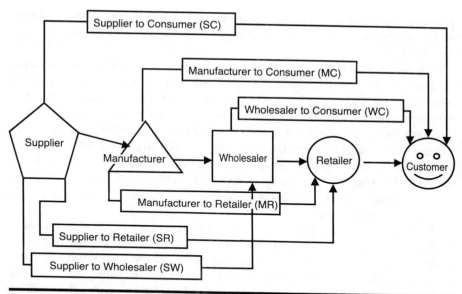

Figure 6.5.   Supply chain complexity.

scorecards, and activity-based management. Design effectiveness is dependent on understanding how to apply these tools combined with technological enablers. Connectivity is a critical component of the supply chain because of its increasing complexity. Solid process design and management are enhanced with Internet and intranet that are facilitated by e-mail and other electronic tools that will link suppliers, manufacturers, wholesale distributors, retailers, and customers on a real-time basis. A variety of tools and platforms not only drive the supply chain, but form the foundation for ensuring compliance and governance within integrated solutions.

ERP ADVANTAGE

ERP is an acronym for *enterprise resource planning* system. There are a number of solutions designed to fit different types of operational structures and industries. Essentially, these systems embody all of the accounting, planning, and control systems used by companies on an enterprise-wide basis to manage literally all facets and elements of the business. These systems are used to provide customer service, control over production planning and scheduling, and inventory management. The ERP concept evolved from material requirements planning and manufacturing resource planning systems. Many companies moved to implement new systems as the 20th century drew to a close as a response to Y2K fears.

All too frequently, management did not fully understand the complexities of ERP systems and the organization-wide effort required to effectively utilize these systems. Accordingly, many of these systems were—and continue to be—implemented without proper training and effective process management. The underlying databases, such as bills of material, inventory accuracy, and linkage to accounting systems, contained excessive errors and were supported with weak process controls. One of the glaring examples of poorly implemented ERP systems was the Goodyear Tire & Rubber Company situation, which required an $89.2 million restatement of financial reports due to a botched implementation.

Management frequently thought that implementing the latest and greatest ERP system was a quick plug-in and bolt-on that would solve all the company's problems. In fact, the opposite scenario frequently occurred. Now that Sarbanes-Oxley requires reliable financial reporting systems and controls, companies are facing new challenges to fix broken systems and implementations. The problem is that companies lost sight of the basic foundations that drive and provide the critical data needed for effective real-time reporting. Solid process design and financial controls are essential ingredients to creating a competitive advantage through the utilization of planning, scheduling, and operational controls. One of the best ways to improve the effectiveness of ERP systems is to provide training to the controllership function and other key functional teams on how to use their systems more effectively.

Competitive advantage from business process management or corporate performance management begins with a foundation of reliable data. When companies use reliable data developed from reliable processes, they are able to create the foundation for better management that translates into compliance and governance.

CRM TO SALES FORCE AUTOMATION

Customer relations or relationship management is called CRM. The processes for maintaining relationships with customers provide necessary feedback about needs and requirements. In an age when the customer has taken center stage like never before, the ability to transfer customer preferences and intelligence is a necessary component for survival. CRM becomes a process for gaining the following information:

- What products does the customer want?
- What is the customer willing to pay for the product or service?
- What level of quality does the customer expect?
- How fast does the customer want the product or service?

While these are simple questions, the process of collecting and interpreting meaningful information is a daunting task. The ability to accurately collect and disseminate this information is a critical element to competitive and operational effectiveness.

Linked with CRM systems is the collection of actual sales data. Sales data are usually correlated by region, territory, customer, and salespeople responsible. Often this information is collected as a module of the ERP system. While CRM systems gather information on customer demand and satisfaction levels, sales force automation systems compile data on what is actually occurring in the various sectors of the business. Both systems are critical to spotting and tracking trends utilized in developing predictive forecasts that drive business profitability. Effective utilization of data flowing from the sales processes can then be fed to operational elements of the supply chain to respond to suppliers, business partners, and operations people. The speed and accuracy of this information translate into operational effectiveness.

Data from CRM and sales force automation systems are integrated with entity-wide information systems into a warehouse of information facts. This provides the depository of data that can be accessed for making real-time decisions. The performance effectiveness of CRM and other systems is a critical success factor. Success is dependent on the speed of information processing and cleansing the data, combined with transforming the data into scalable and useful information. Enterprise-wide connectivity is also critical and is dependent on efficient and effective business processes that enable the transfer of information. Finally, it then becomes the responsibility of management to use the information in an efficient and effective manner.

There are a number of CRM systems that integrate with ERP systems. Also, many ERP systems have modules that are integrated into the enterprise-wide system. Success is dependent on integration and effective execution by management.

DATA WAREHOUSING

Information emanates from multiple sources and systems operating within an enterprise. Data warehouses exist as vehicles to gather all the critical information components. Gathering data into a single warehouse is one step, but ensuring that the data are cleansed and organized for effective management use is even more critical. If information is not of high quality and timely, its value drops considerably. Those organizations that have clean solid data in a cohesive effective format will gain the advantage.

The process of effective data warehousing is not simply a systems function of gathering information. People and people-related processes are needed to ensure that all the critical data are secured and in the proper format on a timely basis. A component of data warehousing is the concept of metadata. This requires defined processes of documenting the source, business logic, timing, and purpose for the data. Maintaining high quality and timeliness of data provides the foundation for analysis and decision making. Analytics are driven by and acted on by people who determine what and at what levels of the entity information should be accessible. The culture and strategic mission of the entity will drive the visibility of the data and the format in which the data presented.

BUSINESS INTELLIGENCE

Business intelligence flows out of the data warehouse to empowered users of the data to monitor business performance. Information from multiple systems and sources flows from within and outside the entity for transformation into useful and actionable formats. The manner and format in which data are used and distributed vary among organizations. Typical approaches include balanced scorecard or other performance indicator formats. Key performance indicators include dashboards that use a variety of stoplights, gauges, and dials. Technology enables the format and ease with which data can be analyzed and presented.

Prior to Sarbanes-Oxley and the evolution of empowered analytics, business intelligence was limited to monitoring lagging indicators. The scope of business intelligence was traditional functional and departmental emphasis and is now changing to a process management focus. Business intelligence was used for strategic and tactical reactive analysis and lacked the integrated approach needed to represent a vision of the future. Output, typically, was numeric based to present tables and charts. It was a tool for limited use by analysts for strategic analysis.

Now, with Sarbanes-Oxley, monitoring performance on a real-time basis is becoming a necessity. Publicly traded companies need to manage and minimize risks. Section 404 requires internal control systems capable of providing reliable financial reports in addition to compliance with laws and regulations. In the interest of public trust, corporations, now more than ever, are laser focused on maximizing shareholder value. Technology enabled the creation of new tools that are providing for more effective process management and generation of better data on a timelier basis. People and processes can become more efficient and effective with the evolvement of business process management.

BUSINESS PROCESS MANAGEMENT

Business process management (BPM) has evolved from business intelligence and corporate performance management. It is a process-based approach that enables all levels of management to understand, communicate, and monitor the key drivers of business value and monitor the execution of strategic vision. BPM enables and empowers people to optimize the execution of business strategy through the effective design and application of business processes.

Sarbanes-Oxley framed and illustrated the need for BPM, for compliance monitoring, and enterprise risk management. BPM will evolve to meet the need for improved communication, collaboration, control, and coordination within and outside the organization. Real-time disclosure will lead to real-time financial closings that will not be possible without BPM.

BPM goes beyond key performance indicators and provides the capability to access predictive dashboards and scorecards. The execution of strategy is enhanced by BPM because it empowers people and processes throughout the organization. It connects all levels of the organization to streamline the planning and monitoring process. Because it is focused and real time, it provides for effective action and adjustment based on identification and measurement of leading predictive business drivers. Since this is a future-oriented approach, organizations have a more effective tool to define goals and objectives to enable strategic planning. One of the most significant benefits emanating from BPM is the ability to move the budgeting and planning process to real-time rolling forecasts based on actual performance.

Since design and operational effectiveness represent the keys to competitive advantage, BPM enables monitoring and adjustment of process development. Continuous improvement and root cause identification can now become integrated into the ongoing business process rather than as reaction to a crisis. BPM is the way of the future, and according to The Data Warehousing Institute research, only 13% of survey respondents have begun to deploy solutions. Selecting the right measures to gain the entity-wide strategic impact will represent a challenge and an opportunity. Success will hinge on selecting the few vital indicators to gain the maximum impact for creating business value.

7

CONTROL ENVIRONMENT RESPONSIBILITIES

Internal control of an organization begins with the control environment. Control environment is one of the five components of the COSO Integrated Framework. It provides the foundation for an organization's internal control and much more. Control environment and corporate culture are woven together and provide the fiber for continuous improvement. This is an organization requirement extending beyond compliance with the Sarbanes-Oxley Act.

Control environment sets the tone for leadership and the pursuit of reality and integrity throughout the organization. These challenges are explored together with how the motivation of Sarbanes-Oxley blends with management philosophy and the creation of organizational knowledge. The tone of the organization extends from the top to people at all levels of the company. The overall control environment drives integrity, ethical value, and competence of people throughout the company. Beyond internal control, the control environment provides the blueprint for organizational action on a pathway to continuous compliance and improvement.

MANAGEMENT RESPONSIBILITY

Internal control is a process that is effected by people. The foundation begins at the top of the entity with the board of directors, management, and other key people. This is where responsibility for the design and maintenance of internal control begins so that it can be applied consistently throughout the organization. A good system of internal control starts with the right people. It is their responsibility to individually and collectively focus on the proper details to achieve the organization's objectives. The leadership of the entity directly impacts the rest of the organization by what it says and does. These actions drive how the entity's objectives are established and the effectiveness of the components of internal control and mechanisms that are implemented.

Many of the problems arising from the accounting scandals were due to management not fulfilling its responsibility. Greed led those in management to bend the rules without regard to ethics and a code of conduct. Their attitude was "do as I say and not do as I do." Codes of conduct existed but were not followed. Management has the responsibility to ensure the existence and implementation of effective codes of conduct. These codes should provide guidelines for acceptable business practice and expected standards of moral and ethical behavior. These guidelines need to go beyond just legal compliance. When management accepts its responsibility for the design and effective operation of internal control, the control environment then becomes the basis for effectiveness and sets the tone throughout the organization.

Sarbanes-Oxley places additional responsibilities on management with respect to internal control. The legislation requires management to assess, test, and document its evaluation of internal control over financial reporting and compliance with laws and regulations. External auditors are now charged with the responsibility for auditing management's assessment in addition to reaching their own independent conclusion as to its effectiveness. Effectiveness of the control environment represents a new challenge for both management and CPAs since it is not transaction driven. It cannot be tested based on an evaluation of activity-level controls. Evaluation must consider all of the elements of internal control and not just the pieces to ensure overall effectiveness.

The control environment is pervasive because it consists of so many business process activities. The complexity of the multitude of processes requires new approaches to understanding. Some of the points of focus offered by the COSO Evaluation Tools provide some guidance for both auditors and management. Some of the issues that need to be addressed include:

- The existence and implementation of a business code of conduct that provides standards of ethical and moral behavior
- Setting the "tone at the top" of an entity that is communicated throughout the organization both in word and deed
- Evidence that employees understand and follow the code

■ Whether the existence of and compliance with the entity's code of conduct enhance other components of the internal control system

The key to creating an effective control environment is achieving organizational realism. Reality needs to be a priority. When management teams take a realistic view of the entity, they learn how they stack up against the competition, yielding important clues regarding effectiveness. This represents a solid argument for management self-assessments.

ORGANIZATIONAL TONE

Organizational tone is synonymous with culture. The tone of the organization from the top to the bottom and across all segments creates culture based on the actions and deeds of all employees. Effectiveness and reliability of internal control are a component of all elements of an organization. Internal control is more than policies and procedures relative to processing transactions. It is how people work together. This is what drives competitive advantage. Compliance with Sarbanes-Oxley provides a unique opportunity for companies to get their control environment (culture) on the right track.

Elements of organizational tone include integrity and ethical values. Tone answers the questions of how companies set values and reward achievement. When entities place unreasonable demands and pressure on employees to produce short-term results, the control environment becomes polluted and fraudulent or questionable activity results. Ineffective boards of directors will foster environmental conditions that lead to inappropriate behavior by not providing clear and objective oversight to top management. Since management is accountable to the board of directors, the strength and independence of the board, therefore, sets the tone for how the organization conducts its business. Organizational tone, therefore, needs to begin at the board level. Management is responsible for the "tone" that influences the execution of leadership and control activities throughout the company. This drives to the core of control environment. The internal controls will only be as good as the people who design, operate, and monitor them.

Organizational tone is the combination of ingredients that enable companies to nurture a control environment that effectively combats the fraud triangle depicted in Figure 7.1. Fraud tends to be fostered by three principal root causes. When the control environment is guided by integrity and ethical leadership, the three primary elements of the fraud triangle are significantly minimized. Effective internal controls are a primary objective of management and help to explain

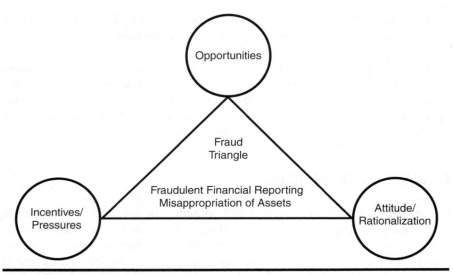

Figure 7.1.   The fraud triangle.

the willingness to self-assess the system of internal control on a regular and ongoing basis. Management integrity and ethical business operations by the mere virtue of effectiveness ensure hiring and training the right people. This helps to diminish incentives and rationalization for fraudulent activity. In short, organizational tone is all about people.

BLUEPRINT FOR ACTION

Just having the right people on the bus is not enough; it is critical to make sure that they are in the right seats. This provides structure to the process. A blueprint that is understood throughout the organization is like a seating chart, so that employees, including top management, know where to sit and the procedures for loading the bus. Evaluation of the control environment needs to consider the appropriateness of the entity's organizational structure and adequate definition of responsibilities.

Creating an effective internal control environment requires communication of all the entity's key roles and responsibilities. Information needs to flow from the top of the organization down into and throughout the operational elements of the entity. It is similar to a military chain of command. The flow of communication needs to contain organizational responsibilities and expectations for all key segments and units of the business. Employees at all levels need to understand what it is that is expected of them and to whom they are accountable. This facilitates the flow of information necessary for effective execution. If a control is not functioning, the effectiveness of the control environment will allow problems to surface so they can quickly be corrected.

The blueprint should indicate the levels of knowledge and experience required for effective execution. It is also important that the model clearly spell out all the key reporting relationships and authority levels. An effective organization will ensure that team members are aligned and capable of adapting to shifts and changes in business and competitive conditions. The control environment model should provide clarity regarding the levels of resources necessary to perform all the responsibilities and an indication of when more or less resources are needed.

A good blueprint contains all of the elements needed to provide effective guidance. The following list is not inclusive, but represents the basic formal or informal components that should be documented:

- Code of conduct
- Personnel policies
- Charter for the board of directors
- Charter for the audit committee
- Disclosure checklist
- High-level map of key business processes at the context level
- Assignment of responsibilities and reporting relationships
- Format for regular ongoing self-assessments to test the control environment

The formality of documentation will vary depending on the size and complexity of the entity. The key is commitment to execution and following up to ensure that the proper tone is being set and followed.

It is one thing to have a code of conduct and another to embed it throughout the organization so that it is clearly understood and followed. A blueprint without action is useless. Employees throughout the entity need to understand the code and relate it to the attitude of management. Management's attitude is the true tone that will flow throughout the entity. Self-assessments of the control environment should test this attitude. The culture of the organization needs to contain a free flow of communication that will reveal sensitive information that would indicate potential problems. There are a number of areas that will provide clues. The tone of executive travel expenses sets the example. Incidents of litigation or investigation by regulatory agencies along with incidents of fraudulent activity will help shed light on the actual tone and how it is established. In view of irregularities or sudden shifts in business conditions, it is important to monitor the actions—or inactions—taken by management and the board of directors. The action elements of the model should contain entity-wide objectives with direction as to how they are planned, executed, controlled, and monitored. It is important to remember that the control environment is pervasive and fluid. The key is realizing the tone established and how it flows down and through the activity-level controls. If there is no clarity throughout the control environment, there is a good chance that deficiencies and weaknesses will emerge elsewhere in the entity's internal control.

ORGANIZATIONAL INTEGRITY

Organizational integrity evolves from ethical values that are followed by all employees throughout the entity. It does not result from an organization chart or specific policies and procedures, but rather from the continuous actions of employees. The actions of employees extend past compliance with laws and regulations. Actions speak louder than words.

Effective communication is the key to building a corporate culture that supports sound ethical principles in contrast to mere rule-following behavior. The creation of organizational integrity flows from the tone set by directors and senior management. Communication of the organization's ethical mission should include codes of conduct and ethical policy woven into the company's strategy. This creates an ethical compass that sends a message encouraging effective ethical and compliance programs and supports good business practices. Objectives of this communication include:

1. Preventing corporate wrongdoing and fraud
2. Creating a positive ethical corporate culture
3. Sending a clear "tone at the top" message
4. Mitigating sanctions and fines under law

The creation of a positive corporate culture will improve the ethical environment and judgment of employees, management, and business partners, and the development of ethical sensitivity will help ensure business practices that are grounded in good ethics. This will foster a foundation for improvement in productivity, quality, and a good reputation. A communication program that sponsors effective organizational compliance based on "ethical principles" in contrast to "rule following" will promote core values and good business practices that achieve compliance as well as a more profitable company.

Good management and leadership will ensure effective business ethics processes. The cost of a poor ethical climate can be staggering because of the resulting loss of confidence in the organization. Examples of the cost drivers from poor ethical behavior include:

- Damaged business reputation
- Declining productivity
- Ineffective flow of information
- Increased employee turnover
- Greater risk of fraudulent behavior

Nurturing organizational integrity is a critical mission that should be driven by both compliance training in conjunction with ethics-oriented training programs. While training is an important element, there is no substitute for involved directors and senior management who walk the talk and demonstrate commitment based on their actions. This will help to ensure an upward flow of communication that involves employees, customers, and vendors.

KNOWLEDGE EFFECTIVENESS

Enterprises are facing intense pressure from constant change and increased complexity, making it a real challenge to remain competitive and still produce results. These competitive challenges make it essential for people to continuously provide innovative solutions to difficult problems. This means applying knowledge to decisions and actions that produce meaningful results. In order for results to be meaningful, it is necessary to apply the right knowledge when it is needed. It also requires having the right people performing and executing in an efficient and effective fashion.

Effective application of knowledge is enhanced when employees take ownership of the organization's mission and code of ethics. It is important for control environments to facilitate the communication of an organization's ethical values in clear and precise terms. This helps to nurture business practices and ethical values in ways that enhance economic performance. Empowerment of employees is a critical and powerful tool for continuous improvement and applying the right knowledge at the right time.

Organizations that are capable of readily accessing the potential of their knowledge capability and capacity build and achieve a competitive edge. A major challenge to knowledge management is the maintenance of an ongoing process of education. No company will ever be capable of hiring all the necessary trained people it needs. Therefore, reducing turnover and preserving the existing workforce is critical. Creating an environment of knowledge effectiveness hinges on maintaining a healthy atmosphere grounded in both compliance and ethics. This condition allows training and communication to flow up, down, and throughout the entity. Building a foundation of ethical employee empowerment not only minimizes all types of business risk but facilitates knowledge management. We will explore knowledge management later in the chapter, but first let's discuss how the philosophy of management and the board of directors directly influences the control environment.

MANAGEMENT PHILOSOPHY

Management's underlying thought, knowledge, and principles guide its actions and decisions and collectively formulate how an organization will react and deal with the maze of opportunities, risks, and threats it faces. Again, management and boards of directors are comprised of people. The quality of people and their training combined with their ethical and moral values set the tone for how the enterprise is managed and strategy is executed. The philosophical compass representing the collective team of leaders determines the organization's attitude toward risk. Risk attitude and appetite impact the control environment and how controls are implemented and monitored. They help us understand why internal control is a people-driven process.

One of the findings to evolve from a study of fraudulent and questionable financial reporting in 1987 recommended that the CEO and the chief accounting officer of all public companies acknowledge management's responsibilities for financial statements and internal control and issue a report discussing how these responsibilities were fulfilled. After the scandals and the passage of the Sarbanes-Oxley Act, some 15 years later we are now struggling to comply with this recommendation. This same study reported that the personnel involved in deceptive reporting did not know or did not realize they were doing anything wrong. These employees ignorantly thought they were acting in their company's best interest. It is clear that when management's philosophy is ethical and is effectively communicated, significant progress can be achieved in minimizing incidents of fraudulent accounting and financial reporting.

Every organization has its own culture and management style. The renewed focus on improving the effectiveness of internal control and risk management creates a new sense of urgency. Management teams and boards need to assess and evaluate their philosophy and style of operations. This should not be just out of concern for compliance, but also to gain competitive advantage and then sustain it. The evaluation process should consider the philosophic approach to risk in conjunction with the economic and regulatory environment in which the entity operates. Re-examination of management's attitude with respect to accounting and financial reporting should be assessed. It might even be appropriate to engage an objective and independent opinion. While the external auditor will look at issues within the control environment, entities should not wait for or rely on the auditor. Management needs to recognize its responsibility and not abrogate internal control to the internal auditors or the accounting department. It is an entity-wide responsibility.

Philosophy and operating style are intangible factors. Some of the areas that should be assessed include:

- Business risk
- Personnel attitudes and turnover
- Attitude toward accounting and reporting
- Effectiveness of organizational communication
- Attitude toward accounting principles and estimates
- Effectiveness of employee empowerment and utilization of knowledge management

This is only the tip of the iceberg relative to potential issues associated with management philosophy and operating style. The key consideration is to realize the pervasiveness of these intangibles and to challenge the effectiveness of how management and the board face reality.

CONTINUOUS COMPLIANCE AND IMPROVEMENT

Compliance with Section 404 requires that management's process for assessing the effectiveness of internal control provide for reasonable assurance of effectiveness as of the end of the fiscal year. This means that the process of assessment needs to be started well in advance of that date. In reality, it means that compliance needs to become a continuous process in order to be truly effective. The concept of continuous compliance should be embraced at the management and board level. This represents the real payoff from Sarbanes-Oxley because assessing internal control effectiveness provides the underlying structure for continuous improvement.

Continuous improvement is called "kaizen" in Japanese. It is a process of steady growth and improvement to overcome resistance to change. The process of improvement is ongoing and can be captured in five primary components, as shown in Figure 7.2. Compliance efforts are translated into improvement opportunities. Management teams that accept the challenge and responsibility for effectiveness of internal control will turn compliance into the creation of improvement opportunity. The five components of continuous improvement as applied to internal control will go the heart of root causes, implementation of solutions, and monitoring improvement. Application of this approach from the control environment and all the components of the COSO Framework can significantly enhance the effectiveness of all business processes.

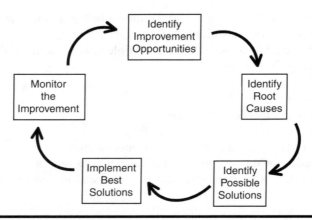

Figure 7.2.   Five steps to continuous improvement.

A continuous improvement approach to internal control will provide better understanding about the internal control throughout the company. This facilitates management's process of managing risk and effectiveness of business operations. Enhancing enterprise risk management extends beyond the management level because the continuous approach creates awareness throughout the organization that internal control is everybody's job.

When management gets into the game and continuously assesses internal control, it makes the job of the internal auditors and external auditors much easier. This translates into reduced audit fees since external auditors can place greater reliance on management's assessment and the level of documentation supporting this evaluation. Attacking root causes and implementing effective solutions results in improved design of internal controls combined with assurance that employees have the knowledge and skills necessary to operate the processes. Communication is another benefactor of the continuous approach and enhances the entity's application of knowledge management.

CORNERSTONE OF COMPETITIVE ADVANTAGE: KNOWLEDGE MANAGEMENT

It is important to realize that maintenance of business processes requires continual effort to monitor and generate improvement. People create and maintain business and operational processes. Achieving and maintaining process effectiveness involves the effort of all employees and the support of management. This effort takes perseverance and a strong corporate culture together with a tried and tested set of procedures to follow. The continuous compliance and improvement environment being advocated needs to be fueled with the support of knowledge management. This is an invisible asset and will not generate any value unless somebody does something with it. Effective knowledge management requires identifying the sources of both explicit and implicit knowledge and connecting them to business processes to create and build value.

Conversion of intellectual assets into value is not easily accomplished. Every company has an abundant amount of information scattered throughout its employees. The problem is maintaining an inventory of where knowledge is located and retrieving it when and where it is needed. A knowledge management system hinges on the sharing of knowledge with employees. When entities understand their corporate culture and have instilled a control environment that embraces a policy of solid business ethics, employee turnover is minimized. Ethical leadership is not just a matter of compliance, but is a foundation for sustaining competitive advantage. This attitude ensures the retention and access of pertinent employee knowledge. When management is conducting continuous self-assessments, it enables the identification of knowledge sources as well as needs throughout the organization. This continuous approach will help to stabilize employee turnover and enhance the retention of knowledge assets and intellectual capital.

Knowledge management will not be effective if organizations lack the processes and structure to support it. Continuous compliance and improvement based on an effective control environment will help provide the foundation needed for knowledge management success to achieve sustained value and bottom-line improvement. Knowledge management hinges on effective business processes. These business processes provide the capability to intentionally structure and collect the right information so that it can be used when and where it is needed. Knowledge is dependent on continuously training people and then retaining them within the organization.

A major objective of knowledge management is to harness information contained within each employee—"tacit" knowledge. This is a pooling of experiences that can be shared and accessed by others within the organization so that they can be leveraged to create value. Software has been created to enhance this process and allow retrieval of key data, similar to an Internet search. This continuous process of learning fits in nicely with the suggested approach to compliance and ongoing improvement. Integration of knowledge management with continuous compliance and improvement builds on existing knowledge and is enhanced by ongoing training and learning. Bolstered by a foundation of good business ethics and leadership that backs up their vision with action, employees will know that their knowledge is valued as a contribution to organizational performance. When entities are capable of effectively harnessing and distributing corporate knowledge, they create committed cross-functional teams that work and communicate together. With knowledge comes power, and when properly applied, it builds internal control processes that mitigate risks and build shareholder value.

INFORMATION TECHNOLOGY ISSUES AND CONCERNS

Managing information in the age of information is a never-ending challenge. Sarbanes-Oxley has changed the playing field and has created many unanswered questions. The legislation has attempted to improve accountability and communication from publicly traded companies. Improved accounting and communication require a foundation that is heavily driven by utilization of information systems and technology. Business transactions are the results of processes that create documentation of invoices, purchase orders, payments, and other output. E-mail and other elements of electronic communication are also components of the challenge. Reliable financial reporting and compliance with laws and regulations require efficient and effective information technology and management. Deficiencies and weaknesses in the IT infrastructure will obviously impact the internal control system.

Sarbanes-Oxley established clear objectives to enhance corporate governance through information and communication. However, the guidance surrounding the area of IT is not detailed and lacks specific direction. The Public Company Accounting Oversight Board (PCAOB) wanted stronger internal controls and corporate accountability. The framework provided as being acceptable to the Securities and Exchange Commission (SEC) was the COSO Framework. The PCAOB makes it clear that auditors need to understand management's information and communication, including the systems and processes. They will also need to understand the flow of transactions, including how they are initiated, authorized, recorded, processed, and reported. This means understanding the extent of IT involvement in each period-end financial reporting process. Without providing detailed steps for how this is to be accomplished, the oversight board recognized the importance of this critical element. The COBiT Framework developed by the IT Governance Institute and sponsored by the Information Systems Audit and Control Association provides direction and insight into the relationship between IT and Sarbanes-Oxley compliance. While it has not been endorsed by the SEC or the PCAOB, it provides excellent information on IT and internal control.

INFORMATION TECHNOLOGY AND INTERNAL CONTROL

We live in the age of information where technology drives information. Information is the key component for conducting business and risk management, which will not function effectively without having the right information when it is needed. Technology is the great enabler of information and how it flows to where it is used. Accordingly, effective design of controls will rely heavily on technology to provide a control environment with the tools required for achieving its objectives. In addition to building an internal control foundation following the COSO Framework, Sarbanes-Oxley has spawned a new frontier of compliance tools. The first step organizations need to take is to define their internal control objectives relative to financial reporting and then assess and document how technology is currently being applied in the internal control system. Conformity relative to Section 404 should be one of the first steps taken by the compliance team.

A major component of the assessment should begin by understanding how IT is managed and organized and its fit into the overall organizational structure. One should look at the entity-wide strategy and then align it with the IT strategy for both technology and applications. Figure 8.1 presents the relationship of how the IT organization fits with both entity-level controls and process-level controls. When evaluating IT entity-level controls, it is important to consider the following steps:

1. Tone at the top
2. Evaluate overall IT controls with respect to risk assessment, communication, and monitoring
3. Identify all the control entities for the IT organization
4. Identify application and data owners

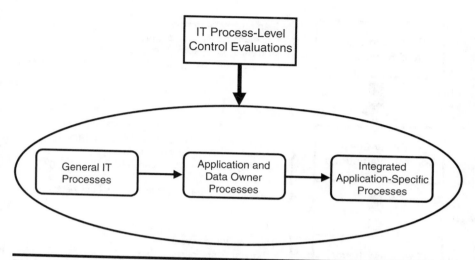

Figure 8.1.   Structure of IT controls.

When evaluating IT processes and controls, it is helpful to refer to Figure 8.2 to understand those steps in the progression from general IT processes to application and integrated processes.

IT has been more deeply embedded into business processes. This occurrence has created greater process dependence on technology, specifically financial reporting processes. Reliable financial reporting depends on the effectiveness of controls related to applications and systems and the integrity of processing the data and information being reported. Therefore, any programmed control must be evaluated and considered regarding its reliability and effectiveness. Additional factors arising from the intensified impact of technology include security and unauthorized access to information and data. Some of these issues include:

- Unauthorized access to data and information
- Inaccurate calculations and processing
- Unauthorized or erroneous revisions to programs

Because of the dependence of financial reporting on technology, the PCAOB has made it clear that management must fully understand the applications impacting financial reporting, together with the associated risks and controls, prior to when external auditors begin their audit process. Auditors will, therefore, be required to conduct more extensive tests than had previously been

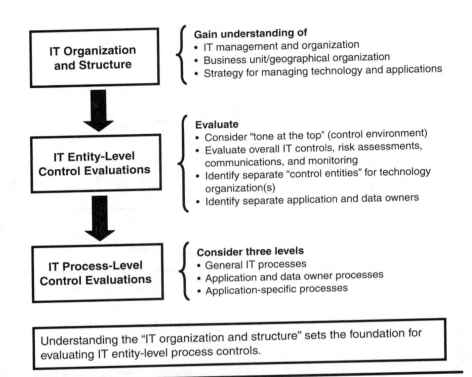

Figure 8.2. Process-level control evaluation.

required. These requirements will be elaborated on in greater depth in Chapter 14.

Each organization has different needs and approaches to technology. Also, companies are typically at different levels of evolution in their technology. Because of this issue, the use of technology will be in a continuous state of development. This means that internal controls and financial reporting will evolve along with technology and its application. Based on its importance and complexity, entities should give IT assessment a high priority. In addition to internal control and financial reporting, technology will play a key role in real-time reporting and effective communication throughout organizations. These considerations should motivate entities to expand their thinking, including clear understanding of the following:

1. Information and records management policies and procedures
2. Leadership support and organizational structure
3. Assessment of the technological environment

Documentation of information and records management is frequently not given adequate priority. It is often taken for granted. Also, the flow of communication and information needs to be solidified to reinforce its importance and support at all levels of the organization. There have been a number of failures within the overall technology environment. Hewlett Packard recently experienced disruption in its order flow that resulted in delayed sales because of difficulties with the integration of an enterprise resource planning (ERP) implementation. If this can occur within a technology company, it is not difficult to imagine the possibilities in less digitally focused organizations. The reliance on digital information will only increase as we move forward in the age of information. Compliance with Sarbanes-Oxley is dependent on the accuracy and trustworthiness of records and information that document business transactions and activities. Without a reliable technology environment, entities will not have reliable compliance and a sound basis for risk management.

ENTERPRISE MANAGEMENT AND BUSINESS PROCESSES

Financial reporting and management processes in today's environment are driven by IT systems. There are a wide range of solutions in use depending on the industry and business environment in which companies operate. Typically, ERP systems are utilized and are totally technology dependent. Enterprise management is comprised of three primary control elements as presented in Figure 8.3. Overall, the company-level controls are pervasive through the enterprise and set the tone down, across, and through the organization. The area of systems planning and company-wide technology environment impact application and general controls. Management and board planning will determine the investment level in technology, which can have a direct correlation to the effectiveness of overall internal control. Failure to provide the necessary technology tools and the associated training in their use represent signals regarding control problems and issues.

From an enterprise-wide perspective, it is important to involve IT leaders with the top level of the organization. Senior management and boards of directors need to have a clear understanding of the technology issues and risks within the entire control environment. Compliance teams also need to include the IT elements of the organization since they will have a material impact on the effectiveness of internal control. IT professionals will need to be integrated into the control environment in order to create a more formalized approach and structure to IT in support of entity-wide internal control maintenance.

Most companies will utilize ERP systems to drive their business processes. When ERP systems are not employed, companies will use a collection of fi-

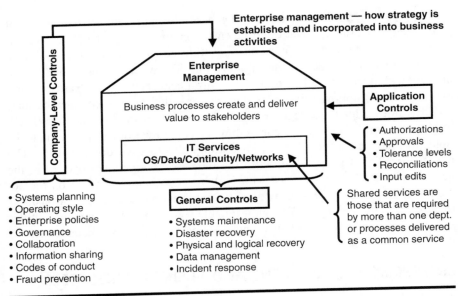

Figure 8.3.   Enterprise control elements.

nancial and operational applications that will support their business objectives. Integration of multiple systems within diverse business units will represent a challenge and a serious problem. Organizations rushed to implement new systems prior to 2000 because of concerns with Y2K. In many instances, implementation efforts were substandard. Management frequently failed to support these implementations with training and effective process management. As a result, problems have surfaced that in many cases resulted in restatement of financial results, most notably Goodyear Tire and Rubber Company. Whatever the specific situation, it is critical that compliance teams place emphasis on aligning their business processes with the enterprise management and reporting systems.

Technology plays an increasingly important role in internal control systems. This correlates with a heightened focus on internal controls and corporate governance. Realization that internal control is process based, flowing across organizational functions, drives home the point that it is critically important to educate and integrate IT people with the organizational structure. Educational emphasis should be placed on the structure and format of internal control required by management and external auditors so that IT can be in a position to effectively support the compliance effort. IT personnel should be provided with understanding of the organization's internal control structure and financial reporting process. From this platform, IT personnel should document and map all the technology-based systems that support internal control and financial reporting. This will provide the basis for assessing internal control and testing, in addition to identifying the risks related to these processes.

Supporting processes within the IT area can be seen in Figure 8.3. General IT controls that are embedded in shared IT services are critical and impact not only the reliability of financial reporting but the viability of the entire enterprise. Shared services will vary from entity to entity and in how they are applied. Components will typically include the type of operating system supporting the organization and the network connecting all the components and business units within the organization. Other components include telephone communication and e-mail systems and the protocol for how they function. Shared services include key elements that are embedded in general controls. For example, systems maintenance, data management, and security are examples of control activities that must be maintained. One other component that has become more real after September 11, 2001 is disaster recovery. While this is an extreme example, there are frequently weather-related issues that will necessitate a carefully developed disaster recovery plan. There are too many instances when management and boards have taken these technology-related controls for granted. Also, chief information officers have not always been given the status and importance at appropriate levels of management as warranted. In an era of disruptive technology combined with an accelerated pace of business, it is crucial that the role of IT be elevated.

Any discussion of how processes impact enterprise management has to include the IT elements of activity controls. It is becoming more commonplace to see controls that are embedded within business processes by design. Effective process design will include digital authorizations, approval levels, and checks on tolerance levels. There are also account reconciliations that are technology enabled. Controls are also created to electronically edit data inputs to correct errors at the beginning of processes. This is all part of the trend toward the automation of processes utilizing efficient integrated technology-based systems. The pervasive nature of technology-related controls mandates that the tone at the top carefully consider and understand technology implications.

THE COBiT FRAMEWORK

The COSO Framework was designated by the PCAOB as being a suitable and available framework for management's assessment of internal control. However, the framework provides minimal direction relative to IT. The IT Governance Institute developed a framework for IT that provides useful direction for compliance with Section 302 and 404 of the Sarbanes-Oxley Act; it is called the COBiT Framework. The institute also published the *IT Control Objectives for Sarbanes-Oxley*. While the COBiT Framework and related information are not the authorized answer to compliance issues and assessment of internal control, they do shed a great deal of light on the significance of IT in the design, implementation, and sustainability of internal control related to financial reporting and disclosure.

The COBiT Framework is very robust. The primary components of the framework are presented in Figure 8.4. We can see how the components of information, planning and organization, acquisition and implementation, delivery and support, and monitoring circulate around IT resources. This framework provides insight relative to developing policy and practice for blending IT controls with COSO control objectives.

COBiT consists of 4 domains that identify 34 IT processes and 318 control objectives. It must be remembered that this framework may exceed or fall short of the COSO Framework and therefore should not be interpreted as the last answer. COBiT's four domains are:

1. Planning and organization
2. Acquisition and implementation
3. Delivery and support
4. Monitoring

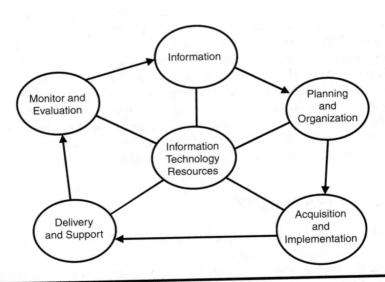

Figure 8.4.   COBiT Framework.

Planning and organization provides for creating a strategic IT plan and all phases of planning and quality, including project and quality management. The next domain deals with administration and implementation and provides guidance on selection of automated solutions, together with implementation and managing changes. Within delivery and support, guidance is focused on defining and managing service levels, security, training, and managing operations. Monitoring extends to processes and the adequacy of internal controls. This domain also deals with gaining independent assurance and providing for independent audits.

Integration of the COBiT Framework into a COSO-based compliance effort makes a great deal of sense. Because of the technology impact on internal controls, organizations can use COBiT to aid in their assessment of design effectiveness from an IT standpoint and then determine control reliability based on documentation and evaluation. COBiT does a good job cross-referencing the IT control objectives for its four domains to each of the five COSO components. Each IT control objective is explained and then matched to the appropriate internal control component. It is beyond the scope of this book to repeat all the elements of *IT Control Objectives for Sarbanes-Oxley* except to reinforce the amount of IT information it contains and its correlation to COSO for practical application to compliance projects. Some of the key IT objectives will be reviewed later in this chapter.

SARBANES-OXLEY COMPLIANCE TOOLS

Sarbanes-Oxley sent every software vendor into high gear to create tools that will help tackle a wide range of tasks to help ease the burden and cost of compliance. Accordingly, there is a wide range of offerings to evaluate and consider. Because this chapter is focused on IT, it is appropriate to explore the capability of these tools. The range of application extends from compliance support and enhanced communication to facilitation of financial analysis and business intelligence. A partial list of vendors is available at www.jrosspub.com. The list was not tested and there are no links to any of the vendors, so it is up to readers to do their homework and exercise due diligence.

Software solutions range from stand-alone programs that provide compliance checklists to complex enterprise-wide applications. Four broad categories of technology tools have evolved for Sarbanes-Oxley compliance:

1. Generic
2. Document management and workflow

3. Business intelligence and data mining/pattern recognition
4. Business process management and measurement (real-time compliance)

Each of the four categories will be explained so readers can determine how the applications might apply to their individual situation.

Generic control tools are primarily used to document internal controls and for enterprise risk management. ERP software contains accounting modules that will provide basic assurance and is not dynamic. Features depend on the robustness of the software package. Some of the more advanced software packages offer built-in diagnostic tools, survey capability, and process documentation. Another feature offered by higher end packages is dashboards and other more dynamic features. Most likely, companies will not switch ERP platforms just because of Sarbanes-Oxley unless they needed to integrate to gain consistency within business units or just happened to be in the process of looking for a new solution. Switching software in the middle of Section 404 compliance is not likely and could force adoption of interim controls to achieve compliance at a point in time.

The generic category also includes communication and collaboration packages in addition to regulatory and technical reference tools. These tools focus on management and storage of digital records plus records management and content monitoring. Communication/collaboration aids in helping to identify audit trails and provide for documentation. Package features range from security over authorized usage to instant messaging and documentation of regulatory compliance workflows. Communication capabilities include virtual conferencing and secure management e-mail. Security software tools, in some instances, provide segregation of duties, antivirus protection, enterprise security, and the capability to update disaster recovery plans. Regulatory and reference tools allow organizations to stay current with regulatory and compliance rules. Each entity will need to survey the offerings and determine products that best meet the objectives of its compliance projects.

Documentation management and workflow tools provide the capability to monitor workflows and processes. The objective is to manage content by establishing internal controls and operating processes via consistent processes using self-defined rules for each business unit. Some of the management tools combine process documentation together with risk assessment in addition to creating and maintaining audit trails. Enhanced capability includes detailed indexing and searching of documents, including e-mail, flowcharts, and numeric data for the purpose of understanding and testing control activities. Also included in the functionality is web-based compliance and collaboration.

Auditors have been using data analysis tools to extract data and test transactional data accuracy for some time. These tools fall into the category of data mining, file retrieval, and pattern recognition. Enhanced analytics resulting from technology innovations provide a wide range of data access and analysis. The software allows data access from ERP, customer relationship management, and other enterprise applications, which enables auditors, financial managers, internal auditors, and other analysts to evaluate transactional data underlying business processes and financial reporting. This means that data can be extracted from the entire array of organizational records from the general ledger, payroll, inventory, information security, and business units. The access capability is enterprise-wide, so that data housed in multiple ERP systems and customized applications can be retrieved and monitored. This extraction capability enables data analysis at the source level to provide data quality and maintenance on integrity. These tools are capable of dealing with unlimited file size capability so that all fields and records of interest can be accessed independent of the applications and processes that recorded the transactions. Organizations are able to embed these tools to provide an audit trail by receiving notification of anomalies and breakdowns in internal controls. The audit tools allow management to compare actual trends and patterns in financial accounts with expected norms to help identify irregularities that might indicate fraud or accounting errors.

Sarbanes-Oxley has created a flurry of technology activity and innovation in an attempt to capture this new compliance market. In many ways, the legislation has taken companies away from investing in noncompliance technology initiatives. The wide range of options has created a patchwork approach, with many companies using a variety of solutions while never hitting the real nail on the head. Internal controls consist of processes that need to be reliable and effective. Some of the technology solutions that have evolved, or are evolving, focus on the need for real-time reporting and intelligence combined with real-time compliance.

Our business environment has been changing rapidly, making the traditional silo functional approach to management obsolete in a world of process-driven innovation. Managers are being challenged to create strategic focus across a wide array of business units and relationships. The demand for agility to remain competitive in volatile markets driven by the speed of innovation extends far beyond the compliance requirements of Sarbanes-Oxley. These factors are the drivers behind the concept of business performance management or corporate performance management, depending on the analyst using the term. In some instances, some have used the phrase performance management to imply scorecards, dashboards, and key performance indicators. Because of the process implications, I think a better description is business process management and measurement to represent a process-centric approach to business decision making that focuses on improving the capability of a business to enhance its insight and improve the effectiveness of its decision-making and overall performance.

Deployments of ERP systems and data warehouses have been implemented by a number of companies. However, the vast amount of data created by these applications is not in a format that provides a consistent and shared view of the business to the wide range of managers that require rapid access to it in a usable format. The concepts will be discussed in Chapters 15 and 16. For now, it is sufficient to realize that a number of companies are moving toward technology solutions that address the needs of strategy-focused decision making and more effective collaboration. Some of the solutions offered have the ability to exchange data with other platforms, in addition to analyzing and modeling data. Included in the software is the capacity to orchestrate applications, people, and partners into executable, end-to-end processes. This process-centric approach enables the management of workflow, process flow, data flow, and monitoring of business activity. This approach places the focus on business objectives and the level of effectiveness required from their business processes. This approach to Sarbanes-Oxley compliance provides a more positive application of continuous business improvement. It avoids the fragmented approach to be in compliance and follows a process-based roadmap that is committed from the top of the organization to a process-based foundation that results in a more effectively managed business.

THE GOVERNANCE CHALLENGE

One of the greatest risks facing companies is safeguarding and protecting their information and information systems. However, the free-wheeling age of information and technology leaves management and boards severely handicapped because of the complexity surrounding the web of systems being utilized within organizations to process information. Information security governance is challenging because it defies understanding. Since knowledge and information represent the hidden asset on the balance sheet and are key components of shareholder value, it is critical that we give information security a high spot on the priority list. In the past, top management and directors have not shown much interest in information security. Now, with a push from Sarbanes-Oxley, it is starting to get more attention.

Since knowledge and information are pervasive throughout an organization, it is critical that information security becomes everyone's job. While information security is an entity-wide job, it begins with management and the board to set the "tone at the top." While it is a process of accountability, it becomes more complex than internal control because of the lack of understanding and the complexity of its underlying infrastructure. The Internet, while a quarter of a century old, has been on the main street of business and commerce for less than a decade. IT has become a core element of literally every business and industry. The cost associated with technology disruption is staggering and goes beyond just being measured in dollars. For example, the cyber attacks that were directed at Amazon.com, eBay, Yahoo, and other sites caused reductions in share values of 17–23% within a three-week period. The combined loss in market capitalization totaled over $28 billion. All too many CEOs and directors think that information security is a simple straightforward fix. This incorrect thinking is why effective information security governance should be moved up on the governance priority list.

The next chapter is devoted entirely to this critical topic. IT and its security in many senses is what internal control is all about. The wake-up call is that it is information which needs to be protected and safeguarded, not just computer systems. Accordingly, it becomes a people process in addition to a technology challenge. Therefore, the topic of information security needs to be elevated to the top of the agenda for management and boards of directors. It also elevates the topic for auditors, both internal and external, to give appropriate levels of attention and focus to IT and its impact on internal control. Management's assessment of internal control under Section 404 needs to become a continuous effort because of the evolvement and pervasiveness of technology and its impact. It is not a fix-and-forget situation because of the dynamics of continuous change.

ASSESSING IT READINESS

Planning and establishing a compliance project is the first step and a critical component in preparing for Sarbanes-Oxley compliance. IT will not impact all of the financial reporting controls and processes, but it will affect a good number of them. Therefore, identification of all key systems and subsystems that relate to the initiation, recording, processing, and reporting of financial information must be documented. This documentation step needs to be accomplished prior to assessing risk associated with the systems.

Documentation involves a number of steps and considerations. Categories of controls as specified by the PCAOB in paragraph 40 of Auditing Standard No. 2 need to be identified and are listed below:

- Controls over initiating, authorizing, recording, processing, and reporting significant accounts and disclosures and related assertions presented in the financial statements
- Controls over the selection and application of accounting policies that are in conformity with generally accepted accounting principles
- Antifraud programs and controls

- Controls, including IT general controls, on which other controls are dependent
- Controls over significant nonroutine and nonsystematic transactions, such as accounts involving judgments and estimates
- Company-level controls, including the control environment and controls over the period-end financial reporting process, including controls over procedures used to enter transaction totals into the general ledger; to initiate, authorize, record, and process journal entries in the general ledger; and to record recurring and nonrecurring adjustments to the financial statements

Documenting the IT impact for each of the PCAOB-designated control types should be part of the process. Identification of significant controls and accounts needs to be developed for both application controls applicable to a specific business process and general controls that apply to all information systems on an entity-wide basis.

Once the IT control applications have been identified, assessing readiness can be determined by following the COBiT Framework to evaluate how IT is aligned to the overall business strategy relative to application of resources and management of risks. COBiT's planning and organization domain provides for 11 action steps that are linked to the five COSO components. Figure 8.5 shows these action steps. Preparing an IT strategic plan involves a number of steps that include risk assessment and the involvement of senior management for developing and implementing both long- and short-range plans that fit the organization's mission. From that platform, it is critical to be sure that these

- Define the IT Strategic Plan
- Define the Information Architecture and Structure
- Determine the Technological Direction
- Manage the IT Investment
- Communicate Management Objectives and Direction
- Manage Human Resources
- Ensure Compliance with External Requirements
- Assess Risks
- Manage Projects
- Manage Quality

Figure 8.5. COBiT planning and organization action steps.

plans are effectively communicated to business process owners and other key personnel within the organization. After the plans have been launched, monitoring and assessing the information systems relative to functionality, stability, strengths, and weaknesses is necessary to provide ongoing support of the entity's business requirements.

Another important component of the assessment is defining the information architectural model and making sure that it is maintained consistent with the long-range IT plan. This model should include the creation of a corporate data dictionary that incorporates all of the organization's syntax rules together with definition of access rules and security levels. Planning and organization needs to consider technology infrastructure, contingency plans, and establishment of both hardware and software plans. Documentation should consider all the organizational roles and responsibility, including quality assurance and supervision. Segregation of duties should be clearly documented, ranging from systems use to network management, administration, maintenance, security administration, and security audit. Policies and procedures need to be established on an entity-wide basis so that personnel understand them and abide by the ethical, security, and internal control standards established and followed by top management.

People and their capabilities represent the lifeblood of organizations. This is especially true of IT due to its rapid pace of change. Retention of personnel and training are essential to maintaining a stable IT organization and platform. Therefore, focus on human resources needs to be a high priority to maintain personnel and provide for cross-training and backup in order to maintain a stable IT work environment. In line with these steps, IT management needs to ensure compliance with privacy, intellectual property, and cryptographic regulations that might apply to the organization.

Management and assessment of risks is an important step in maintaining and achieving IT readiness. Risks need to be understood and managed at an appropriate level for both new and ongoing IT projects. Disasters such as the ERP implementations at Goodyear Tire and Rubber and the issues with order entry at Hewlett Packard are examples of risk that can be managed and avoided with proper attention and focus. A risk assessment approach should define scope, boundaries, responsibilities, and required skills that should be applied to risk identification and mitigation. Management needs to be actively involved in the risk assessment and management process and utilize specialists when and where they are needed. Specialists in security should be employed to address specific and potential threats and IT experts utilized in other situations. The task of risk assessment should include measurement and development of a risk action plan to develop cost-effective controls and security measures. Action plans should also identify risk strategies focused on risk avoidance, mitigation, or acceptance. These strategies need to spell out the parameters and options for accepting residual risk and offsetting remedies including insurance coverage.

The IT function needs to utilize a clear project management framework and process, including responsibilities, breakdown of tasks, budgets, milestones, and checkpoints. Project managers also need to consider assignment of responsibilities and authority. All the elements of project management are beyond the scope of this book, but I do want to underscore the importance of project management as it relates to achieving an effective and efficient IT function.

Quality is a crucial element of defining, maintaining, and implementing IT throughout the organization. Development of a system life cycle approach should be applied to the process of creating, acquiring, implementing, and maintaining computerized IT and systems. The information and communication component of COSO and COBiT encourages a close linkage and coordination between IT customers or users and system implementers. Also, a general framework should be applied to the acquisition and maintenance of the entire technology infrastructure in order to provide high levels of quality and governance throughout the entity. While this represents an overview of areas of focus and ideas for addressing the IT function, a more detailed step-by-step approach can be obtained from COBiT materials on applying the framework and reconciling it with COSO.

IT CONTROL OBJECTIVES

The COBiT Framework provides an IT model that offers management and process owners guidance in addressing Sarbanes-Oxley compliance and facilitates self-assessment following the five components of COSO. A process-based approach is utilized, keying in on both primary and support processes. This makes the approach applicable business-wide and not limited just to IT. Accordingly, business process owners must address all of their activities and link them to deployment of technology where and as appropriate.

Referring to Figure 8.4, recall that the framework has four domains. The objectives fall under the domain of plan and organize in Figure 8.5. COBiT has a total of 34 IT processes, which are presented in Figures 8.6–8.8. Each of the domains has the IT processes segmented into 318 detailed control objectives, providing an inclusive umbrella for managing risk and controlling IT. Since the sanctioned COSO Framework supported by the PCAOB and SEC does not specifically spell out IT control objectives and control activities, this robust framework provides some guidance. I underscore the term guidance since the

Identify Automated Solutions
Acquire and Maintain Application Software
Acquire and Maintain Technology Infrastructure
Develop and Maintain Procedures
Install and Accredit Systems
Manage Changes

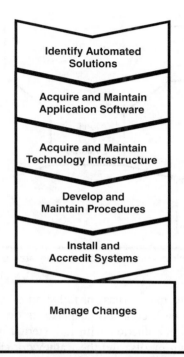

Figure 8.6. COBiT acquire and implement action steps.

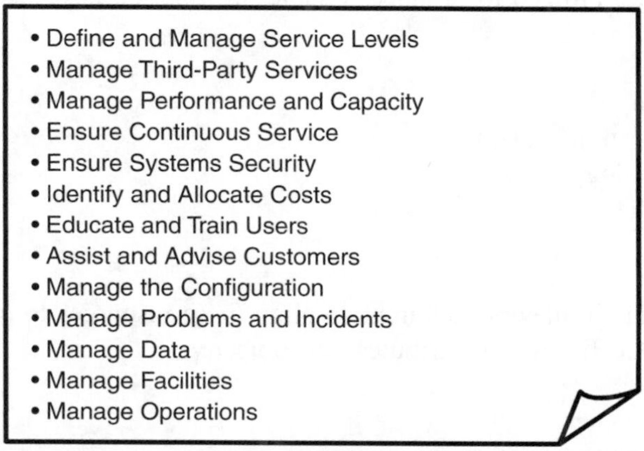

• Define and Manage Service Levels
• Manage Third-Party Services
• Manage Performance and Capacity
• Ensure Continuous Service
• Ensure Systems Security
• Identify and Allocate Costs
• Educate and Train Users
• Assist and Advise Customers
• Manage the Configuration
• Manage Problems and Incidents
• Manage Data
• Manage Facilities
• Manage Operations

Figure 8.7. COBiT deliver and support action steps.

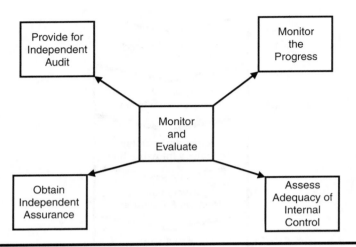

Figure 8.8.   COBiT monitor and evaluation action steps.

COBiT control objectives may surpass or fall short of Sarbanes-Oxley require-ments, and I encourage each company to make its own evaluation on how to apply the framework in conjunction with its external auditors. Each situation needs to stand on its own merits, and the framework should be customized to fit specific unique requirements.

Objectives under the COSO Framework for compliance with Sarbanes-Oxley deal with reliable financial reporting and disclosure, and compliance with laws and regulations. IT will play a major role in achieving these objectives. Re-sources that are utilized to produce reliable information have been pinpointed and include:

- People
- Application systems
- Technology
- Facilities
- Data

The COBiT Framework attempts to align these resources to produce infor-mation with the following attributes and objectives:

- Effectiveness
- Efficiency
- Confidentiality
- Integrity

- Availability
- Compliance
- Reliability

COBiT's process orientation allows for optimization of resources in order to minimize reliance on the individual skills of people in an effort to mitigate risk. Ideally, process objectives offer a level of permanence that balances organization change. Also, process and deployment of IT extends beyond departmental and functional boundaries, involving a wide range of users that will utilize IT specialists to manage the infrastructure. Effective deployment of IT thus provides a foundation for execution of the five COSO components and controlling general and application controls.

The purpose here is to provide insight on the robust capability offered by the COBiT Framework and areas where it offers guidance. Explaining all of the detailed control objectives is not practical. What is important is to direct auditors and practitioners as to where to find ideas for best practices in control implementation relative to IT processes. The delivery and support domain offers direction relative to service levels and managing third-party services. Sarbanes-Oxley does not take management off the hook for responsibility associated with such arrangements, and COBiT provides specific objectives and direction on this issue. The framework also offers assistance relative to continuity of services and systems security.

Monitoring and evaluation of processes is the domain that focuses on assessing the adequacy of internal control. The framework provides steps that should be followed for management to ensure that both IT and internal control processes are adequate, through the application and monitoring of key performance indicators and critical success factors. Further, both operational security and internal control assurance are addressed through self-assessment and audits to provide support that controls are operating as designed. A charter for the audit function calls for receiving independent assurance of critical IT services including independent internal control reviews of third-party service providers following SAS 70 or other independent audit reports. The framework is a useful and helpful tool in providing needed structure and guidance to applying IT objectives to the COSO internal control components and objectives.

CONTROL RELIABILITY

Two types or areas of IT controls have been mentioned: general controls and application controls. General controls usually impact a number of applications and data within the technology environment. They essentially prevent certain events from affecting or influencing the integrity of data or the processing of data. Application controls include controls designed and implemented by respective process and data owners. They also include programmed controls within applications that perform specific control-related activities to check for errors or to validate key information fields.

General IT processes that should be considered critical include those relating to financial reporting and disclosure applications. Examples of general IT processes include:

- Security administration
- Application change control
- Data management and disaster recovery
- Data center operations
- Asset management

Examples of application processes include:

- Security and administration (segregate incompatible duties)
- Access to critical transactions and data
- Business impact analysis/business continuity planning
- Business owner change control

Integrated specific controls for critical financial applications embedded within critical business processes include:

- Application programmed controls
- Access controls for critical transactions and data
- Data validation/error checking routines
- Error reporting
- Complex calculations
- Complete and accurate reporting
- Critical interfaces

These examples offer illustrations of the types of general and application controls that need to be addressed and documented in complying with Sarbanes-Oxley. The key is to determine those controls and accounts that could have a material impact on financial reporting and disclosure. They then need to be identified and documented.

Control reliability needs to be determined and also documented. This provides the foundation for the existence of the control, as well as for evaluating and monitoring effective operation of the control. A component of the docu-

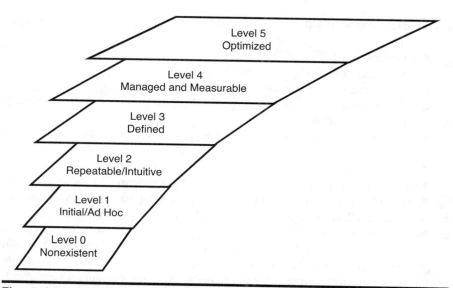

Figure 8.9. COBiT five levels of control reliability.

mentation is the level of control reliability. Documentation needs to include evaluation of control design in addition to its operating effectiveness. Figure 8.9 presents different stages of control effectiveness, which are called the five levels of control reliability. Controls that fall into level 3 and above are those where policies and procedures are in place and documented. Optimized controls are an indication that effective decision making is enabled utilizing high-quality and reliable information. The difference between level 4 and level 3 is usually based on the level of effort required to document and test the control. While levels 3 and 4 will likely pass management's assessment and the auditor's attestation, there is room for improvement. Even level 2 might have controls and procedures in place but lack sufficient documentation and represents an area for remediation. Levels 1 and 0 are both indicative of insufficient controls, policies, and documentation to support management's assertion under Section 404.

Compliance documentation is clarified by the COBiT Framework and supporting material. This insight is helpful since Sarbanes-Oxley does not mandate any specific form of documentation, realizing that it will vary depending on the size and complexity of the enterprise. Company-level controls should include a statement of control and approach that confirms their existence and continued effectiveness over a period time. Activity-level controls should, as a minimum, include the following elements:

- Description of the processes and related subprocesses (including a narrative and/or a flowchart)
- Description of risk
- Size and complexity of process
- Statement of control objective
- Description of the control activities designed and performed to satisfy the control objective
- Conclusions about the effectiveness of the controls based on the results of testing

This represents a basic minimum level of documentation that should be applied to IT-related controls. In addition to the COBiT tools and support material, COSO has evaluation tools and the various software packages and consultants provide input. The key point is that good documentation is critical.

IT has a big impact on internal control, and it is important that CIOs and IT professionals have an active role in Sarbanes-Oxley compliance. This role should not be just a one-time event but rather continuous, ongoing involvement, including representation at the top levels of the organization. IT personnel need to expand their understanding beyond IT and into the implications of internal control and financial reporting. Sarbanes-Oxley is going to be a continuous ongoing process. This represents an opportunity for management, boards, and IT professionals to enhance information security governance as well as build a differentiated competitive advantage.

INFORMATION SECURITY: A CORPORATE GOVERNANCE CHALLENGE

Information security has been elevated in importance because of significant losses from security breaches and the importance of information on the way we live and conduct business. Information driven by technology has a pervasive impact on the infrastructure that supports governments, businesses, consumers, and individual citizens. There is also the ever-present risk of a major cyber attack that could impact the critical national information infrastructure.

There have been a number of legislative initiatives that deal with information security that have been passed, most notably the Sarbanes-Oxley Act of 2002, which impacts publicly traded companies subject to U.S. security laws. In addition, Congress and state governments have passed laws that govern how companies must address the issues of information security. All too frequently, information security is treated as strictly a technology issue when in reality it is a governance concern.

Until the focus created by the financial scandals and Sarbanes-Oxley took the problem to corporate boardrooms, the matter of information security was treated as a technology matter. In many instances, information security still continues to be shuffled aside or delegated to lower level personnel. In December 2001, the National Association of Corporate Directors (NACD) in conjunction with KPMG's Audit Committee Institute published a report titled *Information Systems Governance: What Directors Need to Know* that addressed information and security head-on. This level of visibility is now getting the problem on the radar screen. Chapter 8 created the foundation for understanding information technology and its impact on reliable financial reporting. Information security extends considerably beyond technology to the core of the infrastructure upon which the entire world is dependent.

INFORMATION SECURITY GOVERNANCE

Information security extends beyond safeguarding digital information from hackers and denial of service attacks. Its scope has to include natural disasters, business continuity plans, data classification and retention, backup strategies, and incident handling. Richard A. Clarke, the former National Coordinator for Security, Infrastructure Protection, and Counter-Terrorism, commented that "people think this is a minor problem" that could be addressed with a firewall and password access. This perception is a major component of the issue because people fail to give adequate attention to the problem. Clarke goes on to point out that "the Internet was built without a government or master plan" and "without security as part of the central design." Accordingly, the security of information together with the networks and systems that process it represent a monumental challenge for management. While there has been lots of federal and state legislation, Sarbanes-Oxley represented the most notable wake-up call for senior managers and board members. It was a good thing because the threat of information warfare is real and the investing public is at great risk.

It is a frightening thought to realize that our most important asset is potentially accessible to hackers, competitors, and terrorists because it is swirling through cyberspace in digital format without adequate safeguards. Y2K was another eye-opener for directors and top management. This nonevent at least caused the topic of information security to be added to the agendas of board meetings. The events of September 11, 2001 represented another reminder that business recovery policies and procedures together with information backup systems to restore information are an absolute necessity. Examples of infrastructures that are dependent on continuous operation of IT include:

- Electrical power grids
- Railroads and airlines
- Oil and gas

- Banking and financial systems
- Telecommunication networks
- Information networks

The security of these infrastructures needs to be moved to the top of the priority list and become everybody's job. Top management sets the tone and, therefore, needs to fully understand the issues and how to deal with them.

Thomas R. Horton, co-chairman of NACD's Panel on Information Security, reported that seven of every ten boards delegated responsibility for information security to their audit committees. In surveying the boards, it appeared that information security did not always receive the attention it deserved, but there were signs of increasing awareness. One disturbing piece of information in Horton's article was that "less than two-thirds of survey respondents have ongoing training programs on information security for employees." How are publicly traded companies going to be confident that internal controls are capable of offering reliable financial reporting and compliance with laws and regulations when unknowing gaps in information security could occur? Governance over information security is not going to be a quick fix through the application of an instant Holy Grail. It will require involved management and board members to take action and support it with meaningful policies, procedures, and controls. The following section of this chapter will build on the previous chapter and offer a framework for action that will shed light and offer guidance toward meeting the challenge.

Technology has to become a high-priority component of management's agenda. Governance must include a consistent program of monitoring, assessing, and managing risk to provide acceptable levels of reliability. Only reasonable assurance is possible because absolute 100% information security is just not feasible. The governance challenge will require expanded expertise to maintain the level of knowledge and skill required to realistically assess objectives, risks, and control over security of IT. Management needs to recognize that threats can come from any number of sources, with perhaps the greatest risk occurring from within the organization. Armed with this knowledge, management and boards should raise the priority level and take the necessary steps required to establish a more secure IT environment.

ACCOUNTABILITY AND AWARENESS

Accountability relative to information security starts at the top. This means that top management and boards of directors need to understand security issues and move past the perception that it is a technical problem. Management has to develop an awareness of the people and process steps needed to create a system capable of providing for security of information. This should be a top-down process so that the "tone at the top" is communicated and understood at all levels of the enterprise. Once people understand the seriousness of safeguarding information, they are in a better position to minimize the risks.

Awareness is the first step toward accountability and making information security a component of internal controls and corporate governance. Communication of the importance of information security and what to do about it is crucial. All organizations need to have a plan for making sure that all the right people understand their individual roles with respect to security. This issue is a component of internal control and governance. You cannot have a corporate framework for internal control and governance that does not include technology and its implications. The COSO Framework recognizes the importance of IT, and the Public Company Accounting Oversight Board also understands its impact on internal control. The difficulty is that they do not provide a roadmap or tool kit that spells out the starting point and destination with the clarity required by most organizations.

The Corporate Governance Task Force formed in December 2003 has developed a framework that contains several tools that can be used by organizations to embed cyber security into their governance process. Work performed by the International Organization for Standardization/International Electrotechnical Commission (ISO/IEC 17799) and the Federal Information Security Management Act was utilized to create a framework to guide organizations in their development of an information security structure. I will highlight some of these tools, together with the COBiT Framework and concepts developed by the Institute of Internal Auditors. By applying and blending in these best practices with Section 404 compliance, management can craft effective continuous programs for building a solid information security governance foundation.

Senior management has to develop and create accountability and awareness by establishing specific guidelines, procedures, and policies that should be applied throughout the organization. Security and technology are dynamic and constantly changing. Given these dynamics, management then needs to address the following basics:

- How is responsibility assigned?
- Do people understand their responsibilities?
- Have people and functions accepted their responsibilities?
- Can they respond effectively and quickly when incidents occur?

These are pretty basic questions with universal application to all processes, not just security. Since security and technology are people and process issues, identification of the process and the guidelines for their operation becomes critical. It becomes a matter of what people and processes should and should not do. For these reasons, it is important that the person responsible for IT and security report high enough in the organization to ensure that there is accountability and understanding at the top levels of management. A recent trend is to have CIOs report directly to the CEO. This approach provides greater assurance that technology, business, and governance are more universally applied and understood throughout the enterprise. The key is to find the model. At Microsoft, information security reports to the chief operating officer as a peer, level with the CIO.

Based on incidents of security breaches and in the opinion of many experts, people represent the greatest area of vulnerability. One example provided by the task force was a systems administrator who retained access to the system after being fired, which allegedly cost the company millions of dollars and destroyed intellectual property. Security in essence boils down to ethical use of systems by people, and the greatest risk appears to be people within the organization. Risks are not always from people who knowingly create problems; sometimes they are from personnel who unknowingly place the entity at risk through either lack of training or lack of effective policies and procedures. Training and retention of knowledgeable personnel represent a challenge across the board. It is more critical with IT people because of the rapid pace of change.

STRUCTURE AND INTEGRATION

Sarbanes-Oxley represents a primary motivator for corporations to address governance, of which information security is clearly a component. There are a number of other legislative initiatives that have addressed information security, documented in Figure 9.1. The problem with this legislation is that it has not been a universally accepted framework for structuring and integrating IT and security issues into corporate entities. While Sarbanes-Oxley represents the key driver, it applies only to publicly traded companies, which leaves significant gaps because the issue encompasses individuals, nonprofit organizations, and a host of privately owned companies. We are also dealing with a global economy dependent on extended supply chains and a trend to provide deeper access to services and information. Employees and customers now have real-time access because of the increasing automation of business processes to gain

- Sarbanes-Oxley Act
- Health Insurance Portability and Accountability Act (HIPAA)
- Gramm-Leach-Bliley Act (GABA)
- Federal Information Security Management Act (FISMA)
- Personal Information Protection and Electronic Documents Act (PIPEDA)
- EU Directive on Data Protection (EU Data Directive)
- California Security Breach Information Act (SB 1386)
- Putnam Bill (SEC Reporting)

Figure 9.1. Information security governance legislative initiatives.

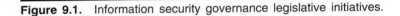

and sustain a competitive advantage. The relationships of this trend are presented in Figure 9.2.

The National Cyber Security Summit Task Force issued a call to action in April 2004 that offers a process (IDEAL) and an assessment tool that organizations can follow to create an information security integration structure. Documenting and discussing all the components of the task force report extend beyond the scope of this chapter and book. It is important to highlight the key

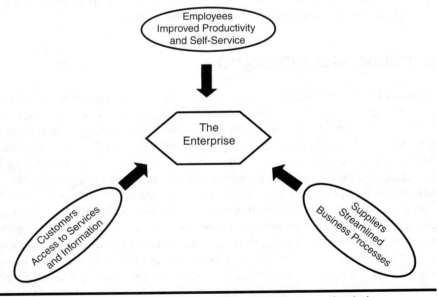

Figure 9.2. Securing digital information in the extended supply chain.

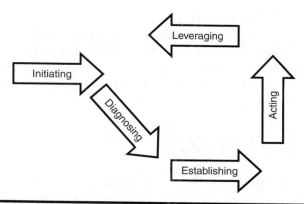

Figure 9.3.   The IDEAL process.

features of the recommendations because they represent a sensible approach to a difficult and pervasive problem. Components of the IDEAL process are presented in Figure 9.3 and were developed by Carnegie Mellon University's Software Engineering Institute.

The task force also developed a framework that can be followed to integrate cyber security into the corporate governance process. Areas of governance addressed by the framework include the following topics:

- Board of directors functions
- Senior management functions
- Authority of the management executive team
- Authority of senior managers
- Responsibilities of all employees and users
- Organizational unit security program
- Organizational unit reporting
- Information security system evaluation

The task force study utilized the COBiT Framework together with accepted security practices spelled out in ISO/IEC 17799. The study also encourages conducting regular assessment as to the organization's business dependency on IT, the risk management process, people, and processes that are components of an information security program.

Creation of the Department of Homeland Security has provided a great deal of traction to information security governance because of the increased awareness to the issues. Also, the task force study recommended that the Committee of Sponsoring Organizations of the Treadway Commission (COSO) should revise its *Internal Control—Integrated Framework* to specifically address information security governance. The recent *Enterprise Risk Management—Integrated Framework* places new focus on managing risk, which indirectly covers information security governance. The reality is that each organization will need to develop programs and assurance tools that best fit its unique situation. There will never be a "one size fits all" blueprint that answers all the questions and addresses all the issues.

CHALLENGE OF E-BUSINESS

E-business has become a key tool in conducting business and for communication between corporations on a worldwide basis. There have been a number of applications that fall into the category of e-business, and almost all of them are Internet based. These applications include electronic marketplaces and exchanges and even the security of the supply chain. We now have electronic banking and processing of cash and security transactions utilizing the Internet. However, the most utilized form of e-business is e-mail. It has become the foundation for corporate communication. All of these electronic tools and applications have created new security and governance challenges. E-mail has become the most used format for corporate collaboration. It is estimated that up to 70% of a typical organization's intellectual property is contained in the e-mail system used for corporate communication. The pressure of regulatory issues from federal, state, and international sources, most notably the Sarbanes-Oxley Act, has created new rules on how and what information corporations need to manage and archive. Record retention and storage have now become major issues affecting corporate governance. In addition, e-mail needs to be a major component of corporate infrastructure because of regulatory issues. Another reason for including it in the infrastructure is the disruption to business resulting from lost access to e-mail. Disaster recovery and privacy now represent legitimate business competitive issues for all mid-size and larger corporations. Some of the possibilities for disruption of service include database corruption, virus attacks, and power failures. The options for backup support include an expensive replication service and emergency messaging systems. These solutions provide backup e-mail and text-messaging contact for employees. The support extends to mobile phones, pagers, BlackBerry devices, and alternative e-mail addresses. This is a critical challenge for businesses that rely heavily on the Internet.

E-mail now provides support and documentation for business more so than memos and reports. Accordingly, document retention is now a major issue because of Sarbanes-Oxley, the Health Insurance Portability and Accountability Act, and the Patriot Act. It is important to understand retention periods, acceptable types of storage, and the techniques for searching and retrieving messages. The need for searching through archived e-mail using specified selection criteria is now a basic business necessity. These basics together with the legal requirements are now forcing evaluation of the policies and protocol for archival and retrieval of messages and for providing an acceptable documented audit trail.

We now realize that somewhere between 50 and 70% of an organization's intellectual capital is floating around in cyberspace in the e-mail system. On top of this realization, we must appreciate the complexity and vulnerability surrounding e-mail. Company employees can expose the system to virus attacks either knowingly or unknowingly. Also, proprietary company information may be forwarded to a person who is not on a need-to-know list. Software applications have been developed that can block both viruses as well as sensitive e-mail messages. While this helps to mitigate mistakes and prevent virus contamination, it cannot overcome deliberate attempts at sabotage and subterfuge. Therefore, a clear corporate policy should be considered to cover acceptable e-mail usage and monitoring, retention, and handling of confidential information.

Extended supply chains and visibility to data represent a major challenge for e-business. Supply chain security is now on everyone's agenda because it facilitates faster processing of shipments between countries. The United States has created a voluntary Customs-Trade Partnership Against Terrorism (C-TPAT) program. This program provides for companies to self-assess supply chain security and agree to government inspections in exchange for faster processing of shipments. This helps to provide for and facilitate the faster movement of products.

In addition to the challenges of e-mail, the other tools utilized for e-commerce demand enhanced levels of security. The reality is that companies as well as individuals are more dependent on the Internet as the foundation for conducting business. Identity theft has become a major threat as a component of white-collar crime. The foundation for accounting and monetary transactions is now more dependent on technology than ever before. This means that IT audits are a necessity. These audits should focus on the major components of IT infrastructure, such as the enterprise resource planning systems, accounting applications, and business intelligence. The audit should also include evaluation of the business continuity and disaster recovery programs. It is likely that the audits will be conducted in conjunction with management's self-assessment of internal control under Section 404. Audits should include a risk assessment and evaluate the major systems that support the critical business processes. If a company does not have an internal audit function capable of evaluating the complexity of IT issues and infrastructures, it will then need to engage outside experts to assist with the evaluation process. The audits should consider the capability of the IT infrastructure to detect and prevent fraud in addition to the quality of the security controls surrounding the system.

ASSESSING AND MANAGING RISK

Information security is a challenge that extends beyond hackers and service denial. It boils down to the critical success factors that contribute to appropriate information security. Management needs to provide a framework for the entire spectrum of occurrences that will subject the organization to risk and the steps required to manage it. Accordingly, it is critical to conduct an assessment of the needs and requirements across the organization relative to the information security assets and information which must be protected.

A security information risk assessment must touch all of the functional areas, including IT, finance, operations, internal audit, sales and marketing, human resources, and other organizational components. The assessment needs to cover the following issues:

- Hackers and terrorists
- Natural disasters
- Business continuity planning
- Data classification and retention
- Backup strategies
- Incident handling

A careful and thorough assessment needs to address what assets must be protected and the extent of protection provided. This boils down to deciding on the level of risk acceptable to the organization, including insurance coverage and the amount of self-insurance. Self-insurance is predicated on determining when the occurrence of risk is so unlikely that specific action is unnecessary and you just take your chances. Since there is a great deal of protection available, it then becomes a function of how much is needed. Hurricanes in certain parts of the country will necessitate a fallback position, while other locations would not have the same level of concern.

A key component of risk assessment is evaluating access to data and controls over what data can be accessed. Consideration should be given to all the perspectives and elements across the organization and should result in the creation of a balanced information security policy. Issues associated with data access deal with applications, firewall security, compliance, and monitoring privacy. The marketing function has to be involved and should be aware of these issues

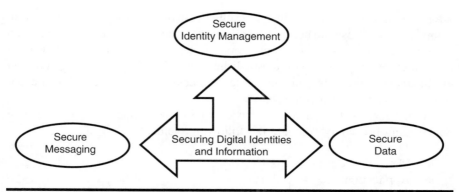

Figure 9.4.   Securing digital identities and information.

in order to balance conflicting objectives. Organizations want marketing and customer service to be as smooth as possible and at the same time preserve privacy and confidentiality of data and information. Figure 9.4 presents the components associated with securing digital identities and information. Risk evaluation needs to factor in the amount of flexibility that should be allowed in setting the level of protection for the organizations versus the degree of risk relative to vulnerability.

Most companies are primarily concerned with hackers and terrorists. This concern has been increasing as more incidents have occurred that created problems and loss of business. The consequences of weak security adversely affect the value of organizations that fall victim to attacks. According to the *Critical Infrastructure Assurance Project* conducted by the Institute of Internal Auditors, the Information Security Foundation provides a benchmark estimate of 2–7% of overall IT spending as a range organizations should expect for IT infrastructure security, but found that it was actually less than 1.5%. Because of the risks associated with information security, it becomes a necessity for top management and boards of directors to take charge and make sure their organization has analyzed its risk and developed a plan to avoid, detect, and mitigate it.

SECURITY ACCESS: HOW SECURE IS SECURE?

There is no such thing as a 100% secure system. However, security can be tightened and made more secure in order to provide greater assurance against the potential vulnerability resulting from conducting business in the age of information. Much of the challenge results in keeping employees honest and in compliance with established policies and procedures. A communication plan should be developed so that the entire organization has awareness of the security infrastructure and abides by the established rules. The key is making sure that management coordinates and integrates polices and procedures that are designed to maintain effective security.

Some areas that need to be considered in the development of effective policies and procedures include the following elements:

- Platform security access
- Application access security
- Network security
- Physical security
- Security of process flow

The elements of platform security access should include permissions and password protocol in addition to systems backup and event logging. Application access should also include account and password protection together with database management and security. Network security must consider steps to prevent unauthorized access via modems and wireless connections. Other issues include device sharing and event logging together with physical security over access to hardware. Finally, care needs to be exercised to provide security over process flows via data transmission. This is a brief overview of the steps that need to be considered in making sure that vulnerability to the system is minimized. Making security more secure should not only be effectively managed but should also be a focus of an audit. The audit should be conducted by the internal audit staff or subcontracted to an outside auditor knowledgeable in IT and information security.

If information security is to be effective, it is critical that everyone in the organization take ownership of the task. It becomes everybody's job and not just the task of a control group. Threats come from within and outside the organization, and cyber risk takes many shapes. Examples of the most common threats include:

- Computer threats
- Computer viruses
- Employee abuse of the network and system
- Financial and telephone fraud

While the above incidents comprise about 80% of the risk, other examples of risk include penetration of the system, theft of information and intellectual capital, sabotage, and denial of service. After reviewing the types of risk, it becomes clear that risk management needs to embrace more than technology. Effective security needs to include people and processes, in addition to effective application of technology because we are striving to protect information assets.

THE INTERNET REVOLUTION

ARPANET was developed by the U.S. Department of Defense in conjunction with military contractors and universities to explore a communication network that was capable of surviving a nuclear attack. It turned out to be an efficient and effective means of communication and is now known as the Internet. It has grown from 3 million users in 1993 to in excess of 200 million today on a worldwide basis. The Internet has evolved into an economic driving force that has become responsible for more than a quarter of all the economic growth since 1993 according the U.S. Department of Commerce.

Households now shop online, and the revolution has spawned an entire multilayer Internet economy. The University of Texas with the sponsorship of Cisco Systems developed economic metrics to measure the impact across four primary economic layers:

1. Infrastructure
2. Applications
3. Intermediary
4. Commerce

Infrastructure includes backbone and service providers together with computer makers. Infrastructure also includes security vendors, fiber optics manufacturers, and networking hardware and software vendors. Applications include consultants, commerce applications, search engines, web development, and web-enabled databases. The intermediary layer includes market makers, brokerages, content providers, and online advertising. Internet commerce includes online retailers, manufacturers selling online, airlines, online entertainment, and professional services.

According to the University of Texas Center for Research in Electronic Commerce, the Internet economy generated over $300 billion in revenue within the United States during 1998 and created over 1.2 million jobs. The job growth has increased to over three million workers, making the Internet economy one of the most important sectors in the world. The Internet is a major contributor to both small and large business growth. Not only do a majority of companies sell their products and services over the Internet, but it has also become a critical component of the communication infrastructure around the world. The Internet drives and fosters innovation and has evolved into a critical component of the world's financial stability. When one understands the impact and importance of IT, then the vulnerabilities and risks become much clearer.

INFORMATION WARFARE

We have seen how the Internet has not only created an economic boom known as the "new economy" but at the same time created a real and potentially catastrophic threat to American security. As the Honorable Charles E. Schumer, senator from New York, stated: "Cyber-security and critical infrastructure protection are among the most important national security issues facing our country." The new economy has become increasingly dependent on the innovation of high-technology goods and services. We have the age of information driven by the continuous acceleration of digital technology and information.

Cyberspace is the crux of e-commerce as well as the foundation of our defense and intelligence systems. In addition, the country's economic infrastructure, such as telecommunications, transportation, energy, and financial services, is dependent on the Internet and digital communication. This realization leaves the country exposed to a wide range of cyber risks. Examples from the Critical Infrastructure Assurance Conference are revealing and provide a new light on the level of vulnerability we face.

Several countries, including Russia and China, are spending billions to enhance their Internet warfare capabilities. Even more frightening is the realization that terrorist cells are also adapting this same high level of cyber warfare capability. Terrorists have the potential to place "sniffers," which are devices capable of stealing information from a computer network. These devices are virtually impossible to detect and are capable of being inserted anywhere. This makes them extremely dangerous due to their capability of stealing and corrupting data. This could potentially sabotage portions of the financial system and produce a Wall Street panic. A similar impact could occur relative to power grids, telecommunication systems, and transportation, such as air traffic control.

We have witnessed the impact of computer viruses, worms, and denial of service attacks on web sites such as Yahoo and eBay. After realizing the vulnerability of our infrastructure, the potential impact from determined cyber terrorists places risk in a different perspective. The danger is real, frightening, and extends well beyond disruption of digital communication via e-mail. Information warfare has the potential to produce a disruption that extends beyond comprehension. The challenge is not just for the government, but also for the private sector to recognize and commit the funds and focus needed to properly address these threats.

INFORMATION SECURITY TOOLS

There are a number of information security tools that can be applied and utilized to minimize and manage cyber risks. One of the primary tools is contained in the COBiT Framework, which was previously discussed. I like this framework because it offers a comprehensive checklist for business process owners as well as insight and direction for users and auditors. SysTrust™ is an assurance service created by the American Institute of Certified Public Accountants designed to provide comfort to management, customers, and business partners supporting a business or activity. This service evaluates and tests whether or not a system is reliable when measured against the principles of security, integrity, and maintainability. Another tool is British Standard 17799, which provides a single reference point for identifying a range of controls used in industry and commerce. The standard is grounded in preserving confidentiality, integrity, and availability. In addition to these tools, there are generally accepted systems security principles (GASSPs) that establish and spell out principles for board-level guidance, functional principles designed for executive-level information management, and detailed principles that guide operational security management. Guidelines established by the Organization for Economic Cooperation and Development and the International Information Technology Guideline developed by the International Federation of Accountants provide additional insight and direction.

What these tool kits collectively boil down to is a full array of information that provides guidance on setting IT strategy and implementing an infrastructure that manages delivery and support of IT services. These tools then provide direction on effective monitoring of IT processes, including internal and external audit. The issue with IT is that management and directors failed to address the issues and problems associated with the growing pervasiveness of digitally based business. Not only has private business not come to grips with the growing magnitude of risks associated with the information revolution, but governments have failed to provide the leadership and funding necessary to cope with the gaps and vulnerability of our information security infrastructure.

Top management, corporate boards of directors, and government collectively need to realize the importance and magnitude of managing information security. It is an ever-changing and evolving process that requires a combined concerted effort across and throughout the entire infrastructure. Threats may arise internally or externally from either intentional or unintentional acts. The types of issues can range from technical to natural disasters. Furthermore, these factors can be combined or mixed with human factors plus reliance on third parties. They all add up to a loss of management control and a major threat to the availability and reliability of information needed to execute the business and economic infrastructure that supports our survival and well being. Yes, there are checklists and tools that will get the job done, but only if they are properly managed.

REAL-TIME GOVERNANCE

Monitoring is the process of assessing and ensuring that all components of internal control and risk management are functioning properly as designed. Internal control is not a one-time event. Controls need to provide continuing ongoing assurance. Business is dynamic from day to day, and perhaps even faster as the pace of innovation and dissemination of information accelerates. Organizational structures shift and change to meet the demands of business. New personnel are hired and others depart. People drive the evolution of business processes and operate them. Management needs to have continuing assurance that processes and controls are functioning as designed.

Management needs to understand the level of effectiveness of internal control across the enterprise. Accordingly, the continuous evaluation and assessment of internal controls is a major component of management responsibility. The degree of assessment and evaluation depends on the level of risk associated with the process controls in place. Monitoring of internal controls is accomplished in two primary ways: ongoing monitoring and separate evaluation. Considering the accelerated pace of business and transactions, the most appropriate method is ongoing monitoring. However, there may be a need to back up and take a fresh look at the processes and controls through application of separate evaluations. Monitoring typically involves some blend of the two approaches. Section 404 requires that management assess the controls it designed to provide assurance for reliable financial reporting and compliance with laws and regulations. This assessment is intended to provide assurance that both approaches to monitoring internal control and enterprise risk management (ERM) are functioning properly.

ONGOING MONITORING

The concept of ongoing monitoring occurs on a real-time basis, responding to the dynamics of changing conditions, and is embedded into the process structure. Ongoing monitoring also includes continuous management and supervisory efforts and actions to check the reliability and accuracy of data and reports. In these instances, operating and support personnel evaluate the output from the business and operating processes. Tools used for this purpose include a number of new software applications that have evolved and were covered in Chapter 8.

Document management and workflow tools are combined with pattern recognition and business intelligence applications. Process workflow applications can alert managers to situations that lock down and provide warnings when incidents exceed the upper and lower limits of process variation. In addition, a variety of software tools are capable of exchanging data in order to monitor functional and performance situations that overlay existing software applications. These new tools have the capability to provide management with data on a real-time basis. Their application has facilitated development of more efficient business processes to optimize the availability and accuracy of data fed to management monitoring systems.

It is estimated that a significant number of companies will evolve toward real-time monitoring and reporting systems under the mantle of business process management or business performance management. I prefer to combine these concepts under the term "business process management and measurement." We will explore these applications in Chapters 15 and 16. Since they fall under ongoing monitoring, it is important to mention them at this juncture. This represents an integrated approach to building compliance and management reporting into the internal control framework so that strategic and operational objectives are met simultaneously as a component of ERM. This provides a new and broader vision of compliance and continuous monitoring together with process improvement, which is illustrated in Figure 10.1. Being able to achieve ongoing monitoring through the utilization of people, processes, and technology provides a unique opportunity for business to capitalize on the demands of complying with Sarbanes-Oxley.

Ongoing monitoring is differentiated from control activities that occur in the operation of the business processes. Some additional examples of ongoing monitoring activities include the following:

Real-Time Monitoring

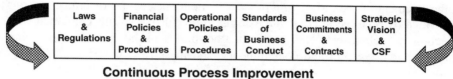

Laws & Regulations	Financial Policies & Procedures	Operational Policies & Procedures	Standards of Business Conduct	Business Commitments & Contracts	Strategic Vision & CSF

Continuous Process Improvement

Figure 10.1. Oversight and ERM.

- Review of operations on an ongoing basis utilizing real-time reports and dashboards
- Consideration of at risk value models regarding the impact on the entity's financial position
- Monitoring input from customers and business partners
- Input from regulators
- Feedback from workshops, training seminars, and other meetings
- Day-to-day feedback from conducting business through e-mails, conversations, and phone calls

While real-time monitoring controls are embedded in the system, it still takes people to react and respond to output. Even embedded digital checks and balances will require a human response to correct input errors. Whether it is a customer response or management review, the process of ongoing monitoring is human based. Customers will provide feedback relative to billing accuracy or issues with quality or service. Management reviews dashboards or key performance indicators based on event or escalation triggers to track trends and magnitude of risk. Comparisons might be made to budgets, prior periods, or target and tolerance ranges. Event or target triggers represent qualitative or quantitative risk indicators that provide timely insight into a variety of risks. Escalation triggers report exceptions whenever certain thresholds are exceeded and provide notification to management on a timely basis. Information can be both financial and nonfinancial, as ongoing monitoring might involve unauthorized access to the systems network or sales data by region or product.

Ongoing monitoring should touch on all elements of a company's system of internal control and management of enterprise risk. The process of ongoing monitoring needs to be a component of the organizational structure and management activities that provide control and identification of deficiencies. Another element of the monitoring process is input and regular recommendations provided by both the internal and external audit functions. This combined with Section 404 self-assessments and evaluations builds a solid foundation for more effective management and containment of business risks.

SEPARATE EVALUATIONS

Even though ongoing monitoring provides most of the feedback regarding the effectiveness of internal control and management of risk, it is important to obtain a fresh point of view periodically. In addition to receiving affirmation on the effectiveness of internal control, separate assessments produce feedback regarding ongoing monitoring procedures. The *ERM—Integrated Framework* outlines approaches to conducting separate evaluations. Section 404 calls for management of publicly traded companies to conduct an assessment of internal controls that impact financial reporting and compliance with laws and regulations. The Sarbanes-Oxley Act and the final Securities and Exchange Commission (SEC) regulations specify that an acceptable framework for internal control be followed and referenced to the COSO Integrated Framework as being acceptable. The ERM Framework offers added clarity on methodology and tools used in conducting the evaluation.

We will blend the two frameworks in preparation for a more in-depth discussion of self-assessments in Chapter 11. The objective of separate evaluations is to make sure that the design of the risk management and internal control system is sound and that it is functioning in accordance with the objectives—in other words, make sure that the system is working properly. Evaluators need to make sure that they understand the system, together with all the procedures and activities, both from an entity-wide perspective and at the activity level. Management is responsible for designing and maintaining the internal control system and therefore will need to dig into the organization and find out from those closest to the action if the system is functioning properly.

Separate evaluations can range from an entity-wide assessment to the monitoring of a specific process. Section 404 assessment is entity-wide, whereas the evaluation of a newly implemented enterprise resource planning system deals with separate monitoring of a new process. The steps include defining the objectives and scope of the evaluation. It is important to select appropriate personnel to manage and conduct the evaluation. The planning process should consider the methodology to be followed in conducting the evaluation and the tools and techniques that will be employed. Creating a project plan for the evaluation is critical and should consider the time line and due dates for completing the work.

The evaluation in many instances might be carried out by the internal audit function since it can bring a more objective perspective in monitoring a company's ERM system and issues. Internal auditors are now being asked to broaden their scope of work beyond the financial segments to include strategic and operational objectives and applications. In addition, internal audit personnel are more likely to have the knowledge and training to conduct the evaluation and to utilize the tools and methodologies needed to test the relevant information associated with risk assessment and control activities. A variety of tools and methodologies are available to conduct effective evaluations and assessments. They include process flowcharting and mapping, benchmarking, computerized tools and audit techniques, workshops and facilitated sessions, and interviews. The evaluation team will have to sort out the approach and methodologies that will produce the desired results based on the scope of the evaluation. The key is realizing that a variety of proven methodologies are available. Evaluators should consider all of the components of the COSO frameworks for internal control and risk management when selecting the tools. Accordingly, consistent application of best practices related to governance, risk management, and compliance is aligned and linked to effective business strategy and operational performance.

DEFICIENCY IDENTIFICATION

A deficiency is a shortcoming or weakness in internal control or risk management. It can represent an adverse impact or an opportunity to strengthen or improve the company. The SEC uses the term "significant deficiency" in a similar context as generally accepted auditing standards (GAAS) use the term "reportable condition." A deficiency in internal control is something that could adversely affect the company's financial reporting process as well as the critical processes that provide data and information in the financial reporting process. In a risk management sense, a deficiency is a condition that represents a perceived, potential, or real shortcoming associated with the achievement of the entity's objectives. Therefore, an opportunity to strengthen an entity's risk management process also needs to be viewed in a similar fashion. Any condition to improve the process represents a reportable condition.

Understanding deficiencies is critical to compliance. Deficiencies can be caused by two situations. Deficiencies can result from improperly designed controls or properly designed controls that are not functioning as intended. The latter are called operating deficiencies. Deficiencies develop because internal controls are processes designed by people and inefficiencies work their way into the processes over time and need to be fixed. This is the reason for conducting both ongoing and separate evaluations in order to identify root causes of problems in the process and correct them. When process deficiencies are identified, they should be redesigned and solutions implemented to correct the situation. Deficiencies in internal control can vary in significance from minor to significant. If the deficiency is significant, it might also represent a material weakness that could create an adverse audit opinion.

A significant deficiency becomes a material weakness when it could produce a material impact on the financial statements. It occurs when there is a high probability that errors or irregularities can produce amounts material to the financial statements and not be detected by employees and the processes. This is a complex process described in more detail in Chapter 14, which discusses audits and auditors. Much of the determination relates to the overall control environment, the nature of the weakness, compensating controls, and the nature of assets at risk. It should be noted that weaknesses relating to fraud are almost always indicative of a material weakness.

Up to this point, our discussion has focused on deficiencies relating to internal control which could impact the reliability of financial reporting. From an ERM point of view, deficiencies are factors or events that could have an impact on the entity's ability to achieve strategic and operational objectives. Deficiencies can relate to identified opportunities to improve the likelihood that objectives can be met or exceeded. Sarbanes-Oxley has focused too much attention on financial reporting instead of driving home the importance of enterprise-wide risk management. The real benefit results from having management concentrate on improving the procedures and processes that determine how the systems function. Management and boards need to provide for effective communication of deficiencies on an enterprise-wide basis by utilizing a solid foundation for identifying and reporting all critical deficiencies that can flow from the evaluation processes that are either ongoing or from separate assessments.

REASONABLE ASSURANCE

Reasonable assurance is a very high level of assurance, but it is not a guarantee that an event will not occur. The concept of reasonable assurance evolves from financial accounting standards (FAS No. 5) which classify likelihood into three categories:

1. *Probable*: The future event or events are likely to occur.
2. *Reasonably possible*: The chance of the future event or events occurring is more than remote but less than likely.
3. *Remote*: The chance of the future event or events occurring is slight.

A significant deficiency is a control deficiency, or combination of deficiencies, that adversely affects the company's ability to initiate, authorize, record, process, or report external financial data reliably in accordance with generally accepted accounting principles. There is more than a remote likelihood that a misstatement of the company's financial statements will not be prevented or detected. In this instance, the misstatement is presumed to be more than inconsequential.

A material weakness occurs when there is a significant deficiency, or a combination of significant deficiencies, that results in more than a remote likelihood that a material misstatement of the financial statements will not be prevented or detected. Deciding if the control deficiency is material should be based on both quantitative and qualitative evaluations and considerations. Qualitative considerations should include factors that influence the financial statement accounts and assertions and consideration of the possible future consequences of the deficiency. A material weakness should be based on its probable likelihood of occurring and its significance relative to the financial statements. Figure 10.2 illustrates the relativity of factors that could produce a material weakness. This determination should consider the effect of compensating controls and whether the compensation controls are effective. Both management and auditors will need to exercise their judgment as to what is reasonable assurance and what is material. When there are questions, it is best to step back and ascertain how another independent objective professional might evaluate the situation and what conclusion he or she would reach.

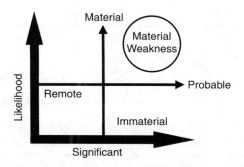

Figure 10.2.   Concept of material weakness.

CONTROL GAPS

Control gaps should be considered as voids in both internal control as well as in managing risks. The monitoring process is designed to identify and categorize risk management deficiencies and opportunities, establish a process whereby they can be analyzed, and create action plans to close the gap. Continuous improvement is the real opportunity associated with Sarbanes-Oxley to go beyond compliance at a moment in time. Figure 10.3 documents the five levels or stages of evolution of risk and control management from early evolvement to optimization. We will now expand on these five levels of development that build understanding of the potential of continuous improvement of strategic and operational effectiveness.

Initially, organizations are dependent on their people to take the initiative to put out fires, as described in level 1. In this state of evolution, organizations have not developed designated process owners capable of managing risk. The organization is people dependent, which carries high risks and the potential for inefficiencies and high costs. Financial and operational reporting and accountability is not rigorous. Limiting personnel turnover is critical to maintaining operational stability relative to the attainment of established objectives.

Level 2 is defined as evolving, whereby the entity is establishing some basic structure of policy together with supporting processes and controls. The organization at this stage is beginning to develop defined roles and responsibilities. Combined with the establishment of authority, the organization is putting into place processes and reporting mechanisms that are starting to provide a higher level of substance and consistency. This stage of development is still highly reliant on people, and gaps in process documentation have not been filled.

Stage of Capability	Description	Attributes
Level 1	Early	Fire Fighting
Level 2	Evolving	People Reliant
Level 3	Defined	Processes Developed and Defined
Level 4	Effective	Quantitative Performance Measurement
Level 5	Optimized	Best Practices — Continuous Improvement

Figure 10.3.   Risk and control management capability.

When we evolve to level 3, we see that the entity has started to advance its development of processes and map the flow of its transactions. At this defined stage of evolution, the organization will typically have identified the risk of errors and omissions, and the controls required to mitigate these risks will have been ascertained. While the known control gaps have usually been identified, there is no assurance that all potential deficiencies have been recognized. The weakness at this level is that the entity is not conducting self-assessments of its processes together with alignment with its internal audit function. However, steps toward achieving focus and direction are in evidence and the foundation is starting to be created for moving to the next level.

Effectiveness starts to gain traction in level 4 as the defined state becomes more quantitative. This is when financial and nonfinancial performance measures provide feedback to management and the board based on controls and risk management practices that are working as intended. At this level, process owners and management are conducting self-evaluations and the internal audit function is aligned to provide assurance to management regarding process effectiveness. The control and risk management frameworks are beginning to provide effective accountability regarding achievement of objectives and control reliability.

Optimization is reached at level 5 when entities achieve the highest state of capability. There is an entity-wide focus on identifying root causes and performing continuous improvement. Best practices are implemented and shared throughout the organization and there is effective responsiveness to changing external and internal conditions. Technology is utilized to document control policies, processes, and real-time reporting. At this level, the entity has effectively aligned its policies, processes, people, technology, and knowledge. This is the desired state whereby organizations employ ERM application techniques to build a foundation for achieving effectively designed processes to enable achievement of strategic and organizational objectives in a cost-effective fashion. This optimized state produces a level of governance, risk, and compliance combined with operational excellence that drives competitive advantage.

Now that we have identified the five levels of control and risk capability, we need to provide the steps required to address control gaps. Control gaps relate to either design deficiencies or effectively designed controls that are not operating as designed. After management has identified the deficiencies, it must develop and implement a solution to close the gap. These action plans should differentiate between design and operating deficiencies, since each situation will necessitate different action steps.

Design solutions should address the company's specific situation and objectives while effectively improving the control weaknesses identified. The revised design should identify specific tasks and the use of resources, consisting of people, processes, and technology, together with a time line for implementation. Operational deficiencies must address clarification of roles and responsibilities and ensure that competent employees are in place to execute the control as it was designed. It is important that management develop measurements and monitoring steps to ensure that design and operating deficiencies are performing appropriately.

When control gaps are identified, a reporting protocol should be in place to ensure that the deficiency is reported to the proper person at an appropriate level within the organization. When serious infractions occur, the chief executive would normally be informed, especially when there is a material financial impact or the event has strategic implications. Internal control deficiencies should be reported to the individual responsible for the function or activity and probably to at least one level of management above the responsible person. However, any incident involving fraud or an illegal act should be channeled to the top level of the organization so that effective action can be taken.

Closing control gaps is even more critical than identifying the gap. The following steps should be considered in following up with corrective action to implement solutions:

1. Assess responsibility for process design
   a. Who is responsible?
   b. What is expected to close the gap?
   c. What will be expected after the gap is filled?
2. Document the revised design of the improved control
3. Design a process-owner monitoring report
4. Ensure alignment of process owner roles with relevant control objectives
5. Align the process owner with performance objectives
6. Determine if the proposed solutions are adequate and ready for implementation
7. Create an implementation plan together with an appropriate time line

After a corrective action plan is established, it is necessary to make sure that any plan includes the development of training together with appropriate levels of documentation. At this stage, it is critical to ensure the buy-in of the process owner relative to the implementation steps developed. In addition to process owner approval and acceptance of the corrective action, buy-in should be obtained from the appropriate level of management, together with a commitment to move ahead with implementation of the solution. To ensure a successful and effective implementation, it is important to provide the necessary training to the process owners and employees responsible for executing and monitoring the improved control activity. After enhancements have been implemented, it is important to continue a positive attitude for application of continuous improvement to the revised process.

DEFINING COMPLIANCE RISK

We will consider enterprise-wide risks in association with real-time governance, but since everyone is riveted on compliance, it is important to deal specifically with those issues. Defining compliance risk begins with understanding material risks. We have to turn to the SEC, which has indicated that a "material weakness" has the same meaning under GAAS and attestation standards. Taking this further, the SEC clarified that both a "material weakness" and a "significant deficiency" relate both to the design and operation of internal controls that could adversely impact a company's financial statements. This can relate to the ability to record, process, summarize, and report financial data consistent with management's assertions in the financial statements.

The SEC's focus is centered on "significant deficiencies" and "material weaknesses." Significant deficiencies may not constitute a material weakness. However, the aggregation of significant deficiencies or a significant deficiency in internal control that could have a material effect on the financial statements based on its severity is what will drive the determination. The key is utilizing and applying the "remote likelihood" rules to situations in evaluating the occurrence of material errors or fraud. A material weakness in internal control is a condition where there is a high probability that material errors or misstatements in the financial statements will not be detected by process controls or employees executing them. This evaluation should consider the overall impact on the financial statements and the financial reporting process taken as a whole.

Three primary considerations influence the determination regarding whether a deficiency or control weakness is material. First, the amount of audit testing performed by the external auditor is a signal that a larger level audit risk exists. This will be evidenced by audit sample sizes and the timing of audit work relative to the closing date of the financial statements. These signals indicate the need to assess the level of residual audit risk and determine if it is acceptable. Second is the emergence of proposed adjustments and the necessity to evaluate the nature of the adjustments and their root causes to determine if they were the direct result of a material weakness. Finally, it is necessary to consider and evaluate the characteristics of the control weaknesses identified.

Evaluating the characteristics of control weaknesses identified should consider a range of factors. We have touched on these considerations at various points, but it is worthwhile to provide a representative listing that includes the following points which will yield some guidance for making a determination of compliance risk:

- Control environment and management attitude regarding internal control
- Consider the characteristics of any identified control deficiencies together with the existence of any compensating controls
- Evaluate the categories of assets and their attributes and how they could be affected by a control weakness
- Consider the presence of other control weaknesses, whereby a combination of immaterial weaknesses could represent a material weakness
- Evaluate the stability of the company's operations, personnel, and systems as a potential for creating a control weakness
- Reflect on past history of the company and the attitude toward accounting estimates and management's process for establishing valuations

Assessing and evaluating potential weaknesses should become ingrained in the monitoring processes so that weaknesses can be fixed and control gaps are closed quickly. The last thing a company wants to face is the reality of having a material weakness and not having adequate time to correct the situation prior to year-end. Effective continuous improvement is vital to a solid program for governance, risk management, and compliance, which is the key to avoiding disclosures under Sections 302 and 404.

BENCHMARKING COMPLIANCE

Benchmarking extends beyond compliance and is a tool that furnishes an entity with the critical information that provides the foundation for managing value. The fundamental issues underlying Sarbanes-Oxley, in reality, are much more than compliance. Benchmarking identifies best practices and to be effective should become an approach of continuous improvement that helps to identify both weaknesses and opportunities. Six Sigma programs incorporate benchmarking into their tool kit as a means of providing valuable information about process effectiveness. Internal and functional benchmarking provides valuable insight relative to understanding how processes are functioning and also what processes are capable of achieving. Internal control is driven by processes and people, which underscores the importance of benchmarking as a risk assessment and continuous improvement tool.

Many companies utilize benchmarking as a separate evaluation technique to see how their internal control systems measure up to other companies. There are a number of ways to determine which companies have "best practice" or "world-class" systems and processes. One obvious way is through reputation based on word of mouth, articles, press releases, and input from consultants and CPAs familiar with such companies. When looking for examples, do not be afraid to switch industries. For example, an order entry model to follow might be a mail order company such as L.L. Bean to provide an illustration of how to establish a process that meets "world-class" standards. Another example is Dell Computer, which is known for its high standards of operational excellence and ability to manage its supply chain. There are a number of emerging solutions that have developed from the enactment of Sarbanes-Oxley, and it is critical to do your homework regarding these solutions.

Benchmarking can be applied to many situations and applications. In the setting of compliance and risk management, we would expect that the focus would be on work processes and operational or strategic opportunities. Consideration of deficiencies as opportunities for potential improvement places a new dimension on the meaning of benchmarking. There are a variety of different reasons to conduct benchmarking, and Figure 10.4 identifies the types of information and applications that a company might select.

Benchmarking techniques help to assess a risk relative to the likelihood of occurrence and the degree or level of its impact. These techniques are applied internally and industry-wide. This risk assessment tool enables companies to develop insight and impact based on the experiences of other organizations. It extends beyond identifying process deficiencies in the performance of compliance testing. It is one of the foundations for continuous improvement because it identifies opportunities.

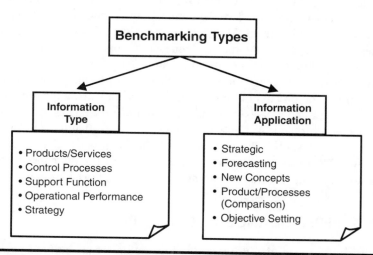

Figure 10.4. Application to benchmarking.

CULTURE AND CHANGE

A component of the monitoring process is separate evaluations that include control self-assessments. The effectiveness of control self-assessments is dependent on the willingness of management and boards of directors to use these tools to their full potential. My workshops put me in touch with professionals from across the country who indicate management's reluctance to engage in the spirit of self-assessment of internal control. There appears to be more of a trend to just achieve compliance than to employ Section 404 assessments as a continuous improvement opportunity. There are frequent examples where management engages an accounting firm to perform the internal control compliance steps and then hold itself above the real issues and meaning intended for management assessment.

Corporate culture is a challenge and a frustration. The reality of corporate culture rests on the culture and training of management and the boards of directors. It even influences the attitude of external auditors, as they have evolved to an environment of avoiding risk at any cost. The result is that we have "do-nothing auditors and managements" that do not want to rock the boat that carries their compensation. Boards are still comprised of independent "good old boys" who were not trained in the discipline of empowered employees and continuous improvement. Participants in my workshops indicated that if they did conduct self-assessments, management was excluded from attending because of fear of reprisal. The tone was a feeling of frustration regarding the narrowness of attitude toward change and the risks associated with it.

Change is a component of competing for the future and requires corporate leadership that is willing to adopt the elements of managing risk in a dynamic global economic environment. Many executives have expressed frustration with the necessity to have the government legislate an approach to self-assessment, which in reality they should have been doing as a best business practice in the first place. At least the legislation brings change and creates movement in the right direction. The process of conducting self-assessments helps organizations see to themselves and creates potential opportunities for change that can move the organization forward. A reality of Sarbanes-Oxley is that it provides a sense of urgency as a result of the alternative to noncompliance. The frameworks offered by COSO provide direction not only toward building more effective internal controls but also for managing enterprise-wide risk.

LINKING PERFORMANCE AND VALUE

Monitoring is a process that provides the foundation for an entity to understand its activities and how they are performing relative to objectives. Ongoing monitoring is really the critical component to ensuring that all of the business processes are functioning as designed and that they are operationally effective. Efficiently designed and operationally effective business processes will yield the best risk response decisions that produce shareholder value. Performance measurement is a key component of ongoing monitoring that helps to ensure continuous generation of value.

Organizations need to pursue continuous application of strategic development and then align these choices with effective execution that translates to creation of value. Monitoring provides the necessary components for evaluating performance. Performance measurement includes the use of financial and non-financial metrics that indicate the status of both leading and lagging indicators of progress. A big part of successful performance measurement is the selection of the proper metrics. Performance measurement extends beyond compliance and encompasses development of strategy and evaluating strategic alternatives.

Metrics based on development of strategic objectives help alert organizations to potential operational surprises and to identify potential opportunities. The feedback process also helps in the identification of risks facing the enterprise and appropriate risk responses. Performance measurement and monitoring is also critical in providing information that allows management to evaluate capital needs and requirements and facilitates allocation of capital to those opportunities capable of producing the greatest value. This process enables leaders to make better decisions relative to risks facing the organization and allows plans to be transformed into results.

REAL-TIME GOVERNANCE

Many of the initial compliance efforts have included utilization of software capable of providing real-time compliance. This represents one of the best developments to evolve out of the Sarbanes-Oxley legislation. The new software products can overlap other software and provide a source for smooth interaction with other software and systems. The objective is to provide real-time monitoring of processes in order to provide management with optimized information and potential compliance problems. In addition to real-time dashboards that monitor sales and operational data, the tools also track business processes and signal early warnings of potential compliance risks.

Future trends in performance measurement and monitoring of compliance risk have a variety of names ranging from corporate performance management to business process management. Successful deployment and application of these tools will require more than purchasing and implementing software. Effective utilization requires empowerment of management teams to utilize a framework of ERM focused on business objectives and a solid foundation of business processes. The shift to these new technology-based tools requires management of culture change grounded in integrity and ethical values. Companies that resort to manual quick fixes and patchwork solutions will be unable to sustain lasting value and a competitive edge in light of the acceleration and pace of business innovation.

The new real-time compliance tools utilize data warehouses to capture information that is fed from all the legacy enterprise resource planning, customer relationship management, and other systems utilized by organizations to manage and monitor their business operations. From the data stored in the warehouses, it is possible to organize and analyze them to detect patterns in financial data for the purpose of improving the accuracy of information and internal controls. Through the use of business intelligence tools, corporations can monitor business process data and report using dashboards that provide management with real-time feedback relative to business and process conditions. This provides a risk monitoring, assessment, and response capability that allows managers to respond dynamically to changing business conditions. Fluctuations in revenue, expenses, cash flow, production, and customer demand allow companies with effective business processes to react and respond quickly to change. This responsiveness provides the foundation for business performance excellence.

11

SELF-ASSESSMENT

Section 404 of the Sarbanes-Oxley Act brings new reality to management teams with the realization that they must assess the effectiveness of their internal controls. While there are a number of provisions of the legislation, Section 404 provided the most dramatic impact compared to other sections because of the extensive amount of change. Beyond the requirement for management to conduct self-assessment of internal controls were the new audit rules whereby external auditors provide an attestation of management's assessment. These revisions specify that internal control evaluation and monitoring are now components of the audit reports. These reports contain management's internal control report and the auditor's report on management's assessment in addition to the audit opinion on the financial statements. We will address the issues and challenges created by management self-assessments together with their audit implications.

These changes represent new territory for both management and auditors. The internal control gaps that have been exposed over the past few years led the Securities and Exchange Commission (SEC) and Public Company Accounting Oversight Board (PCAOB) to place heightened emphasis on both effective design of internal control and the operational effectiveness of the control system. When the regulations were issued, they did not provide guidance other than indicate that the COSO Framework was an acceptable, suitable, and recognizable framework. This left management teams and auditors with considerable room on to how to conduct the assessment and the attestation. Insight and guidance on the COSO frameworks have been provided. Now it is time to discuss the elements and execution of self-assessment.

MANAGEMENT ASSESSMENT OF INTERNAL CONTROL

When the Sponsoring Organization of the Treadway Commission (COSO) developed the original *Internal Control—Integrated Framework,* it felt strongly that "building in" controls can directly affect an entity's ability to achieve its goals and objectives. In this sense, it was felt that senior management was responsible for ensuring that the controls it established were being maintained and operated at a high level of effectiveness. This implied that management would periodically assess its control system because this represented a "best business practice." Following this approach, it is important to realize that internal control is process based and developed by people. Therefore, it is subject to the dynamics of constant change. Since systems become evolutionary, it is important to monitor them in a variety of ways, as discussed in the previous chapter.

There is a great deal of precedent for self-assessment in both the United States and Europe. The Baldrige Award for Operational Excellence is based upon management conducting a self-assessment and scoring the results. This award was initiated in 1987 based on the support of Malcolm Baldrige, who was secretary of commerce from 1981 until 1987. The award was motivated by the total quality management movement and further motivated based on the concern that U.S. companies would not be able to effectively compete in a global market without achieving and maintaining the highest levels of operational excellence. Figure 11.1 presents the seven categories of management

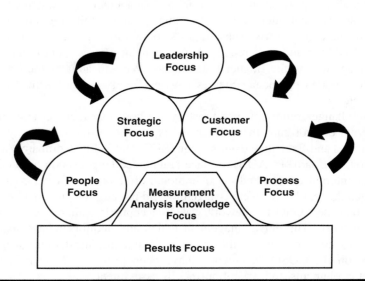

Figure 11.1.   Seven categories of management focus.

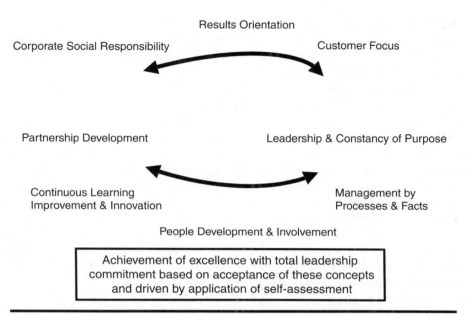

Results Orientation

Corporate Social Responsibility   Customer Focus

Partnership Development   Leadership & Constancy of Purpose

Continuous Learning   Management by
Improvement & Innovation   Processes & Facts

People Development & Involvement

Achievement of excellence with total leadership
commitment based on acceptance of these concepts
and driven by application of self-assessment

Figure 11.2.   European Foundation for Quality Management Framework.

focus upon which the self-assessment is based, with varying levels of points assigned to each of the seven categories. This platform extends beyond the scope of the COSO Integrated Framework and the requirements of Section 404. In addition, the European Foundation for Quality Management (EFQM) is based on a self-assessment similar to the Baldrige Award. The EFQM assessment structure is presented in Figure 11.2. These two examples offer guidance on conducting self-assessments and further illustrate their potential benefits beyond a compliance assessment.

However, for Section 404, the self-assessment needs to take a different direction from traditional self-assessments. Many companies have struggled with how to tackle the challenges of Section 404. One of the best illustrations of a Section 404 self-assessment emerged from one of my Sarbanes-Oxley workshops. One of the participants was an internal auditor with General Electric. General Electric is well known for its application of Six Sigma, and it applied a similar approach to Sarbanes-Oxley. Six Sigma follows a project management format which General Electric used in organizing its management assessment of internal controls. It opted for early compliance and completed its first assessment a year ahead of the compliance deadline. Compliance teams were formed across the organization and were used to conduct self-assessments in workshop fashion in conjunction with interviews and surveys. General Electric employed all of the self-assessment tools and made sure its external auditor was on board with its approach and methodology. Early communication with the auditor is extremely important, so the project effort is focused on the same areas as addressed by the auditor.

Some companies have basically handed off responsibility to CPA firms or consultants to perform the work versus conducting their own self-assessments. All this approach achieves is compliance and does not meet the intent of Section 404. A self-assessment needs to begin with the end in mind. Section 404 has the objective of evaluating the design and operational effectiveness of internal controls. A complete section is devoted to assessment planning and another to the self-assessment process, with insight on the tools and techniques that can be employed to provide management with continuing benefits from the process. Since management has responsibility for designing and maintaining an effective internal control system, it only makes sense that management should want to regularly evaluate the processes to ensure that they are performing as planned. It is critical that management's assessment maintain evidential matter to provide reasonable support for management's conclusions regarding the effectiveness of the internal controls.

AUDITOR ATTESTATION OF MANAGEMENT'S ASSESSMENT

When dealing with the auditor's role relative to management's assessment, it is important to understand that PCAOB Auditing Standard No. 2 is an audit of internal controls over financial reporting that is performed in conjunction with an audit of the financial statements. The PCAOB states that "one audit cannot be separated from the other." The underlying purpose of this requirement is to provide shareholders and the investing public assurance that they can rely on management's description of the company's internal control. The SEC and PCAOB feel that this renewed emphasis on accuracy, reliability, and fairness of financial statements will provide restored trust in the financial markets.

The focus on evaluating internal control is expected to achieve benefits, such as identify opportunities for improving ineffective procedures and reduce the cost of processing accounting information. It should also result in fewer financial restatements and reduce litigation costs. These benefits will only occur if management actively participates in the assessment process. External accountants will engage in expanded testing and documentation, since it must be able to determine that the internal control system is adequate. This is a step beyond agreeing that management's self-assessment process for determining that internal control was effective. Auditors need to be satisfied that management's conclusion is correct by conducting their own tests of internal control effectiveness. Audit Standard No. 2 provides for an integrated audit of both the financial statements and internal control.

The starting point for the integrated audit is with management's assessment. This provides the auditor with assurance that management has a basis for reaching its conclusion over internal control and also provides support for the audit opinion. Management can significantly impact the cost of the audit by providing extensive support and documentation of its assessment, which will enable the auditor to rely, to a greater extent, on the work performed by management. Management's assessment does not relieve the auditor from obtaining a thorough understanding of internal control. This understanding should include the performance of walkthroughs to support the auditor's understanding of the process flow of transactions, the design of controls, and whether they are operating effectively. Walkthroughs should include performing procedures such as making inquiries of and observing the personnel who are actually performing and applying the controls used to produce the transactions and supporting documentation for the financial reports. Auditors will be responsible for confirming their understanding of the effectiveness of internal control design and determining that the controls are operating as intended. Because of this emphasis on obtaining a thorough and complete understanding of the internal control processes and operation, it is crucial that audits be conducted by appropriately experienced auditors. This implies that auditors will be more capable of making qualitative evaluations and assessing the variety of business risks that could have a material impact on the financial statements.

When entities are planning management's assessment, it is important to understand the audit approach that will likely be taken by auditors in applying Audit Standard No. 2. Auditors will begin by identifying "relevant" assertions, such as the existence of assets and liabilities and occurrence of transactions. This process will include the identification of all significant processes and major classes of transactions. Auditors will be required to test and evaluate the effectiveness of how controls are designed and their ability to provide reasonable assurance regarding the financial statements. This step includes the determination of whether the controls would be effective as designed and also whether the necessary controls are in place. This requires inquiries of company personnel, observation of the controls, and walkthroughs in order to evaluate control capability. Auditors will be asking whether the controls are likely to prevent or detect financial misstatements or fraud if they operate according to their design.

The next requirement for the auditor is to obtain evidence and documentation relative to the operating effectiveness of the controls identified in association with the relevant financial statement assertions. Accordingly, the auditor will perform tests of the identified controls to determine that they are operating effectively. These tests will also include an appropriate mix of inquiries, inspection of relevant documentation, and in some instances reperformance of the application of the control. A key point of understanding here is that auditors will focus on the relevant assertions, since these are the points of focus where misstatements are most likely. Accordingly, this emphasis will enable the auditor to focus work on the most necessary controls.

Each year's audit must stand on its own, so management must realize that the auditor will rotate tests to cover different areas each year. When performing tests, auditors are allowed to utilize evidence obtained at different times of the year with the understanding that it must be updated since the audit opinion is as of a point in time at fiscal year-end.

The auditor is allowed to use the work of others, including internal auditors or other company personnel and third parties that management may have engaged. A component of the audit standard is that the auditor is required to understand the results of procedures performed by others and consider the results in designing the audit approach used in forming the audit opinion. While relying on the work of others, the auditor will still be required to perform tests and other inquiries. When testing the controls in the control environment, the auditor will not be able to rely on the work of others. Essentially, the auditor's own work should provide the principal evidence for the audit opinion. Understanding the auditor's responsibilities is important to planning and conducting management's assessment.

LEGISLATIVE INTENT

Originally the SEC wanted to have management report quarterly as to the effectiveness of internal controls. This should be a clear signal as to the intent of the Sarbanes-Oxley Act that management is responsible for the effectiveness of internal control and financial reporting. The belief is that the act will improve internal control structures, strengthen audits, and reduce the chances and occurrence of financial statement errors and misstatements. There is little question that the legislation has the intent of reforming the financial reporting and disclosure process as we know it.

Management and the board are on the line and fully responsible for setting the right tone and for maintaining an effective system of internal control. Many of the frauds that resulted in financial restatement rested on management's ability to exploit and manipulate weaknesses in internal control. Therefore, management is required to express an "adverse" opinion if a material weakness is uncovered. Section 404 is based on the premise of restoring investor confidence through the improvement of internal controls and placing responsibility on management for addressing a new standard of excellence for preventing and detecting fraud.

The new standards clearly spell out new requirements and expectation from management and places auditors in the role of enhanced independence. Auditors must attest to the following four management responsibilities:

1. Accept responsibility for the effectiveness of the company's internal control over financial reporting
2. Evaluate the effectiveness of the company's internal control over financial reporting using suitable control criteria
3. Support the evaluation with sufficient evidence and documentation
4. Present a written assessment of the effectiveness of the company's internal control over financial reporting as of the end of the company's most recent fiscal year

Management's documentation needs to address the five COSO components that we have previously documented. While many management teams and boards have expressed frustration regarding the cost and effort associated with compliance, the reality is they should have been doing this in the first place as a component of sound control and risk management practice.

THE SELF-ASSESSMENT PROCESS

Self-assessment is an entity-wide tool and can employ a variety of techniques. It is a process that facilitates and enables buy-in on business objectives and a technique for evaluating the effectiveness of business processes and internal controls. Utilization of self-assessment is an approach that requires cooperation and participation. It requires organization-wide cooperation all the way from management to employees on the front line. Self-assessment techniques improve business processes using a participative and collaborative approach. Prior to Sarbanes-Oxley, management was responsible for internal control, but external auditors conducted the evaluation. Now, management cannot pass the buck to outside specialists—management must be responsible for designing and implementing the controls and then assessing both the design and operational effectiveness of those controls. This represents a big change. Self-assessments require that management and knowledgeable work teams familiar with the details of the controls evaluate the adequacy of these controls.

Self-assessments involve people actually working with the controls to conduct the evaluation of the risks and controls in place. These team members and management have responsibility for assessing the effectiveness of both the design and operation of the controls, which represents a major shift from auditors evaluating the controls. Since these process owners work with their own procedures every day, they are far more qualified to conduct an evaluation than auditors who are only on-site for a short period of time. In effect, the process owners are the real experts and have a better grasp of the problems, risks, and solutions for potential process enhancement. In addition to enhancing the quality of the evaluation, self-assessments represent a more effective technique for having management and employees take ownership of their process responsibility in contrast to overreliance on auditors. This aligns responsibility for internal control with ownership for evaluating and maintaining adequacy of the controls. This approach produces a stronger level of commitment to control, operational effectiveness, and risk management.

Before expanding on the self-assessment process, it is worthwhile to gain a more thorough understanding of why the time and effort to utilize this methodology improve the control environment of an organization. Prior to Sarbanes-Oxley, there was a lack of organizational awareness regarding the role of internal control in achieving strategic and operational objectives. Involving personnel in self-assessments provides motivation to employees to take greater care in designing and implementing effective controls and engaging in a continuous improvement process. Self-assessment workshops provide a focus on where to concentrate emphasis and resources relative to high-risk areas. They also enable assessment of the qualitative issues that are difficult to assess using traditional audit techniques.

Self-assessments typically utilize multiple facilitated team meetings. Facilitated workshops usually contain 6–15 people and are led by a trained facilitator, with a scribe to record results of the meeting. The composition of the personnel participating in the workshop will be assembled around processes for Sarbanes-Oxley compliance and follow the COSO Framework. This entails taking objective-based and controls-based approaches. Identification of the key risks and controls is done prior to the workshop by the assessment team. The workshops are employed to evaluate and document controls, including mapping the business processes. Not all companies will utilize facilitated self-assessment workshops in complying with Sarbanes-Oxley. However, those that do employ them will be in a position to gain significantly greater business benefits through the continuous improvement process focused on the personnel best positioned to contribute ideas.

Other approaches to self-assessment include one-on-one interviews of key process personnel, together with questionnaires and surveys. Some organizations are likely to employ all three techniques. Depending on the entity, it is probable that all three techniques will be utilized as appropriate. Interviews are employed when the culture of the organization is not conducive to honest and open dialogue. This approach has the advantage of asking open-ended questions to create a dialogue that produces more information than will emerge with the other two techniques. Time is frequently a consideration when employing interviews in situations where personnel cannot be spared from their duties for the blocks of time required by facilitated workshops. Another consideration is organizational culture that is not supportive of open communication and empowered employees.

Surveys and questionnaires are used in complex organizations that have multiple layers of departmental and functional structure and response from a large number of participants is desired. They would also be used where there are multiple business units. Questionnaires are difficult because they require skill in developing appropriate questions. A challenge with questionnaires and surveys is the tendency to suppress awareness of fraud or significant deficiencies because anonymity precludes drilling down into specific issues and opening up a dialogue. This means that key issues can be missed. General Electric used all three methods.

My preference is to effectively blend the use of all three methods. In smaller organizations, I find that the use of one-on-one interviews provides the key to identifying issues and root causes of problems. After the primary issues have been identified, we employ the facilitated workshop to gather the best input from those closest to the action to gain buy-in and ownership of potential solutions. Sarbanes-Oxley requires documentation, and this invariably means mapping the key processes. Also, the workshop will usually consist of personnel from cross-functional boundaries, which aids in understanding and improving communication.

Workshops have five primary formats:

1. Objective based
2. Risk based
3. Control based
4. Process based
5. Situational

In instances where the organization is following the COSO Framework or a similar framework, workshops would be objective based. The assessment would include workshops that concentrate on identifying controls that are in place and any residual risks. Are the controls properly designed and are they effectively operating as designed and intended? In other instances, workshops will need to concentrate on identifying risk and the associated control activities required to manage them. Control-based workshops place emphasis on how well the controls are working and may entail interviews and process mapping prior to the workshop so the workshop team can focus on assessing control effectiveness. Process-based workshops are employed to correct identified deficiencies or conduct business process improvements. Situational workshops are usually functional or departmental driven relative to opportunities and constraints to enhance departmental objectives. Facilitated workshops and assessments represent time and commitment, but they are worth it because of the potential benefit they provide.

ASSESSMENT PLANNING

Compliance self-assessments should begin by organizing them as projects under the direction and supervision of a senior executive. It is highly recommended that one of the certifying officers be responsible for leading the project. Any good project plan starts with establishing objectives and then building a critical path that includes checkpoints and progress milestones. Begin with the end in mind and consider the amount of time the external auditor will require to complete the work prior to year-end. This will provide a fairly accurate time line regarding the starting point after considering the amount of time required to complete the assessment steps. Also, communicate with the external auditor regarding requirements and expectations in order to avoid surprises after completing a good deal of the assessment work.

Development of any project plans should include setting the scope and preparation of action steps, including the completion of a profile and framework for planning. Senior management needs to understand the assessment process and be committed in terms of what it will do and how it will impact the company. From a Sarbanes-Oxley perspective, consideration needs to be given to disclosure procedures and disclosure information required by SEC rules and regulations. This tightens the focus relative to the scope of the COSO Framework. Figure 11.3 illustrates how alignment from business strategy and policies flows through the organization and business processes to the systems and data supporting financial reporting.

This compliance framework helps to lay the foundation for building an assessment plan by identifying and narrowing the scope of the assessment. A Section 404 assessment will apply the COSO Framework and link each of the COSO components and its attributes to the points of focus described in the *COSO Evaluation Tools.* This is illustrated in Figure 11.4 and further amplified in Figure 11.5, where financial assertions are linked to each of the COSO components. This provides a foundation for creating an organization profile that

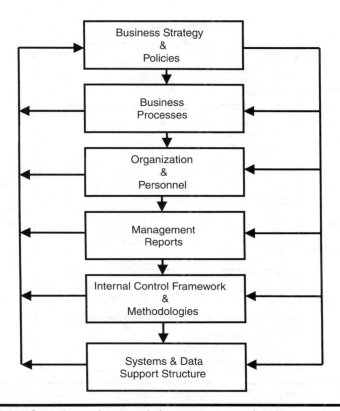

Figure 11.3.   Compliance framework for assessment planning.

focuses on financial reporting and compliance with laws and regulations and achieving the assessment objectives.

Design of the project plan should be broken up into stages to address and evaluate the financial reporting processes. The four stages of the project should include the following steps:

1. Determine the "as is" state and identify all relevant processes
2. Evaluate and document all the critical processes and controls
3. Develop solutions for identified deficiencies and control gaps
4. Implement the solutions for the gaps identified in step 3

The components of the project plan by stage are presented in Figure 11.6 and illustrate the focus of each phase of the assessment project. During the first

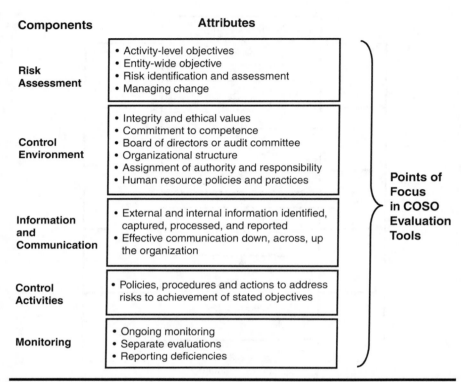

Components	Attributes	
Risk Assessment	• Activity-level objectives • Entity-wide objective • Risk identification and assessment • Managing change	
Control Environment	• Integrity and ethical values • Commitment to competence • Board of directors or audit committee • Organizational structure • Assignment of authority and responsibility • Human resource policies and practices	**Points of Focus in COSO Evaluation Tools**
Information and Communication	• External and internal information identified, captured, processed, and reported • Effective communication down, across, up the organization	
Control Activities	• Policies, procedures and actions to address risks to achievement of stated objectives	
Monitoring	• Ongoing monitoring • Separate evaluations • Reporting deficiencies	

Figure 11.4. Application of the COSO Framework in a Section 404 assessment.

two stages, companies will identify and document their processes and fix the deficiencies by implementing solutions in the second two stages. Attacking the compliance process through utilization of a project approach will provide a foundation for management's assessment report in addition to providing for continuous improvement. Effective communication is critical in executing the project plan and achieving benefits beyond compliance. Establishment of a communication plan and a process for involving the assessment team will help to ensure that the self-assessment effort stays focused and on schedule.

THE ASSESSMENT TEAM

Developing a solid assessment team will provide the formula for continuous improvement beyond compliance. Management needs to realize that it is responsible for the design of internal control and effective enterprise risk man-

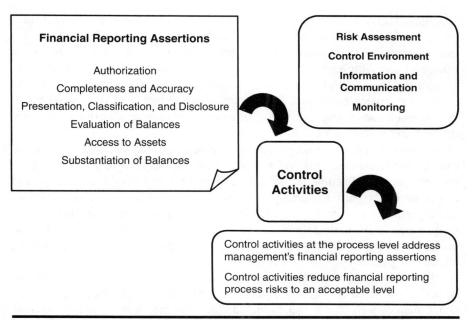

Figure 11.5. Alignment of financial reporting assertions with component of control activities.

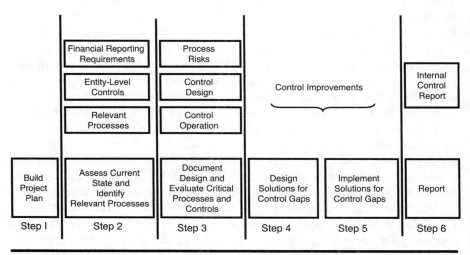

Figure 11.6. Stages of a Section 404 compliance project.

agement. Therefore, the assessment team needs to be linked to all the appropriate functions and business processes with feedback mechanisms so that top management and the board receive the benefit of the self-assessment. Since the primary issue with Sarbanes-Oxley is reliable financial reporting and compliance, it makes sense to have the chief financial officer or controller take responsibility for project leadership. This will help ensure that the CEO receives self-assessment feedback and, vice versa, the assessment team needs to have assurance of the CEO's commitment to the process.

Some companies may feel the need for assistance and support from external experts and resources. This will likely be the case if a company does not have the necessary level of internal resources. A number of CPA firms have viewed this as an opportunity to participate in the Sarbanes-Oxley space without conducting audits and attestations of management assessments. Utilizing a CPA firm or other third-party expert may be a necessity; however, caution should be exercised to avoid delegating management's responsibility. In other words, attempt to gain benefit from the self-assessment process.

Because of the financial reporting implications, the accounting function will be actively utilized on the assessment team, as will key operational personnel. Other team considerations should include the chief information officer, internal audit, and the organization's business unit managers. Other functional specializations that will be helpful in the self-assessment process will be human resources and legal counsel. Depending on the size of the organization, the self-assessment team might be organized so that it reports to a steering committee comprised of certifying officers, business unit leaders, and major functional managers. Some organizations have relied on the internal audit or outsourced internal auditors to complete the compliance work, thus bypassing the spirit of self-assessment. I prefer a self-assessment team that includes knowledgeable second-tier managers and process owners because they are more likely to provide the feedback management requires in order to issue a meaningful assessment report. Not only does this approach provide a platform for training and mentoring for second-tier management, but it also yields critical input needed for effective enterprise risk management. By utilizing its own personnel, versus outsourced internal audit people from a staffing or CPA firm, a company engages personnel with better knowledge of the business and the processes. One approach to effective use of outsourcing is to have the contracted firm facilitate assessment workshops or assist with interviewing and questionnaires.

Should management personnel participate in facilitated workshops? This is a question that many companies will need to answer. The answer will vary depending on the culture of the organization and the attitude of management. It will also be impacted by the skill of the facilitator directing the assessment workshops. Extreme care must be exercised to prevent management from taking over the workshop and creating an atmosphere of fear of retribution or retaliation. If it can be handled properly, the assessment workshop will provide real growth and learning opportunities for management. Those in management will need to be capable of looking at themselves and reflecting through the eyes of employees. This experience might not always be a pleasant one. I can think of no better way for management to communicate an effective "tone at the top" than by actively participating in the real spirit of the self-assessment process. Both the COSO and the COSO Enterprise Risk Management Framework are clear in their support of management participating in self-assessments. The Baldrige and EFQM self-assessments rank leadership high in the allocation of self-assessment points, which represents additional support for management participation.

ASSESSMENT TOOL KIT

In my consulting practice, one of my specializations is conducting operational assessments. After conducting countless assessments, it was natural that I would develop a training program to teach CPAs how to perform these engagements. This program evolved into a self-directed assessment that organizations could apply themselves and derive benefits similar to those from independently conducted assessments. My self-directed assessment program was one of the factors that led me into this book and Sarbanes-Oxley compliance. The program contained a tool kit to assist organizations in their planning and execution of self-assessments. I have since enhanced the tool kit with Sarbanes-Oxley-specific planning issues and questions that need to be addressed in a Section 404 assessment. This section discusses components of the tool kit and application of the COSO Evaluation Tools.

Self-assessments can have a wide range of applications and scope. Relative to Section 404, management teams are concerned first and foremost with compliance as defined by the SEC. However, the process does afford them a variety of possibilities to extend the scope beyond financial reporting and evaluating the effectiveness of strategy and operational efficiency. First, let's address financial reporting and compliance for Section 404. The key elements of the Sarbanes-Oxley tool kit include a checklist that enables the management team to develop a project plan with defined objectives, critical path, critical success factors, milestones, and assignment of checkpoints. In conjunction with the project planning process, the management team must identify the issues associated with defining key financial reporting elements. The tool kit checklist covers questions assessment teams need to consider in the assessment and in documenting results. It drills down to determining what can go wrong and also assessing risk associated with possible errors and omissions. These questions will help guide the assessment team with its project planning and setting the scope for the assessment.

The COSO Evaluation Tools consist of a pro-forma risk assessment and a control activities worksheet that the assessment team can utilize in applying the five components of the COSO Integrated Framework. The Evaluation Tools detail "points of focus" for the five COSO components. The worksheet can be completed for each activity, providing identification of the objectives, risk factors, and likelihood of occurrence. Objectives can be identified by three categories:

1. Operational
2. Financial
3. Compliance

The points of focus are broken into activity-level and entity-level objectives and are provided in a Word document file that teams can use to tailor to their specific assessment issues. The Evaluation Tools also provide a "generic business model" that assessment teams can use to model their documentation and business process mapping efforts. In addition to the pro-forma blank tools, the *Evaluation Tools* provide a filled-in version that is helpful in understanding how to apply the framework. Information on acquiring the tools is available by accessing the COSO web site.

Self-assessments will probably evolve after the deadline for Section 404 compliance passes and companies start to be comfortable with minimum levels of financial reporting compliance. My version of self-assessment goes past minimal Sarbanes-Oxley compliance and drills into strategic and operational issues whereby companies can evaluate their levels of performance excellence. This is more in the spirit of the Baldrige and EFQM assessments. One of the tools in the kit includes a self-directed assessment team survey that consists of over 250 questions assessment team members can utilize to evaluate the organization on a wide range of strategic, operational, leadership, and cultural issues. Also included is a full range of operational questions following checklists I developed from conducting operational assessments. The tool kit provides a SWOT framework for the assessment team to prepare an evaluation of the organization's strengths, weaknesses, opportunities, and threats. This approach offers organizations a platform for formulation of strategy and execution, operational excellence, and approaches to enterprise risk management.

GOING BEYOND COMPLIANCE

Executives and board members of public companies together with CPAs and consultants have been engaged in a flurry of activity as the final compliance deadlines for Section 404 approached. There has been concern not only for the added cost of compliance, but also for the amount of time required for compliance effort. Risk-averse CPAs and concerned managements in many quarters feel that the legislation went too far and was overreactive. One of the comments that emerged from my training workshops was that while the spirit of self-assessment was fine, compliance teams were spending too much time retesting when they should have moved on to more fruitful endeavors. This may be one of the areas where some re-examination and re-evaluation are needed so that management, boards, and employees are focused on meaningful self-assessment rather than compliance for the sake of compliance.

Based on my work with assessments and self-assessment, it is clear that significant benefits can accrue to the management teams that employ and leverage these tools. Yes, it is important that we have sound internal control systems. Much of the effort on the part of many companies has stemmed from performing compliance steps that should have been done as a component of best business practice. It has become clear that many companies have never mapped their critical business processes, to say nothing about application of either the COSO Integrated Framework or COSO Enterprise Risk Management Framework. There is significant benefit from application of these concepts and tools. Much of the challenge is getting back to good leadership and management practices. The answer is not simple or easily achieved. It takes hard work and asking tough questions. Perhaps the most difficult challenge is facing the reality of what excellence is and what is required to succeed in a competitive global economy.

Most of the mountains of material I have reviewed and read regarding Sarbanes-Oxley is narrowly focused on the legal and accounting issues associated with compliance and a higher standard for governance. We need to understand more about strategic and operational objectives. Management teams and CPAs need training relative to strategic execution and achieving operational excellence. What better school to attend than participating in self-assessment and application of continuous improvement? Malcolm Baldrige had the right idea about what was required to achieve operational and performance excellence back in the mid-1980s. This is precisely why the Baldrige Award is based on self-assessment. The SEC and PCAOB followed that spirit in developing standards and rules for management self-assessment. There is much more to be gained than pure compliance with the Sarbanes-Oxley Act. The true benefit lies in the application of self-assessment for the purpose of enhancing the effectiveness of the organization and achieving a competitive advantage through application of improvement opportunities that are seen through the lens of critical awareness and reality.

NEW MEANING
OF INDEPENDENCE

Sarbanes-Oxley has changed the meaning of independence across the business landscape. This chapter explores the ramifications of these sweeping changes and their implications for the future. While much of the impact related to the independence of boards of directors and audit committees, there were also significant changes in how and in what external auditors conduct audits and the services that could be provided. These revisions have necessitated rethinking across the entire accounting profession and the businesses they service.

One of the most profound impacts of the legislation was rules creating more independent boards of directors. Because of these changes, management teams have had to adjust and change how they have traditionally performed their responsibilities. Most of the press has been on the cost of compliance in terms of both dollars and human resources. However, it appears that the complaining has outshadowed the potential benefits that companies and investors can gain from embracing the possibilities that the legislation provides.

NEW RULES OF THE ROAD

Auditors of public companies and their clients have been forced to readjust their relationships relative to services. The close relationship of Arthur Andersen and Enron was responsible for creating a lack of independence that contributed to the ensuing scandal because of the amount of consulting and other nonaudit services that were more valuable than auditing. Now the emphasis has shifted to auditing because a number of services are prohibited under Section 201. The prohibited services include:

1. Bookkeeping or other services related to financial records
2. Financial information systems design and implementation
3. Appraisal or valuation services
4. Actuarial services
5. Internal audit outsourcing services
6. Management functions or human resources
7. Broker or dealer, investment advisor, or investment banking services
8. Legal services and expert services unrelated to the audit
9. Any other service that the Public Company Accounting Oversight Board (PCAOB) determines by regulation is impermissible

However, firms can engage in any nonaudit services, including tax services, which are not described in the list of prohibited activities. It should be clarified that firms can provide these services, but not to public companies where they are performing the audit.

Some of the other new rules also drive at improving independence of audit firms and the partners supervising the audits. For example, audit firms are required to rotate lead auditors and review partners every five years to avoid getting stuck in a rut. Also, audit firms are required to retain audit work papers for a period of seven years. In addition, they must provide for a concurring or second-partner review and approval of the audit report.

These new rules will affect the way management teams utilize auditors. While the auditors can help, they have to be careful not to violate any of the prohibited services rules. Excessive assistance could be interpreted as implementing or strengthening controls. Auditors need to make sure that any assistance provided does not diminish their independence. These rule changes close the door for firms providing audits but, on the other hand, create opportunities for CPA firms and advisors that traditionally did not serve public companies. Many companies will need help with their controls and implementing accounting systems, thus creating new markets while improving the quality of the audits being performed. Another area of opportunity is assisting companies interested in being acquired by publicly traded firms.

CPA firms also have to deal with the PCAOB setting new audit standards in place of the American Institute of Certified Public Accountants. The new audit standards and the PCAOB are discussed in Chapter 14. The new rules require that auditing firms be selected by the audit committee and not management, which represents a major change for everyone. Old relationships will never be the same, requiring readjustment by all the players participating in the game.

MANAGEMENT'S NEW ROLE AND RULES

Besides certifying financial reports and conducting assessments of internal control, the legislation has shifted and revised how management works and responds in a number of ways. Management can no longer select the external auditor, as this responsibility has been shifted to the audit committee, comprised of independent board members. This is a change that has multiple ramifications in how management handles its relationships with the board of directors and with the external auditor. The good old days where management exercised considerable control over the audit relationship are gone. Now management has to tackle new challenges with accounting treatment and disclosure, in addition to assessing internal control on a continuous basis. In addition, the new emphasis placed on board independence and governance has changed the playing field relative to board interaction and involvement. This means that management decision making will undergo greater scrutiny from multiple directions and under new microscopes. Major changes and adjustments will be required by all the players in the game.

Another rule change impacting management teams relates to conflicts of interest. As a result of the Tyco abuses, corporations can no longer provide loans to executives. Section 402 prohibits the extension of credit in the form of personal loans either directly or through a subsidiary. There are some exceptions, which include an open credit plan, home improvement loans, and credit cards. However, the terms for these exceptions cannot be more favorable than what would be offered to the public. The rules are also very specific for changes involving directors, officers, and principal shareholders. Beneficial owners must be disclosed. Beneficial ownership is categorized as ownership of more than 10% of any class of security. The disclosure must be made within 10 days after becoming a beneficial owner, director, or officer.

Officers need to be more careful about their actions because the Securities and Exchange Commission can bar "unfit" officers and directors and also has the authority to freeze their pay. As we saw with Xerox, officers may be required to disgorge bonuses and profits from security transactions. Dealings with the auditor also have come under tougher regulations as officers, directors, and others cannot lie or fraudulently influence auditors. The penalties include fines of up to $5 million and prison terms of up to 20 years. Without question, the new rules are catching everyone's attention, particularly those who have to abide by them.

THE NEW AUDIT COMMITTEE

Audit committees represent a critical component of the Sarbanes-Oxley corporate reforms, and they now have new and expanded responsibilities. As stated earlier in the chapter, audit committees are now required to be comprised of independent directors and are the gatekeepers of honesty and trust in financial reporting. Their new roles place audit committees in a unique position of balancing relationships with management, the outside auditor, the board, and outside regulators. This new responsibility is no small challenge.

Requirements for the audit committee specify that each member must be a member of the board of directors and independent of management, with at least one of its members designated as a "financial expert." The meaning of independence includes any consulting arrangements with management. The "financial expert" requirement will be explained and discussed in the following section. As included in its revised job description, the committee will be directly responsible for appointing, deciding on and arranging compensation for, and overseeing the work of the external auditor. The committee also has the authority to engage additional advisors and experts to the extent it deems necessary. Relative to overseeing the independent audit, the committee must be watchful that the auditors do not provide any prohibited nonaudit services.

In conjunction with oversight of financial reporting and accounting treatment, the committee is also responsible for directing the internal audit function and the chief audit executive. Administratively, the internal audit function could report to a key member of the management team, such as human resources, but clearly the audit committee needs to be responsible for the direction and oversight. A component of that responsibility would include the hiring and review of the chief audit executive. The relationship with the internal audit function is critical since it will enable the audit committee to keep abreast of potential risks facing the company as a result of reviewing the internal audit reports together with their findings and responses. Also, by meeting with the internal auditor, the committee will gain input regarding management, external auditors, and the internal control system and its effectiveness.

The magnitude of the audit committee's new role is critical and has far-reaching ramifications. In addition to oversight of the audit responsibilities, the committee needs to be sensitive to management, particularly the chief executive officer, the chief financial officer, and the accounting function. Executive sessions need to be held with the CEO, CFO, and controller regarding financial statement issues, incidents of fraud, and the existence of any off-balance-sheet transactions. Executive sessions would also be held with the external auditor and the chief audit executive.

Because of the oversight relative to financial reporting, the committee members will need to keep themselves current on all developments associated with financial reporting, financial disclosure, and generally accepted accounting principles. In addition to staying current, the committee members should seriously consider continuing professional education as an option. Beyond current financial reporting, audit committees need to be vigilant as to auditor independence and the occurrence of any prohibited nonaudit services. A permissible nonaudit service is tax, where having the external auditor provide support makes a great deal of sense, especially for complex multinational organizations.

Before leaving the discussion regarding audit committee responsibilities, we need to touch on Section 301, which refers to what is commonly called the "whistle-blower provisions." The audit committee is required to establish procedures for receiving and handling complaints regarding accounting, internal controls, or audit matters from employees or others. The committee is required to keep confidential and anonymous any submissions or concerns from employees regarding questionable accounting or auditing matters. The audit committee has responsibility for retaining and tracking complaints, regardless of the source and the status of the investigation. Complaints could come from a variety of sources including customers, vendors, shareholders, and other parties. This could be and has been a very sensitive topic for a number of boards and represents another item on their expanded list of new responsibilities.

FINANCIAL EXPERTS REQUIRED

In addition to the independent requirement for audit committee members, there is an added prerequisite that at least one of the committee members have financial expertise and characteristics relevant to fulfilling the financial oversight responsibilities. These provisions are spelled in Section 407 and require that a company disclose that it has an "audit committee financial expert" and the expert's name. The intent of Section 407 was that such an expert be well versed in the functions of the audit committee, in addition to having an in-depth knowledge of accounting and financial statement issues and disclosures. The financial expert must have the right blend of experience so as to be able to ask the right questions regarding the completeness and accuracy of the company's financial statements. This is a much narrower view compared to the traditional person with knowledge of financial matters and capital and risk management.

It was interesting to receive feedback from CFOs attending my Sarbanes-Oxley compliance workshops regarding audit committee financial experts serving on their boards. They expressed the opinion that the presence of highly qualified financial experts elevated the capability of the board and contributed new ideas that had a very positive impact on the company. In fact, it appears that boards have gone beyond the requirements of Section 407 by engaging multiple audit committee financial experts on the board. CFOs and controllers expressed a feeling of comfort that they had additional support in dealing with governance issues.

It might be helpful in providing some clarity to identify some of the attributes that characterize a financial expert as the term applies to the audit committee situation. In our early discussions, we saw examples of corporate boards of directors that were essentially "asleep at the wheel." The intent of Sarbanes-Oxley was to create reliable financial reporting and governance that would secure the trust of the investing public. The primary vehicle was an independent audit committee that understood auditing and accounting and would not be hoodwinked. Audit committees need to provide leadership and guidance over the financial reporting, accounting, and auditing process. This means that at least one audit committee member should have firsthand experience with auditing and accounting and should have functioned as either a CFO or a controller.

Starting with this foundation, the financial expert must have experience preparing financial statements and their evaluation. The expert should also have experience with audits of public companies. This means that financial experts should have an excellent grasp of generally accepted accounting principles and internal controls. The guidelines recognize that people have other relevant experience, and these factors should be considered based on the facts and circumstances for each situation. The specifications for members of the audit committee are high as their job has been elevated and they represent the key to restoring public confidence in the accounting and financial reporting process.

AUDIT IMPACT AND MEANING

Sarbanes-Oxley audits have taken on a new meaning based on the impact they will have all across the business landscape. The impact is felt not just by companies that are complying with the new rules but also by auditors who have had to revamp their approach to conducting audits. The implications of the new audit standards are discussed in Chapter 14. Our focus here is on management teams and boards relative to the challenges and opportunities the standards will create for them. Many of the companies complying with Section 404 are struggling to get the job done on time. Also, many have failed to embrace the opportunities created by self-assessment. It is important to gain a better sense of these issues and challenges as we consider the longer term impact and meaning of Sarbanes-Oxley.

A participant at one of my recent training workshops mentioned receiving a letter from the company's auditor, PriceWaterhouseCoopers, indicating status regarding compliance with Section 404. This led to a spirited discussion regarding the number of companies likely to receive a comment regarding deficiencies and/or a material weakness in the audit report. The class reached a consensus that perhaps as many as 10% of reporting companies would have to disclose a material weakness and that 40% of reporting companies would have deficiencies. While this was a very imprecise estimate, it nevertheless provides some indication about the state of internal control processes of public companies.

A more statistically sound sample of compliance readiness was provided by a survey conducted by ACL Services and the Center for Continuous Auditing. It revealed that companies were struggling to comply with Section 404 and were not confident of their ability to maintain compliance past the initial filing deadline. CFO.com reported that PriceWaterhouseCoopers indicated that only 20% of its clients are on schedule to complete their internal control reviews. The same article went on to indicate that a good many companies will report material weaknesses. This article supported the feedback I was receiving at my workshops.

Let's examine what these findings mean. Companies reporting material weakness run the risk of having their credit ratings impaired and perhaps some loss of market capitalization. A credit downgrade could increase the cost of raising capital. Material weaknesses fall into different categories, and when entity-wide controls are weak, it can place a company between a rock and a hard place, because auditors will be unable to work around the weakness, resulting in an adverse or unqualified opinion on the financial statement. The reality is that many companies have weak control environments, characteristic of poor board oversight and weak management. Sarbanes-Oxley was enacted to alert the investing public to these situations and bring confidence to the financial reporting process.

When we see the initial efforts toward compliance fall short for many companies, it supports the hypothesis that management teams face a significant challenge to get their internal control processes in order. While not universally true, my observations have indicated the failure of top management to understand the impact of continuous improvement of business processes. There is an overwhelming tendency to opt for short-term fixes instead of facing the reality of what it takes to build sound reliable controls that, in the long run, create a profitable competitive advantage. Boards of directors need to move past the boundaries of oversight and raise the bar for management teams to grasp the challenge of rethinking the opportunities of continuous improvement. They need to provide training for themselves and their employees on the new framework for enterprise risk management.

THE FUTURE IS NOW

By the time this book is read, most companies will be into the "beyond" stage of initial compliance with Sarbanes-Oxley. This section focuses on issues that need to be confronted as we settle into the new rules. It is my belief that the detailed testing prescribed by the PCAOB will require some adjustment and redirection. My soapbox regarding the benefits of continuous improvement of processes will fall on deaf ears until we reach a level of practicality with respect to redundant testing and retesting. It is important to get people refocused on valued-added activities that have emerged from the COSO Enterprise Risk Management Framework dealing with strategic and operational implications of managing risk.

Companies need to re-examine the Sarbanes-Oxley tools that are being used to facilitate compliance. An overwhelming number of tools have been created by software developers, some better suited for the job than others. Regardless of how the initial compliance effort was accomplished, it is important to step back and re-evaluate the tool kit and select effective comprehensive solutions that are best suited for each individual situation. The range of options was discussed earlier, and we will expand further on the implications of real-time reporting and business process management. Before going back and chopping wood with the same dull axe, it makes sense to find compliance solutions that are supported by companies that will be around in the future.

We need to realize that compliance is not just about software tools but is about improving the management and governance process. CFOs will likely take on an expanded role not only relative to facilitating understanding the financial implications of managing risk but also with respect to business, strategic, and operational issues. Auditors also need to adjust to conducting effective audits through the utilization of audit teams that have received appropriate training and experience in conducting attestations of management's assessment of internal controls. Management teams likewise must immerse themselves in the process of continuously applying the techniques of self-assessment and evaluation. Once everyone realizes the opportunities (along with the hard work) associated with the components of Sarbanes-Oxley compliance, I think we will begin to achieve profitable compliance.

BOARDS GO TO SCHOOL

Even beyond the audit committee, boards as a whole need to improve their understanding of financial statements and internal controls. Some companies have already started a process of educating board members. The National Association of Corporate Directors offers a wide variety of training for board members and aspiring board members on a wide variety of relevant topics designed to elevate the level of board performance and enhance corporate governance. This is critical, since from my perspective boards should set the standard for management, and there has not been enough focus on training to cope and stay abreast with the evolution of concepts needed to sustain performance excellence.

Board members no longer have the luxury of receiving perks as a component of being a member of the "good old boy club." They are on the cutting edge of providing leadership and guidance to the restoration of credibility in accounting, financial reporting, corporate governance, and leadership. Board members not only face greater responsibility, but also face grave risks for failure to properly execute their stewardship trust and confidence. In other words, they are on the front line and a sure target for litigation if something goes wrong. As a CPA, I am required to complete 40 hours of continuing professional education each year in order to maintain my licenses. Boards of directors should not be exempt from a similar level of training.

After the financial crisis resulting from the numerous scandals, it started to become apparent that some board members did not understand the financial data or even how to read and analyze a financial statement. The complexity of business is increasing at an accelerated pace, which is making it mandatory that directors receive the required education necessary to fulfill their responsibilities. Some of the topics directors need to consider in their learning curriculum include:

- Understanding financial numbers and statements
- Improving audit committee performance
- Executive compensation
- Mergers and acquisitions
- Changes occurring in the marketplace
- Strategic planning and execution
- Enterprise risk management
- Information technology and related issues of security governance
- Effective board interaction and decision making
- Challenges of leadership, ethics, and governance

This is not a complete list, but it covers some critical areas that are changing and shifting on a dynamic basis. As you can see, the meaning of independence has taken on new dimensions for boards of directors.

STRATEGIC EXECUTION

Most of the compliance scramble has been focused on testing and documentation relative to reliable financial reporting and legal compliance. Some organizations have utilized the full arsenal of self-assessment tools, but most have not taken advantage of the potential opportunities that exist within the control frameworks. One of the objectives of the COSO Integrated Framework is operational effectiveness. The release of *Enterprise Risk Management—Integrated Framework* in September 2004 added a strategic objective together with objective setting, event identification, and risk response. While these attributes are not specified by the compliance rules and the audit standards, they are factors and challenges where management and boards need to elevate their priorities.

Some of my workshop topics include corporate performance management and strategic and competitive analysis. These workshops provide me with wonderful feedback that covers a wide variety of organizations from all corners of the country. Some of the findings reveal that there is a wide gap between knowledge and understanding relative to strategy and how to execute it. Associated with this void is the determination as to which performance measures should be utilized throughout the company. The self-assessment process represents a perfect opportunity for organizations to communicate from top to bottom and vice versa. Some of the challenge is educational, and this can be partially addressed through the assessment process. Execution and measurement of strategy can be elevated through management and board involvement.

Trust of the investing public will return very quickly when people begin seeing the maximization of value resulting from application of an effective enterprise risk management program. Internal control is an integral component of enterprise risk management, and it is management's responsibility to design and maintain effective controls. Rather than stop at reliable financial reporting, management should be serious about applying all the elements provided by the framework. Strategic execution requires the alignment of risk and strategy that will utilize a balanced scorecard to measure performance from a variety of perspectives. By stepping beyond the scope of the assessment for the sake of compliance, management and boards have an opportunity to minimize risk and build shareholder value.

Expanded management involvement reduces the chances for operational surprises and losses, because it enhances management's ability to identify potential risks and establish effective responses. Because the process puts management and employees into an environment that improves communication, the organization can more effectively take advantage of opportunities and improve its deployment of capital in more responsive ways. While the balanced scorecard helps to create strategic focus, it does not necessarily guarantee strategic execution. This is where the concept of continuous self-assessment as a component of the audit process helps to provide a two-way feedback process that leverages success and value creation. By going beyond compliance as a static event, management and boards can create a foundation that is pervasive and inherent in the way the business functions.

RETOOLING AND RETRAINING

This chapter identified the new independence associated with Sarbanes-Oxley as providing sweeping new changes to the business environment. Management assessment of internal control and independent boards of directors combined with new audit standards and rules represent a great deal of change. This is forcing management teams to become involved in areas that are new to them, and some have complained that the effort required is excessive. I agree that some adjustment of the balance is needed. However, shortcomings lie in the need for management to retool its thinking about how to manage application and selection of the tools required to get the job done.

There is an abundant array of methodologies available focused on process flow, designed to improve the effectiveness of strategic application aligned with operational excellence. My book *Dynamics of Profit-Focused Accounting* presents all of the major methodologies and tools in a single volume. The problem is breaking down the functional silos and departmental barriers to achieve more effective utilization of empowered cross-functional teams. The legislative impact of Sarbanes-Oxley is forcing the assessment of internal control, which many executives may ultimately see as an opportunity once the compliance dust settles.

Training and education represent the answer, but you have to get management committed to take the time and spend the money to make the transition. Much of the challenge lies in the outdated concepts of management accounting and application of the same old tools in the same old ways. Business process management and measurement is beginning to evolve, and software and technology are enabling it. However, it takes time and human willingness to embrace change. It is my belief that training and facilitated self-assessment can produce significant competitive advantages for the management teams willing to take the time and effort to get their processes right and continuously improve them. If directors are engaging in continuous professional education, then management teams should embark on a retraining effort that will help elevate their capability.

13

THE CASCADE EFFECT

A common misunderstanding about Sarbanes-Oxley is that it has very little impact on privately held companies and, therefore, we do not need to be concerned with it. I attended a recent Sarbanes-Oxley update presentation sponsored by the Research Triangle Chapter of the National Association of Corporate Directors. One of the speakers focused on several reasons why privately held companies were experiencing a "cascade effect" instead of what he thought would have been a "trickle-down effect."

So let's take a look at some of the "cascade effect" issues and factors. The primary reasons to give consideration to some level of Sarbanes-Oxley compliance is that it is good business practice. We will see that some private companies have a broad base of shareholders who will insist on some level of assurance. These issues will be described together with steps that private companies are taking to enhance their internal controls. In addition to good business practice, privately held companies are faced with legal and other reasons that will drive them to mirror the practices and techniques being applied at publicly traded companies.

JUST GOOD BUSINESS

Underlying the Sarbanes-Oxley legislation was good internal controls that would provide for reliable financial reporting and compliance. It makes sense that privately held companies would require the same level of internal control assurance as public companies. Why should there be a difference in adopting best business practices that are employed by the leading companies? Best business practices are benchmarked all the time and set the standard for others. The

Toyota Production System is a model that every other company in the world has been attempting to duplicate. Internal control models are no different. In fact, there are many Sarbanes-Oxley similarities to Toyota, such as mistake proofing the system and employing process controls that will produce reasonable assurance with no deficiencies.

Good governance and effective business processes are the same regardless of company ownership. Companies are looking around and seeing the standard of excellence being set higher as a result of the new regulations. What I see as obstacles and objections are the levels of nonvalue-added testing that may not be necessary. This will likely settle down as we evolve into greater understanding of what is needed to comply and what makes sense. Management self-assessment is a process that has been nurtured by the Baldrige Award for some years. Now, with the new standards that require such assessment, we are seeing forward-thinking management teams that are embracing these techniques to improve their businesses.

Frameworks for internal control extend beyond internal controls to risk management and establishment of strategic objectives. Many privately held companies are observing the benefits and opportunities that come with adopting these frameworks. Many private companies have directors and officers who are also involved with public companies. This is creating a spill down to private companies. Private companies that have good management teams are not going to stand around and wait for lending institutions, customers, and other regulators to tell them what to do. They will be proactive and set the tone. One incentive for adopting the new standards is that the cost of liability insurance for officers and boards of directors will be more available and affordable.

The standards for audits and financial presentation are being established by the Public Company Accounting Oversight Board (PCAOB) and Financial Accounting Standards Board. Two standards is not a workable situation. Private companies are going to see pressure from third-party stakeholders to achieve consistency in both internal control standards and financial reporting. Heat will be felt by accountants as some states begin to adopt laws and regulations regarding work paper retention and other requirements. Sarbanes-Oxley has established a standard for internal controls and management discussions and analysis, and management teams and directors of private companies will find it difficult not to adopt the spirit of its message.

EXIT STRATEGY

Any company contemplating a public offering of its stock will need to consider becoming compliant with the new regulations. Any company that has not started its compliance efforts should begin immediately. By following the approaches provided for compliance, private companies can position themselves to be ready when the appropriate time arrives. An additional consideration that private companies need to evaluate is the composition of their boards of directors. Rules for calling for independent boards of directors will drive companies to begin the search to fill positions and restructure boards as necessary. Compliance efforts may also mean restructuring the internal teams needed to conduct the work, including the development of an internal audit department.

Exit strategies do not always mean a public offering. There are a number of privately held companies that have a strategy to be acquired. If this is the case, it is important to put in place the necessary controls and perform the assessment steps required to comply with the provisions of the Securities and Exchange Commission (SEC) and PCAOB. Frequently, companies tend to put off succession plans and exit strategies. Reasons for procrastination are numerous because owners fail to think ahead. They fail to understand the amount of time required to become compliant with Sarbanes-Oxley. When a company is ready to put a deal together, there may not be much of a window for a selling company to respond. This is particularly true of public companies on an acquisition track. Their tolerance to wait an extended period of time for a company to become complaint with all the sections of the legislation is not going to be an option. Financial presentation and internal controls are going to represent key issues to a public company making the acquisition since it will have a subsequent impact on its financial presentations. This means that a noncompliant company can lose its window of opportunity.

A number of private companies are funded by venture capitalists or institutional investors. These funding requirements are nudging private company officers and boards to adopt the new governance standards being met by public companies. These companies represent potential issuers of public offerings. In the case of an IPO, a private company becomes subject to the provisions of Sarbanes-Oxley as soon as it files a registration statement. Therefore, it is critical for companies to have their governance and compliance house in order. Some private companies have registered debt securities which require them to be compliant with the regulations.

THE FRAUD TRIANGLE

A very strong reason for private companies to consider application of some components of Sarbanes-Oxley is the fraud triangle. Fraud risk factors and the fraud triangle were introduced in Chapter 7. Fraud occurs when risk factors are prevalent. While fraud appears in companies of all sizes, it is more likely to occur in smaller private companies that have not applied a focused approach toward internal controls. Because of this tendency, it makes sense to apply the best business practices offered by the new standards.

Misappropriation of assets occurs for a number of reasons, and highest on the list is the ease of misappropriation that usually results from inadequate internal control, allowing the theft to occur. Other reasons that provide incentives for fraud include the incentive or pressure to steal as well as employee attitude. Employee attitude arises from relationships emerging out of the culture of the organization whereby employees feel that they are owed the money that they steal. Sometimes factors that occur within the company drive employee attitudes to get even. Employees may feel they have justifiable reasons because of failure to be promoted or to receive a raise. Whatever the reasons, companies typically set themselves up for the theft by having large amounts of cash, inventory that can be easily removed and sold, or fixed assets that are not carefully identified and controlled.

When it comes to internal controls, smaller companies tend to become lax and fail to implement the necessary control framework and procedures that effectively safeguard assets. Some of the more common failures of internal control include inadequate segregation of duties and poor management oversight. Other reasons include poor human resource policies with respect to hiring, poor documentation for transactions, and weak information technology controls over automated records. Whatever the reasons, the theft could have been prevented through establishment of a sound system of controls and a supportive control environment. It also helps to have monitoring systems that discourage employees from committing fraudulent acts.

Fraud can occur from misstatements arising from fraudulent financial reporting or misappropriation of assets. Good internal controls are designed to protect against both types. Fraudulent financial reporting usually occurs when there is a combination of incentive or pressure for misstatement of financial results to occur combined with an associated opportunity and rationalization for misstatement. Opportunities evolve from an ineffective control environment supported by ineffective management and weak internal control. The incentives or pressure producing misstatement is frequently created by economic, industry, or operating conditions. This situation is then rationalized by an attitude that it is either okay or the misstatement can subsequently be corrected. Rationalization is when individuals convince themselves that the fraudulent act fits within their personal code of ethics. When third-party expectations are unusually high, combined with risk of personal loss or opportunity for gain, companies are at risk. Sarbanes-Oxley sets new standards for ethical behavior and governance that will help prevent such situations.

Misstatements arising from fraudulent financial reporting are intentional acts designed to deceive users and readers of the financial statements. Fraudulent financial reporting can result from manipulation, falsification, or alteration of financial records or supporting documentation used to prepare financial statements. It can also occur from misrepresentation or omission of events, transactions, or other significant information supporting the financial statements. Finally, financial statements can become misleading through the intentional application of incorrect accounting principles, classification of transactions, or inadequate disclosure of financial information.

THE NEW BENCHMARK

Publicly traded companies are required by legal necessity to abide by the Sarbanes-Oxley legislation. But what about other organizations and privately held companies? Will they respond to the new benchmark? Other companies that might be affected can range from large to small privately held companies, including family-owned businesses. Also included are nonprofit organizations, where the impact might be felt more quickly than in for-profit organizations. This latter category covers a wide array of organizations, including colleges and universities, charitable organizations, hospitals, churches, labor unions, and professional associations. Because of the public interest in these categories of organizations, it appears that they will become subject to the new standards of governance and controls more quickly than will other types of private companies.

A new model for governance and accounting has been created by the Sarbanes-Oxley Act and will eventually be the roadmap for all companies, both public and private, to follow in their pursuit of governance and good accounting practices. Lenders and businesspeople working with public companies are starting to see the benefits created by the new standards. In addition, the advantages that result from independent directors and audit committees will be applied to privately held companies and nonprofit organizations alike. When dealing with the "beyond" aspect of compliance, I think we will see private companies adopt those provisions of the standards that make good business sense.

In considering the new benchmark, it is important to examine the types of demands that private companies and nonprofit organizations will expect to receive. One area of pressure is likely to come from lenders and insurers. Lenders can be expected to include Sarbanes-Oxley conformity and governance as a component of loan covenants. Likewise, insurance companies in some instances will make conformity a requirement of policy renewals in an effort to reduce their risk. Another example is private companies doing business directly or indirectly with government agencies. The SEC already impacts private companies that have public debt, and Section 404 applies in those instances. A number of private companies have large numbers of outside shareholders, absentee owners, or public companies that own shares. In these instances, companies are being required to add disclosures and control standards to satisfy the demands of their shareholders. Nonprofits are the most likely organizations to be encouraged to comply because of public trust, board members with public company backgrounds, and the tendency to utilize public bonds to raise capital.

A variety of elements of the new benchmark are being adopted and applied. Audit committees are being reshuffled and upgraded to achieve greater independence, and these steps will provide greater organization-wide impact toward improved governance and internal controls. Another Sarbanes-Oxley provision being adopted by private companies is financial statement certification by officers. The prohibited services provisions of the act are being adopted, and audit committees are reaching out to outside advisors as opposed to automatically going to the external auditor for expanded services. The emphasis is being redirected back to auditing and establishment of independence. Other steps include upgrading of accounting principles and the establishment of internal audit functions. Executive compensation is also coming under scrutiny, and the whistle-blower provisions are being enforced. While there does not seem to be a widespread trend toward management assessment of internal controls, it would appear that it will be only a matter of time before the Section 404 regulations will start to take hold. When considering "beyond" implications of Sarbanes-Oxley, the assessment component offers management teams the greatest benefit once they gain understanding of how to effectively apply the tool.

THIRD-PARTY ISSUES

Privately held companies will begin to feel quiet pressure from third parties as to the degree of compliance effort they need to adopt in the face of Sarbanes-Oxley. Much of the focus will come from venture capitalists, bankers, insurers, vendors, and customers because of the best practice standards established by the new guidelines. After two-plus years of existence, the components and standards for internal controls and governance created by Sarbanes-Oxley are well known to investors, partners, and interested third parties. While there are complaints about the rigorous testing and redundancy associated with detail testing forced by Section 404, the overall spirit of good internal control, governance, and mitigation of risks is accepted as the new standard for how good business is conducted. There is no question that many third parties will likely demand some level of adoption of the new standards to help provide transparency, integrity, and accountability. Embracing the elevated new standards can have a material impact, either directly or indirectly, on the valuation of a privately held company, because its governance practices and financial presentations are considerably more reliable than those companies that have not adopted the new standards for best business practice.

I have given my workshops to a cross-section of private companies, and for the most part all of them were in the process of adopting some components of the standards. These companies were clear about minimizing the risk to shareholders and establishing a risk management framework that allows them more affordable insurance for officers and directors liability. In addition, shareholders and business partners of the company realize that officers and directors are more knowledgeable regarding the operations and financial matters of the company as a result of adopting the corporate governance practices. Good governance also works to the company's advantage when raising funds from venture capitalists and angel investors. This extends to attracting outside directors and strategic partners for the business. Establishment of good corporate governance practices makes it more likely that independent directors will consider and accept board positions because of the minimization of risk to both the company and the director individually.

Exit strategies will play an important role in deciding to adopt the new corporate governance practices and standards. Early adoption of the standards can have a direct effect on the valuation of a company by allowing it to get to market in a more timely and efficient time frame. Failure to take a proactive attitude toward adoption of the standards can have a negative effect on marketability and share valuation. When the exit strategy is acquisition by a public company, the same rules apply. Early adoption of the standards will make a big difference in executing the exit strategy and frequently can be a deal breaker.

Early adoption of the new governance standards should start with selecting appropriately qualified independent directors. Creating a board of directors that is not comprised of founders, friends, and management will go a long way toward creating trust with shareholders and potential investors. Both the NYSE and NASDAQ have detailed definitions for independence that apply to members of boards of directors of public companies. A private company should review the composition of its board on an annual basis relative to its market and industry. Companies that receive guidance from independent directors with industry expertise will benefit greatly from the breadth of experience and independent perspective as they move closer to executing their exit strategy. Even without an exit strategy, private companies that regularly receive effective independent insight will benefit from such input that translates into enhanced shareholder value. In addition to having a board comprised of independent members, private companies should establish, at a minimum, an audit committee, a compensation committee, and a nominating committee. The PCAOB has been very focused regarding the audit committee and how it functions. Private companies that adopt similar provisions for establishment of audit committees will benefit according to the effort and focus they provide to these areas. The tone is set at the top, so starting with a solid slate of independent directors makes a lot of sense. Taking the effort and spending the money now may save a great deal more later on. Creating the right tone on the board of directors will go a long way toward creating the right control environment.

COPYCAT LEGISLATION

One of the fears associated with Sarbanes-Oxley was that states would begin creating legislation that would attempt to expand on the original act and extend the reform concepts to private companies, nonprofit organizations, and accountants. The American Institute of Certified Public Accountants has addressed this concern with a study of state issues related to the Sarbanes-Oxley Act. This study advocated taking a reasoned approach to reform at the state level by providing uniform laws that would not go overboard in legislating private companies, nonprofit organizations, and accountants. As of this writing, there have been almost 20 attempts at copycat legislation in a dozen states, with no end in sight.

The most aggressive legislation is being offered by California and New York. California's legislation requires a CPA performing an audit for any corporation (private or nonprofit) to report to the audit committee all accounting policies used during the audit together with alternative disclosures and treatments discussed with management. It also requires a corporation to disclose if it has adopted a code of ethics for its senior financial officers and increased the penalties for violating the Corporate Securities Law of 1968 from a maximum of 5 years in jail to not more than 20 years and a fine of $10 million or both.

In New York, Attorney General Eliot Spitzer proposed a series of reforms in an attempt to strengthen the state's corporate accountability laws. The proposal includes providing whistle-blower protection for employees reporting illegal activities, protecting against fraud relating to nonprofit corporations, addressing misconduct by corporate officers, and improving the oversight of the accounting profession. Spitzer called for accounting reforms to go beyond the Sarbanes-Oxley Act to include firms that do not audit publicly traded companies. Legislation was introduced to require nonprofits with $1 million in gross revenues and $3 million in assets or with audited financial statements to establish audit committees that will be responsible for overseeing the auditors. Other legislation was introduced covering increased penalties for corporate bribery and receipt of corporate bribes. The bill required that the president, chief executive officer, chief financial officer, or treasurer verify the corporation's annual report, in addition to encouraging designation of executive committees and audit committees.

Other pieces of legislation introduced prohibit auditing firms from having consulting contracts with the company being audited and require creation of audit and compensation committees comprised of independent board members. Another example requires CPA candidates to pass a separate exam in professional ethics and expands continuing professional education requirements for CPAs. New Mexico wants stricter control of conflict of interest standards for CPAs. These are representative of new restrictions that were proposed. Clearly, it is likely that the impact from Sarbanes-Oxley will be extended well beyond the federal parameters to include a number of wide-ranging restrictions for private companies, nonprofits, and CPAs. We now have new standards for conduct, internal controls, and governance, and it should be quite clear that the impact will be widespread and with far reaching consequences for all organizations.

INTERNAL AUDIT CHALLENGES

In addition to building board of director competency with independent members, the next challenging task for private companies, including nonprofits, will be to establish internal audit capability. Many companies, both private and public, just do not have the necessary internal resources to staff and manage an internal audit function. In addition to the resource challenges, it is important to realize that the internal audit function needs to report directionally to the audit committee. This latter issue can complicate the formation of an internal audit function, since creation of independent audit committees comprised of qualified and experienced members can take some time. When faced with these obstacles it makes sense to step back and take first things first, meaning that resource evaluation is the critical issue. Following this scenario, companies need to address the audit committee on a priority basis, because this component will help to establish an objective standard for corporate governance.

There are some good options for establishing an internal audit function that will help create a control environment capable of addressing financial and operational risks. The options include hiring a consultant or temporary audit professional to get the program moving on a short-term basis. Aligned with this option is outsourcing the function to a CPA firm or other consulting firm skilled in internal auditing. This latter option can make sense for a firm that has not solidified its independent audit committee and may not have a clear objective of the internal control risks facing the company. While the CPA firm used to perform the internal audit function will not be able to perform the audit work, it will likely have the expertise to guide company management on the best approach for identifying risks and provide direction on the establishment of an audit committee. Ideally, establishment of the audit committee would be preferred since it can help a company create a focus on controls and financial reporting.

The new governance rules of the road include separating prohibited services that could be performed by the external auditor. This is an area where the audit committee can provide direction and guidance. One of the challenges for companies will be to compensate and empower the audit committee in order to gain the desired benefits from the governance initiative. This chapter provided insight into approaching compliance and adopting best practices for governance and internal controls. It is one thing to say this is what we are going to do and still another to take the necessary action steps to implement the full program. In addition to the steps mentioned above, it is suggested that companies look at materials and programs offered by the Institute of Internal Auditors (www.theiia.org), which has a wide range of services that can be useful.

LOOKING AHEAD

When we look down the road, it is quite clear that good governance is here to stay, and the requirements for private companies and nonprofit organizations will fall into the compliance mold created for public companies. Since the standard for best practice will set the tone, those companies that say the Sarbanes-Oxley requirements do not apply to them will be a minority. In fact, failure to create a stronger control environment can expose organizations to unnecessary risks and place them at a competitive disadvantage. Nonprofit organizations will either be forced into compliance with the rules by law or run the risk of having their reputations damaged by loss of trust resulting from poor financial management. Internal control assessment and adoption of best practices will become mandatory to maintain effective fund-raising efforts.

The risk of fraud for smaller, less sophisticated companies was documented earlier. Application of the concepts and principles of the COSO Integrated Framework of internal control can be effectively adopted and followed by smaller organizations. The framework clearly spells out steps for applying the tools to small to mid-sized companies, so size is not an excuse. It would seem that voluntary early adoption of the higher standard for governance, internal controls, and financial reporting represents an opportunity.

In the early stages of adopting the new governance standards, it is becoming clear that all companies will be impacted in some form by the new rules. It will take time for the rules to take hold and for all companies, private and public, to see how to comply and benefit from the new benchmark standards. Private company adoption of the governance standards will initially be to create independent boards of directors and establish an internal audit function. We can also expect to see more corporate officers certify financial results and create a code of ethics to guide conduct and set the tone for the organization. A latter stage of compliance will emerge when companies begin applying the standards created by Section 404 and self-assess the design of their internal controls and operational effectiveness. Audit standards are being set by the PCAOB, and the differences between audits of public and private companies will blend together. When this level of compliance begins to gain traction, companies that embrace the true spirit of self-assessment will reap the multiple benefits of continuous improvement in addition to increased market valuation. Higher market valuation and acceptance by shareholders and investors will accrue, based on recognition that a company adopted and maintained a control environment that meets the highest standards of excellence.

NEW WORLD
OF AUDITING

In any book on Sarbanes-Oxley, it is important to take a look at the changes that have occurred in auditing from multiple perspectives. From my point of view, I think it was about time for new rules and standards. Not everyone will agree, but one thing is clear: it is a different ball game. The only constant that I see is that there will be continuing changes emerging as the business world and the accounting profession struggle to cope with their new environment and rules of engagement.

This chapter will help to clarify how the rules are set for complying with the new standards of governance. We will take a look at where we are and also attempt to gain some sense of the future. This journey will help to clarify the new auditing standards and accounting principles and to answer some of the questions that have been gnawing at the back of people's minds. There are multiple facets of the legislation that businesses, managers, directors, and auditors need to understand as they evaluate risk and make decisions. It is not the same old standard, and more changes can be expected as the initial compliance efforts begin to unfold. We will start with the new independent oversight body and move forward from the rule setters to how auditors will apply the new standards and what might be in store for us in the future.

INDEPENDENT OVERSIGHT

One clear objective of the Sarbanes-Oxley Act was to create a board that would be responsible for administering the oversight of audits of publicly traded companies to protect the interests of the investing public. The oversight board was named the Public Company Accounting Oversight Board, more commonly called the PCAOB, and came into existence in October 2002. Funding of board activities is provided by support fees charged to each publicly traded company based on the size of its market capitalization. The board consists of five members appointed to a five-year term, and only two of the board members can be or can have been CPAs.

As part of its role, the PCAOB is responsible for registering and inspecting auditing firms performing audits of publicly traded companies. Auditing firms that audit 100 or more public companies are subject to annual inspections, and firms auditing less than 100 companies are subject to inspection every three years. The PCAOB is responsible for setting audit standards and quality control standards, ethics, maintaining independence, and other standards associated with preparing audit reports. In addition to conducting inspections of auditing firms, the PCAOB is also responsible for investigations, applying disciplinary procedures, and applying appropriate sanctions on auditing firms when necessary. Each firm registered with the PCAOB pays an annual fee that covers the cost of conducting its inspection. At the time of this writing, there were 1419 firms registered with the PCAOB and 42 firms waiting for approval.

The responsibility for setting audit standards before the existence of the PCAOB fell to the American Institute of Certified Public Accountants (AICPA). Because of the failure of the accounting profession to effectively set standards for public companies, this job is now entrusted to the new oversight board. The AICPA still has the job of setting standards for private companies, and it has the challenge of minimizing differences and avoiding confusion. A new standard for governance and internal control has been created by Sarbanes-Oxley, so it will not be surprising to see the two standards begin to blend together. The establishment and setting of standards for conducting audits represents a major departure from the past. The PCAOB has driven a serious stake in the ground on auditing standards, accounting principles, and financial reporting. In addition to overseeing auditing firms, the PCAOB is also administratively responsible for the Financial Accounting Standards Board (FASB), which is the body responsible for setting generally accepted accounting principles (GAAP). These topics will be elaborated on in greater depth in later sections of the chapter.

It is important to put the mission of the PCAOB into proper context, as its objective is to instill confidence in auditing and financial reporting in the minds and perceptions of the investing public. Perhaps instilling confidence should be phrased as "restoring public confidence." This means more than just a check-the-box approach to internal control and financial reporting. It is all about "tone at the top" and providing the professional discipline required in managing and minimizing business risks within the ranks of auditors and for management and boards. The best way to fully understand the significant impact of the oversight board is to comprehend the sweeping revisions that have transpired since the enactment of the legislation. How the new audit standards are being applied and the tone of the message being sent to achieve true independence and professionalism from auditors will be described. Detailed information and updates on all activities and pronouncements from the PCAOB are available at www.PCAOB.org.

TWO SETS OF AUDIT STANDARDS

Along with Sarbanes-Oxley came the concept of a different audit combined with management's assessment of internal control. Our focus here is to clarify the two audit approaches. We will also explore audit reports issued to private companies, along with the differences between them and audits of publicly traded companies. The new audit is in reality two audits that cannot be separated for publicly traded companies. Audit standards for privately held companies do not include a requirement for a management assessment of internal control, which is required by Audit Standard No. 2 under Section 404.

When viewing the new audit opinion rendered for a public company, investors know that management has self-assessed its design of internal controls and tested and documented its operating effectiveness. A reader of a private company's financial report has only the assurance from the auditor that the financial statements are presented in accordance with GAAP, with no mention of or reference to the strength of internal controls supporting the statements. The AICPA is responsible for audit standards for private companies. The PCAOB is the standard setter for audit reports of public companies. In fact, an audit report of a public company could be presented in accordance with GAAP and contain the disclosure of a material internal control weakness. The question has to be asked if a material control weakness should be excluded from private audit reports when good business practice for public companies requires the disclosure. When we have two standard setters, the next question is how and when we close the gap.

The issue of restoring the public's confidence extends beyond publicly traded companies and drills down to credibility of the accounting profession. Setting audit standards for public companies has been removed from the self-governance of the accounting profession. We have seen a new benchmark created for best business practices as a number of private companies move to adopt elements of Sarbanes-Oxley. Accounting is a regulated profession, and the tone of new rules created for public companies and accountants serving those companies will be felt by private companies and accountants serving those companies. Accountants have always reviewed internal controls as a component of their work. These reports were the subject of management letters, which were frequently not taken very seriously. Maybe private companies, in the eyes of some, should be excluded from management self-assessment and auditor attestation of management's work. Based on the extensive amount of work I have conducted in the private sector performing assessments, I would suggest that management and accountants would derive significant benefits from this disciplined approach. Accountants and companies that fail to reach for the highest standards of excellence and performance across the board will fall short of earning people's trust lost during the spate of corporate scandals.

AICPA: REGAINING LOST RELEVANCE

Prior to the establishment of the PCAOB, the AICPA was responsible for setting technical accounting and auditing standards for the accounting profession. It also provided the guidance and direction for examinations leading to licensing for the profession. However, it is important to realize that licensing is regulated by each state, so some variation can creep into the process. Accounting and auditing standards were a critical responsibility of the AICPA for all companies prior to the PCAOB and now only provide guidance relative to private companies. Accounting standards are set by the FASB, which is under the direction of the PCAOB. Peer reviews were also a function of the AICPA.

We can clearly begin to see where a shift in relevance has occurred with the emergence of Sarbanes-Oxley. Now the waters are murky as the AICPA sorts out its new vision and mission. The organization is focused on supporting its members and the public interest. While its role is no longer that of a primary standards setter, it is providing guidance and direction in supporting its members in areas of ethics, education, and high-quality services to their clients. The organization has a total membership that exceeds 350,000 nationally and internationally, so when we look at the reach of the organization, there is no question that it is broad. Its membership uses the wide range of technical and other materials offered as work aids and support in providing a broad range of services. The materials and support services are too numerous to mention here, and I suggest visiting www.AICPA.org for a complete summary of all the information, technical support, and materials offered.

Since the enactment of the Sarbanes-Oxley Act, the AICPA has been forced into new roles and the adoption of new strategies. There has been a full effort to provide hot lines and other support areas relative to the PCAOB and new compliance activity. One of the initiatives that has been extremely helpful is the creation of information and guidance on audit committee activities. *The AICPA Audit Committee Toolkit* created by the Audit Committee Effectiveness Center offers a wealth of information relative to the audit committee and its role. Also, the AICPA's Center for Public Company Audit Firms provides an abundance of current information relative to compliance issues and questions.

Effectively, the AICPA has evolved into a partnership role with the PCAOB by helping to assist its membership to regain public trust and provide information and initiatives that support the challenges encountered in complying with the new legislation. While one of its roles has been redirected to the PCAOB, there has been a major thrust by the AICPA to provide objective advice and promote the issuance of reliable financial information in an efficient and accountable fashion. The reality of the Sarbanes-Oxley impact has motivated the accounting profession to earn the highest level of trust by providing the lead in attracting good capable people into the profession and setting a high standard for ethics and governance. In addition to earlier mentioned initiatives, the institute is promoting high-quality audit standards in a number of specialized areas, such as employee benefits and public company audit issues relating to private companies and not-for-profit organizations.

One of the key new standards issued by the AICPA is SAS 99, which focuses on how auditors address fraud relative to the delivery of services and specifically when dispatching audit responsibilities. Also, a number of smaller firms and practitioners are working with public companies on complying with Section 404, and this reality is being addressed by the AICPA in providing assistance and valuable input. Another AICPA initiative is the publication of the *Enterprise Risk Management—Integrated Framework,* issued in conjunction with COSO, which provides a guideline for managing and identifying risks and opportunities that boards, top management, and others can follow in enhancing shareholder value. The AICPA has also taken the lead in business reporting by establishing the Enhanced Business Reporting Consortium, which will be launched in 2005, to improve the quality, integrity, and transparency of information used for business decision making. There is a long way to go in regaining the luster that was tarnished as a result of the Andersen implosion and the financial scandals that descended on the accounting profession. The joint efforts by the AICPA and PCAOB represent the first steps in the journey to regain relevance lost by the accounting profession.

FASB AND GAAP

It is important to provide clarity regarding the functioning of the FASB since it operates under the authority of and with funding by the Securities and Exchange Commission (SEC). The FASB has the responsibility for establishing financial accounting for publicly traded companies. This role has taken on greater significance since the enactment of the Sarbanes-Oxley Act in 2002. Since the FASB operates under the umbrella of the PCAOB, the authority to set standards has effectively been shifted away from the accounting profession. While the accounting standards handed down by the FASB are for public companies, there is clearly a common tendency for private companies to adopt these standards. There are several issues with respect to differences in GAAP between public and private companies, which will be addressed in a later section. Our purpose here is to create understanding and clarity surrounding the setting of accounting standards by the FASB.

The FASB consists of seven full-time board members that serve for a five-year term. Board members are required to sever all connectivity and affiliations with the firms they served while they are fulfilling their terms on the board. The board members come from diverse backgrounds and are required to have knowledge of accounting, finance, and business. Since the board is setting accounting standards for public companies, board members must be sensitive to maintaining the trust of the investing public and readers of financial statements. The current composition of the board includes a mix of former public accountants, educators, security analysts, and financial executives. In addition, the board has a staff of approximately 40 professionals and support personnel.

The FASB is responsible for developing accounting concepts in addition to setting standards for financial reporting. Its mission is to establish and improve standards of financial accounting and reporting, in addition to the education and guidance of the investing public, auditors, issuers, and users of financial information. In order to accomplish its mission, the FASB has created the following action steps:

- Improve the usefulness of financial reporting
- Ensure that standards are current and reflect business and economic conditions
- Use the standard-setting process to improve significant deficiencies in financial reporting
- Promote convergence of standards with the International Accounting Standards Board (IASB)
- Enhance common understanding of the nature and purpose of information contained in financial reports

The FASB operates in an open forum in order to achieve an orderly process for setting standards that is not swayed by particular special-interest groups.

The purpose here is to provide a general understanding of what the FASB does and how it goes about the process of establishing and maintaining standards for accounting and financial reporting. Some of the areas of focus for the FASB include small business issues, governmental accounting standards, simplification, improvement of U.S. standards, and international convergence. Current discussion of all of these topics can be found on the FASB's web site at www.fasb.org. The board has an advisory council called the Financial Accounting Standards Advisory Council, comprised of over 30 members who provide a broad representation of preparers, auditors, and users of financial information. Also, the Financial Accounting Foundation is responsible for selecting the members of the FASB and its advisory council. Accounting is at a critical juncture because of the changes being forced on a traditional profession that has struggled with shifting paradigms and business conditions. The FASB is at the vortex of helping to cope with and accommodating the complexity of the many issues associated with providing understandable and meaningful accounting and financial reports. Since financial statements need to be presented in accordance with GAAP, we need to understand who sets the standards and how the process functions.

PRINCIPLES-BASED ACCOUNTING

In any discussion of auditing and changes in the application of accounting principles, it is important to understand differences in how accounting standards are set across the global environment. It is also critical to understand that the rules-based approach that evolved with U.S. accounting standards is one of the factors that led some companies involved in the financial scandals to interpret the standards for the purpose of achieving their own objectives. Enron and others employed financial engineering techniques to further their personal accounting objectives and avoid reporting on economic reality. Further, the U.S. accounting standards have not been in conformance with International Financial Reporting Standards (IFRS) and International Accounting Standards (IAS). These standards are predicated on an approach that requires both the preparer and the auditor to step back to evaluate and consider if the proposed accounting is consistent with the underlying principle. It is strongly felt that if such a principles-based approach had been in effect, the Enron scandal would have never happened. The Sarbanes-Oxley Act of 2002 required the SEC to conduct a study of the adoption of a principles-based accounting system within one year of enactment of the legislation.

A principles-based approach to setting accounting standards, in contrast to current U.S. GAAP, means that principles would apply more broadly and there would be less interpretative and implementation guidance for applying the standards. This means that more commitment from both preparers and auditors will be required to resist pressures for following the principles in contrast to resorting to a rules-based approach. Greater professional judgment will be necessary to comply with the spirit of the principles-based standards. One of the primary obstacles to implementing principles-based standards is the lack of a clear and consistent framework. The FASB is in the process of considering the feasibility of a framework similar to that developed by the IAS, which is *IAS 1 (Revised): Presentation of Financial Statements*. The FASB's proposal dated January 3, 2003 identifies the following issues where the new framework would provide guidance:

- Materiality
- Going concern
- Professional judgment
- Accounting policies
- Consistency
- Presentation of comparative information
- Override situations to avoid misleading presentation to convey economic reality and substance

The proposal indicates that there would be very few exceptions to the principles and more situations where similar transactions and events are recorded on a comparable and consistent basis.

A principles-based approach will take a great deal of effort and result in additional costs. The FASB indicates that, in the absence of additional guidance, some organizations could become *de facto* standard setters, leading to abuses not consistent with the intent of the standards. Also, broader standards will be easier to understand and implement. Additionally, the increased use of professional judgment will help to convey the economic substance of the transactions and events being reported, because there would be a reduction of the accounting engineering involved to structure transactions. Clearly, the FASB is headed in this direction because it feels that the result of adopting a principles-based approach would be high-quality accounting standards that will improve the transparency of financial information. Additionally, principles-based standards will produce less detailed presentations capable of being more responsive to the changing financial and economic environment of the 21st century. Since the IAS operates on a principles-based accounting platform, adoption by the United States will facilitate convergence with the FASB and the IASB and others responsible for IAS. While it is clear that principles-based accounting represents the future, there is no doubt that coping with and adjusting to the process of transition and change will be a major challenge all across the board. Fear factors will include being second-guessed by regulators plus a concern for potential litigation and retaliation. Traditional accountants will require some serious doses of education and retraining.

AUDIT STANDARDS FOR THE NONAUDITOR

Before Sarbanes-Oxley, the audit report required that the financial statements be presented in accordance with GAAP along with appropriate footnote disclosures. Now we have new rules of the road, and auditors are auditing not only the financial statements but management's assessment of internal control. The PCAOB to date has issued three new audit standards, the details of which can be accessed and downloaded from its web site. Audit Standard No. 1 deals with References in Auditors' Reports to the Standards of the Public Company Accounting Oversight Board. Standard No. 1 accepted the AICPA's Statement on Auditing Standards No. 95: Generally Accepted Auditing Standards. Essentially, new audit reports will state that they were conducted in accordance with the standards of the PCAOB. Audit Standard No. 2 deals with auditing internal control over financial reporting, and Audit Standard No. 3 covers audit documentation. We will discuss these new standards in more depth, especially Audit Standard No. 2, which deals with an audit of internal control.

Audit Standard No. 2 represents the biggest change to both preparers and auditors because it deals with compliance under Section 404, which requires management to assess internal controls over financial reporting. Auditors are required to audit management's assessment of internal control. It is helpful for preparers to understand the audit requirements since this will provide guidance on how to conduct their assessment and prepare for the audit.

Key elements of Standard No. 2 require the auditor to evaluate management's assessment of internal control. During this process, the auditor must obtain an understanding of internal control, including performance of walkthroughs and identification of significant accounts and relevant assertions. A critical component of the audit is the testing and evaluation of the effectiveness of the design of the controls in place. After evaluating control design, the auditor must then test the operating effectiveness of the control. There is much more to the standard, and the major facets and elements of this new requirement will be described.

We have discussed the COSO frameworks, and the PCAOB makes it clear that this is an acceptable framework to be used for management's assessment. Moving further into the application of the standard, it addresses company-wide controls, including tone at the top and management's risk assessment process. When applying the standard, it is critical to identify the significant accounts in order to determine what and where to test. Some of the factors that should be taken into consideration include the following:

- Size and composition of the account
- Susceptibility to loss from errors or fraud
- Volume of activity
- Nature of the account
- Accounting and reporting complexities
- Exposure to losses represented by the account or account group
- Likelihood of contingent liabilities
- Existence of related party transactions
- Changes in account characteristics from the prior period

After consideration of significant accounts, the major transactions that are significant to the company's financial statements need to be identified. These should be broken down into routine transactions, those that are not routine, and transactions developed by estimation.

Auditors and management must then determine and identify the major processes for the company. These can be segmented into the following categories:

- Capturing input data
- Sorting and merging files
- Making calculations
- Updating transactions
- Master files
- Generating transactions
- Summarizing, displaying, or reporting data

Once these steps have been accomplished, it is then critical to understand the flow of transactions, including how they are initiated, authorized, recorded, processed, and reported. From this juncture, auditors need to identify the points within the process at which a misstatement, especially fraud related, might occur. Auditors then must identify the controls management has implemented to address and avoid these potential misstatements. Identification of controls that management has implemented over prevention or timely detection of unauthorized acquisition, use, or disposition of assets is also a required step in the audit process.

After the significant accounts and processes as well as the controls that management has implemented have been identified, auditors must evaluate management's own assessment and documentation of internal controls. The more clearly management documents its internal control over financial reporting, the process used to assess control effectiveness, and assessment results, the easier it will be for auditors to make their evaluation. While auditors can place some reliance on the extent and quality of management's assessment, they still need to obtain their own independent understanding of the internal controls. Auditors are required to confirm their understanding of the process flow of transactions and design of controls and identify any point at which a potential misstatement could occur.

During the walkthrough, auditors can frequently gain simultaneous understanding of the transaction flow and identify and understand the controls in place. The walkthrough process is critical in executing Audit Standard No. 2 and requires the utilization of more experienced auditors. This provides auditors the opportunity to ask client personnel key questions about the controls and how they are being applied. Areas to investigate include the following:

1. What do you do when you find an error?
2. What are you looking for to determine if there is an error?
3. Auditors should observe if client personnel are merely following listed procedures and controls.
4. Inquiries should be made regarding the types of errors identified.
5. When an error is found, how is the error resolved?
6. If no error is found, is this because of good preventive controls or because the person performing the controls is overqualified and is able to overcome a control deficiency?
7. Personnel should be asked if they have ever been requested to override either the process or the controls, and if so, why it occurred and what happened.

When evaluating controls, either through the walkthrough process or in testing, auditors need to identify the points at which errors or fraud could occur. One of the AICPA statements on auditing standards, SAS No. 99, deals with the steps that audit teams should follow in this regard. Considerations by the auditor should include the nature of controls implemented by management together with the significance of each control in achieving the objectives of the control criteria. Stated another way, how many controls are required to achieve specific objectives? When evaluating risk that controls might not be operating effectively, auditors should consider the following:

1. Changes in volumes and nature of transactions
2. Changes in the design of controls
3. The degree to which the control relies on the effectiveness of other controls
4. Changes in key personnel who perform the control or monitor performance

5. Whether the control relies on performance by an individual or is automated
6. The complexity of the control

When evaluating internal control, there needs to be clarity that management's responsibility for the effectiveness of the company's controls over financial reporting is expressed at the level of reasonable assurance. Management needs to evaluate the controls using reasonable control criteria and support its evaluation with sufficient evidence and documentation. Finally, management should present a written assessment of the effectiveness of the company's internal control over financial reporting as of the end of the most recent fiscal year.

Understanding the testing and evaluation of operating effectiveness in addition to control design is another facet of the internal control audit. The word testing is important because it is a function that must be performed by the auditor and it takes on greater significance under Standard No. 2. Testing means to thoroughly examine and explore the necessary authority and qualifications of personnel to perform controls effectively. The tests should include a mix of inquiries, observation, and reperformance of the application of the control. Inquiry is obtaining information, both financial and nonfinancial, from knowledgeable people within the company. It is important to consider the skill and competency of personnel relative to the sensitivity of the control to prevent errors or fraud and to support the inquiries with appropriate documentation as evidence. In addition to inquiries, it is important that the auditor actually test the underlying documentation used by or generated by performing the control. Testing also needs to consider adequacy over time in addition to the "as of" specific dates using appropriate cutoff procedures. In response to the question about the extent of tests, the answer is until sufficient evidence is obtained to determine if the company's internal controls are operating properly. Auditors will be required to vary the tests from year to year in addition to the size limit or amount of transactions tested.

The experience level of auditors will need to be more advanced than in the past. A higher level of professional skepticism will be demanded during the testing process. There needs to be a greater awareness as to the possibility of fraud or financial misstatement. Just believing that management is honest is no longer good enough. Auditors need to document their tests with more than hunches and relationship with management. Testing must be supported with real and hard evidence that controls are reliable. While auditors can rely on the work of others, including internal auditors or other third parties, they still need to conduct their own independents tests and evaluations.

Considerations in evaluating management's assessment need to include the control environment and the integrity and ethical values of the company. Auditors will need to evaluate the company's commitment to competence. Another factor auditors will consider in their evaluation is the level of participation by the board of directors and the audit committee. Auditors need to inquire regarding the assignment of authority and responsibility, along with human resources and other policies. Evaluation of management's assessment needs to consider the scope of the assessment, adequacy of work programs, documentation, supervision and review, whether the conclusions reached by management were reasonable and appropriate, and whether the reports were consistent with the results of the work performed. While this summary does not identify all the considerations and factors touched on by Audit Standard No. 2, it does hit the key elements.

CONTROL DEFICIENCIES

Control deficiencies are defined in Audit Standard No. 2 and are important enough to warrant a separate discussion. A control deficiency exists when the design or operation of a control does not allow management or employees, in the normal performance of their duties and functions, to detect or prevent a misstatement from occurring on a timely basis. A deficiency in design exists when a control required to achieve the control objective is missing or the existing control is not properly designed, causing the control objective to be missed. Deficiencies in operation result when a properly designed control fails to operate as it was designed or when the person performing the control does not have the necessary authority or qualifications to perform the control effectively. It is important to realize that these two factors—design and operating effectiveness—need to be met to avoid a deficiency.

A significant deficiency is a control deficiency, or a combination of deficiencies, that can affect the company's ability to initiate, record, process, or report external financial information on a reliable basis in accordance with GAAP. The deficiency occurs when there is *more than a remote likelihood* that an inconsequential misstatement of the company's annual or interim financial statements either will not be prevented or will not be detected.

The term remote likelihood follows FAS No. 5, which spells out the following three categories:

1. Probable means that a future event or events are likely to occur
2. Reasonably possible is when the chance of a future event or events occurring is more than remote but less than likely
3. Remote is when the chance of a future event or events occurring is slight

Understanding the distinction of remote likelihood in the context of defining a deficiency is very important.

A material weakness occurs when a significant deficiency, or a combination of significant deficiencies, exists where there is more than a remote likelihood that a material misstatement of the annual or interim financial statements either will not be prevented or will not be detected. Materiality must be evaluated by utilizing both qualitative and quantitative considerations. From a qualitative standpoint, the evaluation needs to consider the nature of the financial statement accounts together with the financial statement assertions. Consideration also needs to be given to the possible future consequences and impact of the deficiency. When evaluating deficiencies, auditors should reflect on the effect of any compensating controls and whether those controls are effective.

In deciding if deficiencies represent a material weakness, a number of factors and considerations need to be weighed. Reference to Figure 14.1 can be of some help in weighing the variety of factors that impact whether or not a deficiency is a material weakness. This is an important consideration because material weaknesses need to be disclosed, whereas a significant deficiency does not require disclosure. Factors that should be weighed in concluding that a deficiency is a material weakness include the following:

■ Nature of the financial statement account
■ Susceptibility to fraud

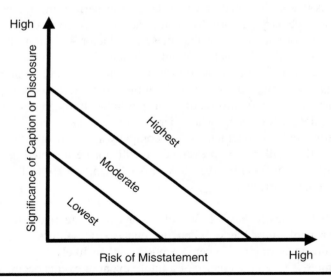

Figure 14.1.   Material weakness considerations.

- Subjectivity, complexity, or extent of judgment to determine amount
- Cause and frequency of known or detected exceptions for the operating effectiveness of controls
- Interaction of the deficiencies
- Possible future consequences of the deficiency

When making the decision on a material weakness, the evaluation should consider the significance of the deficiency, including the level of detail and degree of assurance that would satisfy prudent managers in the conduct of their own affairs. Would another manager reach a similar conclusion that such transactions were necessary to allow the preparation of financial statements in conformity with GAAP?

In any situation where a material weakness exists, management is precluded from concluding that the company's internal control is effective. One or more material weaknesses require disclosure of all material weaknesses that exist at the end of the company's most recent fiscal year. If there were material weaknesses during the year, management must have changed the internal control to eliminate the material weakness sufficiently in advance of the "as of" date and satisfactorily tested the effectiveness over a period of time in order to make the representation as to effective internal control. Any deficiency involving fraud will almost certainly result in a disclosure of a material weakness. Also, a company with weakness in its control environment, especially the tone at the top, is more likely to face situations where a material weakness could exist. Each company needs to address the issue of materiality and material weakness based on its individual situation.

NEW WORLD OF GOVERNANCE

A new component of the audit process under Sarbanes-Oxley is the role of the audit committee. Previously, it was the norm for audit firms and management to have very close relationships, and frequently auditors moved into accounting positions in the company. It was management's job to select the audit firm, and more often than not the board of directors was comprised of management or close associates of management. Because of the scandals and the fallout, new rules of governance and independence were created. The PCAOB and the SEC feel that board composition and responsibilities, particularly the audit committee, will dramatically change the confidence level of the investing public and create a new standard of governance.

Audit firms are now selected by the audit committee, comprised of independent members of the board of directors. Additionally, the audit committee is responsible for the audit, evaluating the auditor, and audit funding. Audit committees can also select other third-party experts for assistance as they deem necessary. In its independent role, the audit committee is also responsible for reviewing any complaints received by the company, internally or externally, about concerns regarding internal controls or auditing issues. This is the so-called "whistle-blower" provision to prohibit retaliation against personnel in instances of alleged fraud or other wrongdoing.

Internal audit functions are also accountable to the audit committee as they become the eyes and ears of the committee about what is going on within the company. The audit committee will likely encourage an atmosphere of professional skepticism between the internal audit function and the CFO and controller. In essence, the audit committee is the keeper of the gate to ensure that the internal audit function is adequately funded and allowed to focus on a healthy evaluation of key components of internal controls and risk assessment.

The SEC has placed a great deal of importance and emphasis on audit committees by requiring them to be independent of management and contain at least one individual who qualifies as a financial expert. Qualifications of an audit committee financial expert are focused on the experience and qualifications to manage an audit and financial function, together with in-depth understanding of preparing and analyzing financial statements and GAAP. The AICPA's *Audit Committee Toolkit* includes an excellent summary on the criteria for deciding on and considering the qualifications and experience required for an individual to be selected as a financial expert candidate.

In short, the good old days when management could select and control the auditor are over. There are new rules of the road that need to be closely followed. Audit committee members of the board have a major role and responsibility to help restore the public's confidence in auditing, accounting, and internal controls. It will take some time for the transition to evolve as both auditors and companies adjust to the process. There is no question that corporate governance has been and will be upgraded by the changes implemented by the PCAOB and the SEC. The key will be attracting and retaining qualified audit committees that will be capable of executing the vision.

BIG GAAP AND LITTLE GAAP

A considerable amount of concern has developed regarding application of accounting standards for large publicly traded companies and smaller private companies. This has led to the terminology known as "big GAAP" and "little GAAP" because of the opinion that different accounting and reporting should apply to large and small companies. This topic has been debated and studied off and on over the past 30 or 40 years with no resolution. Issuance of some recent standards has stirred the debate, along with the complexity and hardship for small public companies to comply with the new regulations. Some businesspeople and accountants felt that FASB No. 150: Accounting for Certain Financial Instruments with Characteristics of Both Liabilities and Equities and FASB Interpretation No. 45 and No. 46 were in many instances not applicable to smaller privately held companies. Financial Interpretation No. 45 relates to guaranteeing indebtedness of others and No. 46 deals with consolidation of variable interest entities. Both of these interpretations were pronouncements that arose out of the Enron scandal. The above accounting principles are illustrative but not inclusive of all the situations where differences of opinion might arise.

Typically, GAAP is meant to apply across the board for all companies without distinguishing between private and public entities. The FASB is the accepted standard setter for both public and private companies and does not provide for different recognition and measurement principles. Included in GAAP are the following basic core elements:

- Recognition of assets, liabilities, equity, revenue, and expenses and associated gains and losses
- Measurement of cost and fair value
- Financial statement presentation
- Financial statement footnote disclosure

The SEC and FASB have been charged with responsibility for improving the accuracy and disclosure of financial information for public companies as a result of the Sarbanes-Oxley Act of 2002. While the legislation does not specifically address privately held companies, we have seen that it certainly has set the standards for best business practice.

A major concern relative to smaller and privately held companies is the increasing complexity of GAAP pronouncements. It is important to recognize the significance of the impact that private companies have on the economy. According to the government, small companies create two-thirds of the jobs and employ approximately one-half of the workers in the private sector. There are approximately 5 million corporations in the United States and only 17,000 are publicly traded and registered with the SEC. GAAP accounting and financial reporting is geared toward external users of financial information and is relied upon by lenders, insurance companies, governments, stakeholders, and others. A significant number of privately held companies are issuing GAAP statements as a result of audits, reviews, or compilations that are relied on by third parties. Complexity and cost of financial statement presentation are valid concerns because of the increased complexity and pace of business. Simplicity and understandability of financial information is a goal for both public and privately held companies.

Sarbanes-Oxley has created a focus on and an awareness of the issues, problems, and potential solutions to financial reporting and internal control. Multiple projects are underway at the FASB to address convergence and transparency of financial information and reporting. We will ultimately see the IAS and GAAP move together as principles-based accounting standards are developed. Along with this progress, we will likely see movement toward fair value measurement that provides greater relevance for financial information. My opinion is that we should not begin developing different sets of standards based on company size or ownership. We need to embrace best business practices and work diligently to train and educate both accountants and users on the use and application of professionalism to create and build accounting relevance into financial reporting and disclosure. It is a big job and a big challenge that will not be the result of an easy and quick solution.

FUTURE ACCOUNTING AND AUDITING NOW

The accounting profession has a long way to go to recover its lost dignity and relevance, but the turnaround has been started. Emerging new auditing standards are being applied as this is being written. The hole that the accounting profession dug for itself will not get filled overnight. At least the profession appears to have stopped the digging and is beginning to tackle the hard issues it faces on the road back to relevancy and creditability. The mechanisms to put the train back on the track are there as the PCAOB takes the lead in setting new audit standards and the FASB begins to build principles-based accounting and financial reporting models. Change is tough, and people—and professions—resist making the necessary transition. Some of the makeover needs to occur with management teams, boards of directors, analysts, and the investing public.

I have a saying that "perception is nine-tenths of the law." As long as there is the perception that financial statements are exact representations of reality and precision, not much progress will occur. Financial statements are estimates based on the best accounting and business judgment available and nothing more than that. The American Assembly used the word "exactitude" based on an article that appeared in the April 2003 issue of *The Economist,* which indicated that too many members of the investing public felt that financial statements portrayed with precision the assets, liabilities, and financial performance of issuers. The profession and the PCAOB face a huge challenge in changing this perception. Everyone needs to realize and understand the magnitude of the transition to more meaningful audits and readable financial statements.

This chapter has attempted to provide a basic understanding of the new audit standards and how they will provide value and benefit. It will take some time to realize the benefits as companies begin to go through the first stages of compliance required by Section 404. The new audits will be conducted by more experienced auditors combined with greater involvement of second-partner concurrence. This trend will continue and necessitate recruitment and training of accountants who have broader business and technology skills. This means taking a different approach to how audits are conducted and the personnel who perform the work. Pure accounting knowledge and training will not be enough, and it will be necessary to utilize audit teams that contain consulting capability in addition to accounting. Application of auditors with forensic training and knowledge will also be a requirement of audit teams. Financial statements and disclosures will need to provide ranges of estimates in some instances and also provide for presentation of industry-appropriate nonfinancial information and data. All of these tendencies and trends will require time and education for both recipients and issuers of financial statements.

Most people feel that the Sarbanes-Oxley Act heads in the right direction, but at the cost of time, resources, and money. In many camps, the feeling is "let's just get compliant so we can go on with life." Management assessment of internal control and the identification of root causes of problems along with solutions is how Sarbanes-Oxley compliance becomes profitable. In line with this concept, the new role of the audit committee will be challenged to cope with and accommodate all the changes being implemented. Upgrading of audit committees will be a necessity to keep the auditors and the audit function on track. This is an area where the PCAOB may need to provide oversight, as audit committees are a critical component of its mission. Finally, the FASB needs to stay the course and make real progress on the development of principles-based accounting and financial reporting standards. Along with these thoughts and suggestions regarding the future of accounting and auditing, it is imperative that the accounting profession—particularly the larger firms—lead the way in attracting the brightest and best people into the profession. Without good people, there will be no future.

This book has free materials available for download from the
Web Added Value™ Resource Center at www.jrosspub.com.

STRATEGY AND COMMUNICATION

During the bubble years of the 1990s leading up to the financial scandals and subsequent enactment of Sarbanes-Oxley, it seemed like the only strategy in the minds of managers and directors was meeting investor expectations with a steady flow of increasing quarterly profits and revenues. Reality set in as failures in corporate governance turned the accounting profession into a tailspin with one scandal after another. Economic reality is not a steady drumbeat of making the numbers every quarter. In fact, the pace of economic conditions and competition is more challenging than ever as balance sheets are comprised of knowledge assets and intangibles. Corporate management is now required to operate and plan on almost a real-time basis. All businesses require a framework for managing enterprise risk that employs greater strategic focus and organizational communication.

At the time Sarbanes-Oxley was enacted, organizations had been morphing along with a wide range of technology tools and applications. There have been attempts at business intelligence dashboards which spawned an array of measurements. Concepts like balanced scorecards have gained traction. There is renewed emphasis on operational excellence and greater emphasis on strategy and its execution. All of a sudden, Section 404 required that management assess internal control and document its assessment and processes. This created the development of more technology tools and solutions to help corporations comply with certification of quarterly financial reports, solidification of internal control, and the requirement for disclosure on a real-time basis.

Compliance efforts have been going forward on a continuous basis. Both auditors and corporate management have been consumed with the effort. With the passage of the first Section 404 compliance date, there needs to be a realization that a structure for communicating and executing corporate strategy and monitoring the future in a predictive fashion will be a competitive necessity. Implementing Section 404 compliance is the first step in building the foundation for a way to manage and measure in the future and is the focus of these final two chapters.

COMMUNICATION OF STRATEGY

A major obstacle for many organizations is the failure or inability to effectively communicate strategy, which in turn creates a state of ineptness. The people who need to understand and execute the strategy have not received the message about what the strategy is and what they need to do in order to make it happen. Managers and employee teams at all levels need a foundation to make the improvements in the organization envisioned by senior leadership and the board. In his book *Performance Management,* Gary Cokins comments that "senior executives do not have control of their organization's traction, direction, and speed." Communication of strategy is about moving the organization in the right direction.

Before you can communicate the strategy, senior management and the board need to determine the strategy. Development of a strategy map as illustrated in Figure 15.1 provides the concept of strategy and value propositions combined with the internal business processes and people applications required for successful execution. Linking the strategy map with a balanced scorecard approach can provide the linkage and alignment of the resources within the organization that will help create traction, direction, and speed. Figure 15.2 illustrates the concept of strategic alignment that will be required to achieve success. It is critical to understand that a balanced scorecard approach is headed for failure unless it is linked with the management processes necessary for strategic execution.

A balanced scorecard approach provides a way for organizations to link appropriate performance indicators and measure their strategy. The balanced scorecard approach to corporate performance measurement and management is described in my first book, *Dynamics of Profit-Focused Accounting.* In addition to describing the major management methodologies, the book explains and describes in detail how to calculate a number of key business performance metrics. It also provides a solid foundation for understanding the underlying concepts of the points being offered relative to strategy and performance management.

When addressing the challenges of communicating strategy and building understanding and traction across the organization, we need to appreciate the

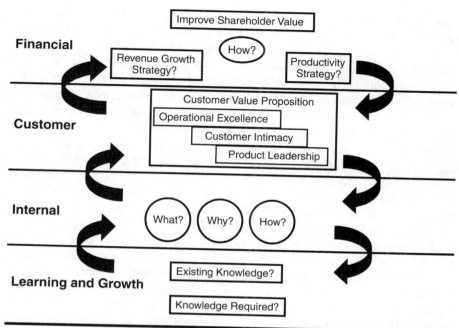

Figure 15.1. The strategy map concept.

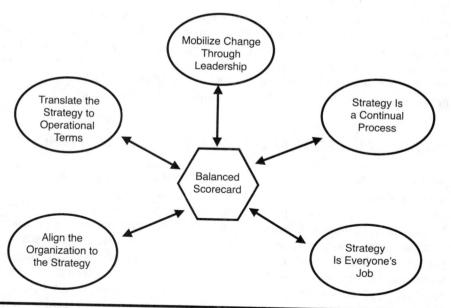

Figure 15.2. Strategic alignment.

opportunity afforded by management self-assessment under Section 404. Compliance under Sarbanes-Oxley offers opportunities for effective communication of strategy during management's self-assessment of internal control. The underlying financial reporting processes being tested offer a foundation for expansion to be linked with performance management tools and measures. This represents a natural extension that fits with real-time reporting required by Section 409 disclosure. Additionally, it provides a way for auditors and management to gain improved understanding of the business. The future of accounting is moving rapidly to the use and application of both financial and nonfinancial measures, and the assessment effort gets everybody into the game. Expanded and improved communication will evolve from the interaction of the assessment process. Communication will not only transfer tone at the top and a code of ethics, but will also enable the strategic missions to be more effectively understood and executed at all levels of the entity.

In addition to establishing a foundation for strategic understanding, managers and employee teams will know which key performance indicators link to the company's strategy. Since the assessment structure has been created for Section 404, its concepts can just as easily embrace strategic execution and the metrics needed to understand the cause and effect relationship of the entity's strategy. The strategy map approach can be visualized more clearly from Figure 15.3 as it portrays the relationship of strategy to objectives, measurements, targets, and initiatives. The assessment approach allows management to get closer to the necessary functions and team members needed for performance management to create solid processes for collecting, transforming, and modeling data into the necessary format for communication to the right users. When such an effective communication process is in place, companies can begin to measure the right things where they need to get better. Measurement starts to get narrowed down to the vital few measures that really count.

LINKING STRATEGIC AND OPERATIONAL EFFECTIVENESS

Operational effectiveness is not strategy and strategy is not operational effectiveness. Operational effectiveness is something that all companies are focused on and takes shape in the application of different methodologies, from lean and Six Sigma to traditional financial measurement. Accountants zero in on lower costs, higher revenues, asset management, and how are we are doing versus last year and the budget. Sales and marketing look at customer feedback, market share, and sales by region, product, and customer. In short, there is an overload of all types of measures and indicators that stream from multiple software and technology solutions that overwhelm management and employee teams. Tradi-

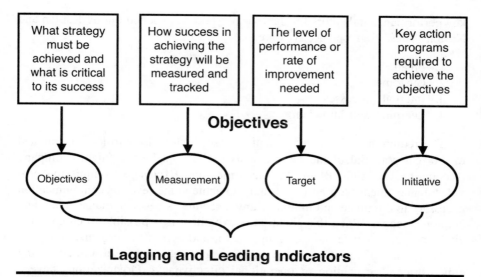

Figure 15.3.   The strategy map: cause and effect relationships.

tional external financial reporting has done little to deflect criticism of accounting-based reports that lead to a perception of precision. It is an illusion that is not grounded in reality. Sarbanes-Oxley was intended to produce more reliable and accurate financial information. While this is a noble goal, it is important for management teams and the accounting profession to begin a transition toward educating statement users on the range of estimation and variability that exists in financial reporting. They also need to begin embracing the concepts of nonfinancial measures or indicators that provide insight into the value of intangible assets such as brand identification, intellectual capital, and knowledge management, which are the invisible assets on the balance sheet. Sarbanes-Oxley is grounded in generally accepted accounting principles, which is driven by earning per share. Again, *Dynamics of Profit-Focused Accounting* provides a good explanation and discussion of accounting profit versus economic profit. During the process of evaluating principled-based accounting and financial reporting, there is some merit to considering the need to overhaul the current approach, which pushes investors toward the quarter-by-quarter mentality.

Refocusing on the simplicity of financial reporting combined with enhancing the value and use of the financial statement will or should create the necessity to link operational effectiveness of the organization with the strategic components of the business vision. These indicators should provide an indication of how well we are doing on what is important relative to executing the strategy. A balanced scorecard approach is more than just slapping together the key performance indicators for the four perspectives spelled out by Kaplan and Norton. These four perspectives are:

1. Financial
2. Customer
3. Internal processes
4. Learning and knowledge

The requirement for management to assess internal control when pursued to the real potential of the requirements spelled out by the Public Company Accounting Oversight Board and Securities and Exchange Commission provides management with an opportunity to achieve the level of communication necessary to eliminate and minimize any disconnects between management and employee teams. When this situation is exploited, it is possible to cascade the vital few performance indicators up, down, and across the organization.

Traditional financial measurements have not been very useful in achieving either strategic execution or operational effectiveness. Organizations have a great interest in implementing lean thinking (lean manufacturing concepts) as a way to pursue competitive survival. Other companies have gone to Six Sigma as a way to control and minimize process variation. Some have applied tools such as activity-based management along with these approaches to achieve operational effectiveness. Operational effectiveness applications take an organization only so far—unless a strategy is linked to the initiative, failure will be the likely outcome.

COSO's new *Enterprise Risk Management—Integrated Framework* has added a strategic objective based on the consensus of the commission that high-level goals need to be aligned with and supportive of an entity's mission. The framework also includes an operational objective to promote effective and efficient use of resources. My advice to management and boards is to leverage the framework and assessment techniques to move beyond compliance to remove any disconnects with employee teams. Entities have a wonderful mechanism available to create and strengthen the linkage of their strategic vision and mission with operational efficiency and effectiveness. Assessing internal control is not a one-time event, and neither are execution of strategy and risk management. Yes, all these suggestions represent hard work and effort, but then success and continuous improvement never come without a price.

GETTING INFORMATION TO FLOW

We are in the age of information, and it would seem an easy task for companies to access and obtain all the critical data needed to manage operations and craft the proper strategy. Unfortunately, the process is not that simple. An abundance of information flows from enterprise resource planning systems designed to plan resources, record transactions, process payroll, manage assets, and invoice customers. Additional planning applications include advanced planning and scheduling systems and manufacturing execution systems.

In addition to enterprise-wide systems is customer relations management to gather data from customers relative to intelligence associated with customer segments, product information, and sales prospects. Customer relations management also tracks customer behavior and customer experiences and provides a foundation for analyzing data. These programs also enable sales force automation, which allows salespeople to manage their contacts and prospect their pipelines. Effective use of customer relations management programs provides the foundation for development and use of predictive forecasts and trends.

Other generators of data include knowledge management programs that catalogue and monitor employee knowledge. Sarbanes-Oxley documentation has provided software for storing and tracking e-mail, as the pervasive application and use of the Internet has generated even more information than internally generated data. Compliance legislation has introduced communication and collaboration software plus document management and workflow tools. Because of the flood of information and data, software developers have created data mining, file retrieval, pattern recognition, and business intelligence tools.

Now that it is obvious that there is information on top of information covering every conceivable scenario, we begin to see the dilemma. How do organizations use all the information available to them and make effective use of the data? The answer lies somewhere between overwhelmed to varying levels of effectiveness, depending on how well a company has its act together. I frequently use Dell Computer in my training classes as a case study example of a company that has figured out how to cope with massive amounts of information and has used strategy, operational effectiveness, and communication to create a competitive advantage. Dell is a company that had little difficulty complying with Sarbanes-Oxley because it already had all of its internal business processes in excellent shape. Dell did not have to reinvent the wheel because it was effectively in place and turning pretty darn well.

While there is an overwhelming amount of data and information, the key is getting it to flow. This provides management and employee teams with what they need to get the right things done at the right time. Companies will continue to struggle to harness the flow of data until they come to grips with the reality that fixing business processes is a tough job that takes time and focused effort. If companies had all their business processes documented and were focused on continuous identification of root causes throughout all corners of the organization, we would not have heard all the Sarbanes-Oxley complaints. My message is that information is not the problem; the problem is management's inability to engage its business processes and employee teams to focus on both strategic execution and operational excellence. Likewise, accountants have not been of much help because of their inability to keep up with the pace of change. We will not improve financial reporting and the flow of information without an all-out effort to make the necessary changes to improve our processes.

RIGHT MEASUREMENT AT THE RIGHT TIME

My training workshops cover a wide variety of topics, but one issue is continuously raised by participants. Participants indicate that they struggle with finding the proper indicators (measurements) to monitor events and track trends. A primary reason for the confusion and frustration is the lack of guidance associated with applying the strategy and value propositions at appropriate levels of the entity. There is no shortage of indicators, so most companies are overrun with data that never gets to the right people at the right time to take the necessary action.

Unless management makes the effort to create a two-way flow of communication regarding strategy and what is needed to execute it effectively at all levels of the entity, we will continue to struggle with the challenge of strategic execution. The assessment framework provides a communication feedback mechanism that allows management to let employee teams understand their mission as well as the indicators that provide leading guidance regarding what is around the corner. Just as important, employee teams are able to let management know their needs as well as the indicators and data necessary for them to execute according to the strategic value propositions identified in the balanced scorecard.

Typically, only a very few indicators will be required. Selecting the vital few is a function of truly understanding what needs to be done to make a difference. When we think of reporting, the tendency is to think of financial measures. In reality, functional employee teams will relate better to indicators that provide them with real-time feedback. A baseline scorecard is presented in Figure 15.4, which breaks down indicators into six primary categories from financial to supplier performance. Once management and employee teams start to take advantage of the self-assessment workshop approach to execute strategy and improve operational processes, they will need to develop some approach for selecting the appropriate indicators. Figure 15.5 presents a performance measurement profile that can assist organizations in selecting the right measurements within the concept of balanced scorecards and their entity's value propositions. From the performance measurement profile, organizational teams can then employ a viable framework for measurement, such as the example pre-

Measurement	This Year	Last Year	Assessment Team Comments
Financial Performance			
Net Sales			
Operating Income as Percent of Sales			
EBITDA			
R&D Cost as Percent of Sales			
Percent of Sales from New Products			
Capital Investment as Percent of Sales			
• % for New Products			
• % for Capacity			
• % for Safety and Environment			
Working Capital as Percent of Sales			
Economic Value Added			
Operational Performance			
Manufacturing Cycle Time			
Performance to Takt Time			
Raw Material Inventory $			
Raw Material Inventory Turns			
WIP Inventory $			
WIP Inventory Turns			
Finished Goods Inventory $			
Finished Goods Inventory Turns			
Total Inventory — Days on Hand			
Product Service Quality			
Defects per 1000 Units			
Average First-Pass Yield Percentage			
Customer Satisfaction			
Customer Satisfaction Index			
Customer Return Percentage			
Delivery Performance			
Average Quoted Lead Time			
Late Shipments			
• Measured in $			
• Measured by # of Parts Affected			
• Measured by # of Customers Affected			
Abandoned Customer Phone Calls %			
Employee Satisfaction			
Employee Turnover			
Absenteeism			
Number of Suggestion per Employee			
Number of Suggestions Implemented			
Hours of Training/Education per Employee			
Safety & Ergonomics			
Injuries			
Medical Costs per 100 Associates			
Lost-Time Accidents			
Supplier Performance			
Supplier's Delivery Performance			
Supplier Defects per 1000 Units			

Figure 15.4. Baseline scorecard.

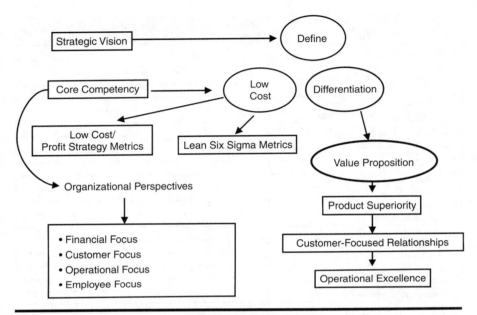

Figure 15.5.   Performance measurement profile.

sented in Figure 15.6. Once the proper indicators are identified, the battle is more than half won since there is an abundance of real-time tools for reporting because the proper focus has been created.

BUSINESS INTELLIGENCE

The evolution of business intelligence (BI) has emerged with advances in technology and software tools to provide for analysis and decision making from intelligence information. The term BI actually embraces a framework that contains a relationship of five primary layers of components:

1. Business layer
2. Administration and operations
3. Data warehouse
   a. Data sources
   b. ETL processing (extraction, transform, and load)
   c. Data warehouses
   d. Data marts
4. Information delivery
5. Business analytics

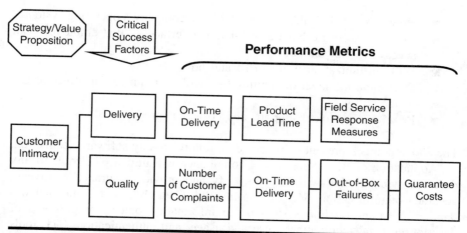

Figure 15.6. A framework for measurement.

Originally, BI was the application of online analytical processing (OLAP) to identify trends, patterns, and exceptions within databases that provided a variety of multidimensional views of data contained within a database. Models were created to help understand and support decision making.

The real benefit of BI is business analytics. Managers and employee teams are able to apply the analytic capability to analyze and ask the questions critical to more effective real-time decision making. When these powerful tools are embedded in the organizational business processes, they can provide the potential for real breakthrough business performance. All too frequently, managers think all they have to do is implement BI and they will immediately experience instant performance improvement. This is a fallacy because without a strategic roadmap aligned with an operationally effective focus there will be no impact. People need to understand that these tools can enhance their performance but will not change the way business is done. When properly used, BI is an enabler of greater business efficiency and effectiveness.

There has been a significant amount of hype regarding the use of BI tools associated with Sarbanes-Oxley compliance. Two areas of compliance where BI tools can be effective are Section 404 and Section 409. Software vendors offer a great deal of puff in the BI arena. While the tools can be effective, it is critical for accountants and companies working on compliance to gain an understanding of both the viability of the vendor as well as the tools the vendor offers. Some basic considerations should at least include the following criteria:

■   Understand the most important functions and features of the software relative to its capability.

- How compatible is the software with the company's operating systems?
- Does the software have a web-based interface so that employees can access the tool online?
- Will customization be required and how much?
- Determine the level of training that will be required for effective use of the software.
- Price, maintenance, support, and cost of upgrades.

The above points represent common sense relative to any software acquisition.

Application of BI to Section 404 compliance will utilize ETL tools to link data via metadata that will help to verify and provide assurance relative to accuracy of information. Metadata is literally "data about data" and includes data from an information system or an information object for purposes of description, legal requirements, use and usage, and authentication. ETL tools extract, transform, and load data into a data warehouse or data mart. Figure 15.7 provides an illustration of how data are moved from systems within an organization and then transformed, cleansed, and loaded into the data warehouse so that analysis of data can occur. This process can be applied to an enterprise resource planning system, an Excel spreadsheet, or a customer relations management system to transform data for subsequent monitoring and analysis. This approach can be used to assist with ensuring accuracy, application of security, and tracking changes. These BI applications can also pull data required for Section 409 reporting to accelerate and speed up the reporting and certification process. They can also help to facilitate using the data to provide real-time feedback and reporting to enhance bottom-line operating performance.

METHODOLOGIES FOR REAL-TIME MEASUREMENT

The crunch of Sarbanes-Oxley compliance has settled in with larger companies as they have had to deal with assessing their systems and internal controls. For the first time, many of these companies have had to document their business processes. When these realities are combined with the pressure of trying to keep pace with accelerating customer demands and competitor innovations, companies are ready to tackle real-time performance measurement. Figure 15.8 portrays the linkage of risk with value. A picture of the approach, methodologies, and framework of the typical components most organizations will utilize is shown in Figure 15.9, from the source systems, data integration and data infrastructure to data access.

We have the technology tools in place for real-time measurement and analysis, combined with the motivation for risk management and building corporate

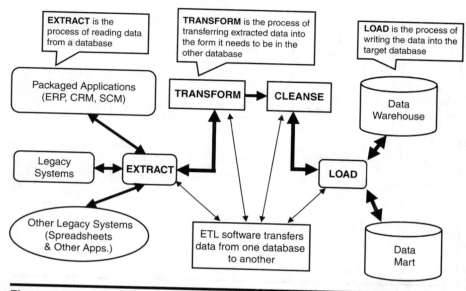

Figure 15.7. Moving and transforming data.

value. BI is a tool that is just beginning to come into its own, and with web access it becomes more potent and offers greater potential. Some of the other methodologies that will likely be employed are balanced scorecards and activity-based management models for planning, forecasting, and strategic analysis.

Until recently, real-time performance measurement has been isolated in individual operational areas and has not been employed on an entity-wide basis.

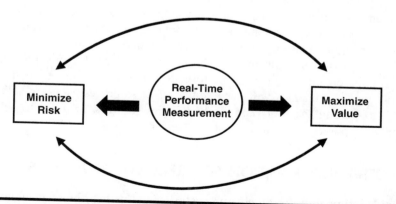

Figure 15.8. Linking risk and value.

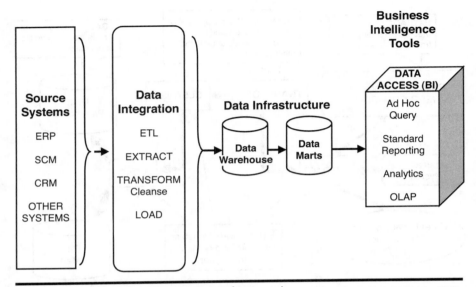

Figure 15.9. Real-time measurement framework.

One example of operational application is retailers making decisions based on sales performance monitored on a real-time basis. Other uses include the military, Internet, and technology applications. A number of corporations have seen new possibilities from the multitude of Sarbanes-Oxley applications, while others had been employing BI methodologies in some form prior to the Sarbanes-Oxley compliance effort. According to the Gartner Group, "fewer than 10 percent of enterprises will have implemented corporate performance management by year-end 2002; however 40 percent will adopt it by 2005." Considering the potential impact it can have on enhancing corporate performance and the link to Sarbanes-Oxley compliance, corporate performance management and real-time measurement and analysis are a necessity for companies striving to create a competitive advantage and enhance shareholder value. Just plugging in software and creating a bunch of performance indicators is not enough to get the job done. Companies will need sound business processes and a solid approach to putting the tools and methodologies to work in order to achieve effective corporate performance management programs.

EFFECTIVE INFORMATION FOR RELIABLE PROCESSES

Effective information for reliable processes should perhaps be reversed to read reliable processes for effective information. What comes first—the chicken or the egg? Sarbanes-Oxley uses Section 404 to require management to conduct a self-assessment of the reliability of the design of internal controls as well as the operating effectiveness of controls that support reliable financial reporting. The assessment is required to ensure that reliable processes are in place to provide reasonable assurance that they will produce reliable information. On the other hand, management needs effective information that the business processes are functioning as intended, and real-time reporting systems are designed to alert the appropriate parties if something is out of kilter. This provides the tool employee teams can use to take the necessary actions to fix broken processes. Workers can either restore the process or situation to normal or exploit the potential of new opportunities. The meaning of self-assessment should go well beyond just financial reporting and embrace strategy and operational excellence, and these concepts will be explored in greater depth during the discussion of business process management in Chapter 16.

Another corollary to risk management is the proposed Capital Accord from the Basle Committee on Banking Supervision for International Settlements, known as Basle II. Basle II provides new recommendations for credit and operational risk and is encouraging banks to increase their sophistication in analyzing and managing risk. Essentially, Basle II wants banks to embrace lessons from total quality management (TQM) from the 1980s. My book *Dynamics of Profit-Focused Accounting* provides an in-depth discussion of TQM. Basle II provides five levels or factors associated with evaluating operational risk:

1. Operational processes
2. Control and risk self-assessment
3. Key risk indicators
4. Loss data
5. Analytics

The analogy is that all business is built on the performance of operational processes and represents the foundation when discipline and consistency are applied to their operation using the concepts of TQM. If all the levels of the foundation are properly applied, then analytics is the last step in allocating losses for capital allocation. This represents a parallel analogy to business performance management as companies attempt to reduce their financial and operational risks using new real-time reporting tools.

TQM is grounded in continuous improvement and identification of root causes. All the technology tools in the world will be meaningless until management teams understand that improved business performance is going to depend on accountability and reliable business processes. The tools will help those companies that also employ the principle of continuous improvement and empowered employees in a proactive manner. Strategic communication will be a key ingredient to sorting through the haystack of data to identify the vital few that truly matter. Success will evolve from application of continuous improvement and using the assessment approach prescribed by the Public Company Accounting Oversight Board. Better dashboards are not an instant ticket to better performance and building competitive advantage. Organizations that learn how to leverage dashboards and real-time reporting to drive effectiveness and enhanced value will gain the secret combination for developing a meaningful enterprise-wide performance management program.

16

BEYOND COMPLIANCE

This last chapter is being written as we enter 2005, which is when many companies began their Section 404 compliance. People have asked me why I am writing a book on Sarbanes-Oxley. They say that "it's going to be over with and all the questions will be answered." Teaching my Sarbanes-Oxley compliance workshop has been interesting, fun, and revealing. Looking back, I am seeing a new era of governance unfold, together with strong attitudes on the rigors of compliance testing relative to Section 404. Much of the attitude on the part of accountants who have been working hard on the program is "Just get us compliant. We want to be done with this stuff so we can go do our job." This attitude also seems to emanate from CPAs and other consultants who have been called in to shoulder the load of getting public companies compliant.

The prevailing attitude seems to be "your glass is either half empty or half full." This attitude represents a widespread shortcoming within organizations and their management teams. Management is hard work, and creating better companies takes time and effort. Better organizations will not evolve from the latest management fad or just plugging in technology and software. My answer to better management, better organizations, and profitable compliance is performance management that encompasses building better business processes. In fact, the journey to performance improvement and reliable financial reporting is a process in itself. The examples used in previous chapters included Dell and General Electric. I can guarantee that their excellence did not happen overnight. Better performance is built over a period of time using the focus of the "flywheel effect" described by Jim Collins in *Good to Great*. As we near the conclusion of this book, I view going beyond compliance as just the beginning. We have seen only the tip of the Sarbanes-Oxley iceberg.

BUILDING A TRUSTWORTHY FOUNDATION

When those in management learn that better organizations and improved performance are built on better processes and not the result of application of the fad of the month, they will have taken the first step of the journey. The Public Company Accounting Oversight Board has clearly spelled out the need for a framework and Audit Standard No. 2 suggested that the COSO Integrated Framework was suitable as a model for the purposes of management's assessment of internal control. COSO went beyond its original framework and provided an enhanced framework for enterprise risk management as a guideline for helping management deal with risks and opportunities affecting value creation and its preservation. Both of these frameworks are grounded in the fundamental concept of ongoing processes that flow through the organization.

Sarbanes-Oxley has provided the foundation for management's assessment, a tool that offers multiple opportunities for profitable compliance. I feel strongly that self-assessments generate great value for companies, but they have not been used to their best advantage. My message is that company leaders need to change their thinking about how to build and create value through better processes. Gary Cokins offers a wonderful comment in his book *Performance Management*; he states that too many managers "believed in the KISS rule (keep it simple, stupid)" but left out "the corollary LOVE rule (leave out virtually everything)." He then goes on to say that "the message is you must dig in a little bit."

Building a trustworthy foundation will require company leaders to dig in a lot to improve their business processes. It is much more than getting compliant—it is what is required to manage the enterprise and create competitive advantage. Enterprise risk management as defined by COSO is worth reviewing:

- It is a process
- It is effected by people
- It needs a strategy setting
- It is applied across the enterprise
- It is designed to identify potential events that could impact the business
- It provides reasonable assurance
- It is geared to the achievement of objectives

By applying these concepts beyond internal control and risk management to all the elements of business process management and measurement, we can begin to realize the potential.

When building a trustworthy foundation, it is important to realize that success or failure hinges on people. Processes are created by people, and self-assessment is one of the most effective ways for improving processes. Building a foundation of continuously improving processes is how companies produce the desired results, minimize the use of resources, and create the ability to adapt to changing customer and business needs. A component of building better processes is the creation of performance measurement processes, which is tied to effective execution of business strategy. When organizations build a foundation based on continuous process improvement, they prepare themselves to handle an accelerated rate of information flow.

ACCELERATED FLOW

When we extend beyond compliance and strive for strategic and operational effectiveness, we can achieve breakthrough results. Accelerated flow translates to shorter cycle times from business processes. Business process management (BPM), or business performance management, focuses on making processes more efficient and effective, which translates to higher profitability for companies that get it and dig in. In addition to reduced cycle time, savings are produced from reducing errors, automating tasks, and producing more output with fewer people. Productivity improvement occurs across the organization, resulting in more visibility and responsiveness from people because of elimination of errors and cost reduction. This approach is similar to Six Sigma, whereby a well-defined and controlled process helps companies deliver products and services literally with no defects. Such capability is significant when compared to companies that have only a three- or four-sigma level of capability.

Productivity improvements occur as the result of implementing process management steps, which range from modeling to optimization. Section 404 requires that companies model their internal control processes, and this is the first step toward creating improvement. Process modeling provides the foundation for understanding the flow of work activities and enables process owners to identify opportunities for improvement. Flow acceleration can be achieved through automation of processes, which helps to reduce errors and shorten cycle times. Management's assessment provides assurance that all processes are being executed efficiently and also provides an opportunity to identify additional improvements. Optimization of processes occurs as the result of continuous improvement and identification of root causes.

BPM along with management's assessment creates opportunities for enhancing efficiency and effectiveness. Some of the common opportunities for streamlining operations include:

- Convert paper processes into an electronic format
- Automate steps through integration with enterprise applications
- Add intelligence to forms, which will reduce errors and omissions

- Incorporate control features that will help ensure integrity of the processes and compensate for human or system failure
- Apply analytics to further evaluate performance for possible optimization and improvement

These represent some of the possibilities that more effective BPM offers for accelerating flow and improving bottom-line profitability.

Accelerating flow requires identifying the critical business processes that either constrain flow or offer the greatest opportunities for improvement. It is important to understand that each business process in some way will define how tasks, people, and applications are engaged in delivering goods, services, or information to a combination of internal and external customers. The business processes also define the rules on how the tasks are performed and how people operate within the organization. We are describing business processes and not specifically internal control, and it is important to see the correlation. Sarbanes-Oxley compliance forced management to assess internal control, which was a best business practice management should have been doing all along.

When evaluating business processes, it is critical to consider the volume of activity through the process. In high-volume processes, even incremental improvement can yield significant bottom-line impact. Another issue is consideration of the steps in the process, since the more people who are involved, the greater the likelihood of errors or delay. This a key component of lean thinking as described in *Dynamics of Profit-Focused Accounting*. Automation becomes a viable necessity, and activity-based management is an invaluable tool for deciding where it should be applied. Even though automation is possible, we still need to consider the people issues. Error elimination provides acceleration, and this requires effective design of control plus operational effectiveness.

Beyond compliance offers many lessons learned from compliance. Acceleration of process flow occurs because it allows employee teams and managers to act faster and respond to conditions more quickly. Improved processes produce more consistent results, and employee teams as well as management have a better understanding of roles and responsibilities. These factors all contribute to a more agile and competitive organization. Strategies get executed faster and operational excellence is increased. Once the organization can accelerate its process flow and create a trustworthy foundation, it can begin to address the speed and reliability of real-time performance management.

CREATING SPEED AND RELIABILITY

After companies get past the initial crunch of compliance effort and reflect on the reliability of their business processes, they will begin to comprehend the possibilities that can result from having critical information on a real-time basis. My purpose in writing a book on Sarbanes-Oxley was to provide insight into how to profit from the compliance investment. The bottom line is that Section 404 provided companies with a blueprint for creating and sustaining more capable business processes. Without this foundation, real-time reporting and analytics are impossible.

A reality of compliance with Section 404 was that it was expensive and time consuming for many companies. It represents a major challenge for companies attempting to meet both the accelerated and nonaccelerated filing dates. A survey by the American Institute of Certified Public Accountants' Center for Public Company Audit Firms listed the compliance challenges of small companies. Some of the issues were as follows:

- Lack of financial and personnel resources
- Lack of segregation of duties
- Lack of knowledge, sophistication, and expertise
- Poor cost-benefit relationship
- Inadequate information technology resources

It seems to me that these challenges represent opportunities for companies to turn the corner of competitive opportunity. Business success is dependent on making good decisions based on the most accurate information and data available. This means enhancing the company's ability to understand customer needs, hire capable personnel, communicate with suppliers, and gather and assimilate critical market data about competitors. The time line to react and respond to changing market conditions is shrinking at a rapid rate. Innovation of new products and services is dependent on speed and time to market. Companies struggling with the above challenges will face other issues such as competitive survival if they are unable to build business processes capable of supporting a real-time analytic infrastructure. Bad data lead to bad decisions, and when the need for speed intensifies and reliability is diminished, then we have a recipe for problems and trouble. Companies need to realize the competitive necessity of having business processes capable of compliance, since it provides them with the ability to integrate real-time data with historic contextual data for more effective decision making and breakthrough profitability. From this realization, Sarbanes-Oxley becomes a blessing in disguise. Change does not occur until people feel the heat, and Sarbanes-Oxley provided that heat.

Once business processes achieve a high level of reliability, companies have assurance that speed of information flow can be increased. This enables the use of real-time analytics. Real-time analytics moves data from an operational system into a back-end application that transforms the information as "fresh" or live to enable the capability for real-time decision making. The concept of real-time analytics is taking information and integrating it with data from other sources so that it can be compared with historical data to detect variation in trends. Evaluation of historical data in real time and merging data streams from multiple sources provide management with critical information, which, when used effectively, provide companies with a significant competitive advantage.

Ability to utilize real-time analytics is enhanced with the evolution of data warehouses and operational data marts. This moves the quality of intelligence to a higher level predicated on up-to-date fresh information. Companies can use this information to track customer needs to upstage competitors and correct operational problems with real-time effectiveness. Management, on the other hand, needs to decide how to integrate these tools into its culture of decision-making style and infrastructure. Technology and a wide range of tools create choices for deploying and making good use of real-time information. Based on my observation, one thing that will be mandatory is an abundant dose of training so that management and employee teams can maximize the potential of the new tools.

BUSINESS PERFORMANCE MANAGEMENT

Because of all the acronyms that are being tossed around, a good deal of confusion surrounds BPM. It is not just business intelligence and a system for maintaining key performance indicators (KPIs). I have tried to set the stage leading up to this discussion that solid business processes combined with application of business intelligence provided management teams with a very powerful tool. The power of the tool will fall by the wayside until there is a management process capable of applying it in effective ways. Some of the other terms floating around include corporate performance management and enterprise performance management. Sarbanes-Oxley has created a lot of heat to close the books faster, make sure data are more accurate, and provide reasonable assurance regarding internal controls. Many companies are applying components of BPM in a variety of ways but have not integrated the tools and the processes capable of producing a competitive advantage through strategic execution.

Business performance management is a process in itself that takes advantage of the technology to enable optimization of a company's strategies and operations. In addition to reporting of financial and nonfinancial data, BPM encompasses budgeting, KPI scorecards, and business intelligence. Earlier we discussed the inability of management and employee teams to execute strategy. The gap between strategy and executing it is huge. Technology is not the hurdle to a successful BPM process; it is people, communication, and understanding. The concept of BPM is not restricted to large global companies and publicly traded companies, although these entities have made more inroads in adopting it because of the need to connect data and requirements for Sarbanes-Oxley compliance.

BPM is a best business practice for companies to drive business value through more effective communication and the ability to monitor critical drivers of business and process data. The Data Warehousing Institute (TDWI), which is a division of 101communications LLC, issued a study on *Best Practices in Business Performance Management and Technical Strategies,* which provides an excellent discussion and definition of BPM. The report says that BPM is *not* what many people usually think it is, including the following:

- Technology solution
- Business intelligence
- Financial reporting
- Dashboards and scorecards
- Forecasting simulations
- KPIs

TDWI states that "BPM is about improving performance in the right direction." This supports the conclusions I have reached from my management seminars. The problem is that most companies struggle to gain the traction needed to understand their key value drivers. They also fail to effectively communicate and use their data to execute strategy needed to create a competitive advantage.

Basically, business performance management enables strategic execution through the application of best business practices. When we have real-time reliable data and understand the mission, BPM facilitates better communication, collaboration, control, and coordination across the entire entity. A properly implemented and executed BPM process will help companies exploit market opportunities, accelerate innovation, and improve business and operational processes. The right information gets to the right people in time to do the right things with the data.

TDWI suggests that BPM is a four-step process that organizations will use to transform strategy into the right action steps executed by management teams and employees. The four steps consist of the following:

1. Strategize
2. Plan
3. Monitor
4. Act and adjust

Figure 16.1.   Balanced scorecard is a strategic management system.

The strategize step is where companies align their strategic focus with their value propositions to identify the key performance drivers. Translating the mission into outcomes is the essence of strategy, which is illustrated in Figure 16.1. This is an area where the balanced scorecard can be effective in formulating the strategy and selecting the indicators of value that need to be monitored. The balanced scorecard concept is presented in Figure 16.2. A well-implemented BPM process becomes the catalyst to notify the right people when something requires attention. The act and adjust step provides employees with the right information to take appropriate action either to respond to market conditions or to fix a broken process. In a continuous improvement environment, a well-executed BPM system provides for real-time identification and correction of root causes.

A BPM system fits well with Boyd's OODA loop concept originally developed for one-on-one fighter aircraft combat. This has been redeployed to business strategy. The concept consists of *observe, orient, decide, and act*. The BPM systems allow companies to observe and organize information within the business environment on a more responsive basis. The more rapid *observe* and *orient* modes can be used to exploit opportunities; the more effective *decide* action can be used to exploit the identified opportunity. This strategic concept is dependent on creating a sense of awareness within the organization to communicate and take advantage of both the strategy and the business performance management system.

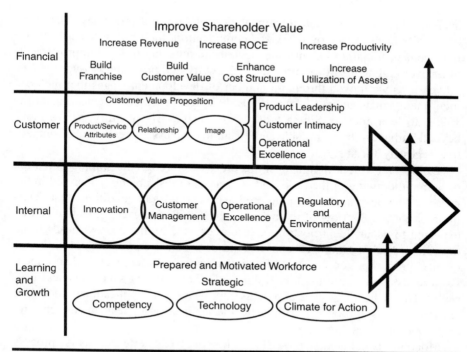

Figure 16.2. Balanced scorecard concept.

The concept of BPM is relatively new and has only begun to emerge as an effective management tool within the last two or three years. Sarbanes-Oxley has heightened awareness of the capability of BPM's potential. Also, software vendors have been rolling out products with enhanced capability. Companies that want to take advantage of BPM have a number of options for how to begin the process. Some companies have followed the enterprise-wide approach; others might take a cross-functional approach to optimization of processes, while still others may opt for a functional approach. Whatever the approach selected, it is critical to evaluate the company culture and its ability to embrace the complexity of deploying a BPM tool and take advantage of its potential.

BUSINESS PROCESS MANAGEMENT AND MEASUREMENT

There is an important distinction between business performance management and BPM. We now have real-time tools aided by technology and the linkage of strategy with performance management, which help in improving the effectiveness and reliability of business processes. BPM is the design, modeling, analysis, improvement, and documentation of business processes. Therefore, companies need to employ BPM as a component of their business performance management initiatives. Companies have been pursuing process improvements in a never-ending effort to improve productivity and profitability over the past 50 years, as we moved through a number of development stages that included total quality management in the 1980s, business process reengineering in the 1990s, to lean and Six Sigma today. Now, in the 21st century, as we move beyond Sarbanes-Oxley, reliable and dynamic business processes are a competitive necessity for survival.

BPM starts with designing business processes through the graphical creation of a digital drawing of the tasks and sequences of tasks being performed in the process. The next step is defining the business rules and conditions that determine or control the flow of the process, along with any exceptions that can be expected to occur. Identification of resources used by the process needs to be documented, along with the expected process performance in time, units, or quality. From this step, the cost of completing each process step is determined. BPM analysis tools are used to design "as is" or "current state" business processes. This is the initial stage of process improvement for application of modeling capability. This approach is similar to the application of lean manufacturing, ISO 9000, and Six Sigma.

Modeling is the next step of BPM. This involves taking the "as is" process design and making a range of assumptions about the amount of time required to perform each task. The cost and the probabilities of various options are injected into the model. Assessment of the model will include locating the bottlenecks or constraints within the process and determining what is required to exploit them. From this point, process improvement can be identified and modeled prior to implementation. The final step is documenting the improved process.

Evolving trends in BPM include application of technology to manage processes literally in real time. Technology applications include dynamic frameworks capable of accelerating the deployment and management of automated business processes. While technology enables the orchestration of application and information technology resources, effective deployment needs to be coordinated with the appropriate human resources. Technology enables the application of the digitized process model through the extension of the functionality of other systems, such as enterprise resource planning (ERP), customer relationship management (CRM), supply chain management, and other management technology applications.

When evaluating and considering the potential of BPM applications, it is important to consider that over the past 50 years organizations have been built on a structural foundation. These structural foundations are frequently referred to as organizational silos. All of the critical operating components such as manufacturing, marketing, finance, human resources, and information technology have been created with layers upon layers of management systems that have no consideration of the cross-functional operational processes. There has been a renewed focus on improving and reengineering business processes. In tackling this initiative, managers discovered that the supporting information technology systems such as ERP and CRM systems contained only about 30% of an entity's business processes. According to a Gardner Group report, the other 70% are either executed on an ad hoc basis or are manual processes.

BPM tools apply their digitized capability to provide rapid process improvement directly to the process level, completely overcoming the complexity of silo-based systems that employ ERP and CRM. BPM systems now have the capability to leverage people and systems supporting functional silos by sitting on top of the underlying applications and data sources. These new applications can be used to analyze any type of process that involves activities, time, cost, events, rules, conditions, or exceptions. The potential for managing, monitoring, and measuring business processes in this fashion is enormous and largely untapped.

BPM analysis and system application is similar to Six Sigma's DMAIC model. A BPM system designs, models, analyzes, improves the process, and determines the cost savings. BPM systems work with both human-centric processes and enterprise-application-centric business processes, such as ERP and other tools that have been described. Basically, the BPM tools provide companies with the ability to create operational innovation of workflows. They then overlay the improvements on top of existing processes to avoid reimplementing new systems, in addition to enhancing process efficiency and effectiveness. This is all accomplished with a significant reduction in the amount of time to streamline and implement the enhancement.

It may seem that we have drifted away from Sarbanes-Oxley, but we need to remember what is beyond compliance. The BPM approach to Sarbanes-Oxley enables automatic detection of identified transactions or activity with a source system as defined by company policy. This in turn provides for automated monitoring of activity of process flow for both analysis and validation of control procedures and transactions. The modeling capability of the tools allows for determining potential accounting impacts of a variety of risk scenarios. Moving back to the OODA loop concept, the BPM system allows companies to adjust and act accordingly. This controlled loop approach can be applied to revenue recognition control processes and other high-risk areas of potential financial misstatements.

FROM COMPLIANCE TO COMPETITIVE ADVANTAGE

Linkage of BPM systems provides a real and potent compliance tool for Sarbanes-Oxley application, and its use will grow as more companies move past the initial stages of meeting the Securities and Exchange Commission deadlines. I believe that one of the primary reasons underlying much of the cost, time, and complaints associated with Sarbanes-Oxley is that business processes were not in good shape at many companies, and management had never addressed many of the problems until legislation provided the necessary heat. From a competitive standpoint, many companies were emerging from business intelligence to awareness of business performance management and BPM. Since July 2002, financial reporting and internal controls have become a priority. Not all compliance teams used BPM tools, but a lot of teams did and observed the potential benefits beyond just internal control and financial reporting.

The compliance applications were described in the previous section. How do companies create competitive advantage with BPM? Automating and optimizing business processes can produce a significant reduction in cycle time that might exceed 90%. Faster cycle times translate into reduced costs and improved customer service. Modeling and optimization of processes produces improved quality. When businesses elevate quality to a Six Sigma level, they can achieve the following magnitude of improvement:

- 20% margin improvement
- 12–18% increased quality
- 12% reduction in employees
- 10–30% capital reduction

This enables accelerated business growth because of the increase in cash flow and the flexibility of doing more with less, which provides more opportunities.

Companies that can generate high levels of innovation in their business processes see a wide range of benefits. Errors are reduced, which saves considerable time and cost through avoidance of lost forms and information. A dramatic improvement in process visibility results, which facilitates employee teams to gain an improved understanding of how the process works and flows, their roles in the process, and the ability to quickly act and adjust based on variations in process output. This visibility provides a foundation for empowerment and cross-functional effectiveness.

During the 1990s, the flavor of the month was business process reengineering, based on Michael Hammer and James Champy's book *Reengineering the Corporation*. This book was a manifesto for a business revolution that did not really gain traction. The desire and the motivation were there, but companies got bogged down with legacy systems and a lack of tools capable of providing the speed and agility necessary to affect innovations that produced new ways of working and accomplishing results. Now work teams have BPM analysis tools that have completely transformed implementation because of technology and software breakthroughs. As a result of their Sarbanes-Oxley experience, many managers are observing how the BPM systems overlay legacy systems and unite the human resource factor with amazing results. While all these slick tools offer tremendous potential, nothing much will happen unless there is effective execution of the entity's strategic vision.

CONTINUOUS COMPLIANCE AND MANAGEMENT

I realize that a lot of CPAs and finance teams are saying, "Wow, will I be glad when this compliance and assessment stuff is over." In reality, the job has just begun. Management needs to realize the potential from self-assessing its design of internal control and determine if it is operating effectively. When companies understand the reality of the benefits from application of better business performance management—and BPM—they will begin to embrace the compliance effort as a tool for creating a competitive advantage. Management's assessment of the adequacy of internal control will be a continuous full-year process.

Companies had a great deal of work to do to get their internal controls to provide reasonable assurance relative to the reliability of financial reporting and disclosure. These same self-assessment techniques can provide management and employee teams with a much better understanding of the company's strategy and business operations. Off-loading responsibility for compliance to a third-party consultant will not provide the insight to business processes and is not a viable substitute for being in the game. Continuous monitoring of controls using some of the tools we have been discussing can be leveraged for greater profitability and competitive advantage. My mission is to have companies achieve breakthrough performance by applying the right tools for the right job. Big challenges for companies large and small will be to overcome disconnects from functional silo thinking and begin adopting cross-functional concepts that will produce better results more quickly.

Management teams and board members will need to be committed to continuous learning and training. There is much to be learned about selecting and applying the right management methodologies. CPAs will need to learn new principle-based accounting principles and the nuances of new audit standards. It is critical to remember that we have layers of bad habits that are the result of functional silo mentality and a tendency to look for silver bullets to fix problems. Effective solutions demand focus, discipline, patience, and hard work. There are no shortcuts to overcoming process problems and challenges.

Hopefully, the accounting scandals of recent years will abate, and the accounting profession will restore its tarnished professionalism. The Public Company Accounting Oversight Board guided us in the direction of an internal control framework that has evolved into a framework for enterprise-wide risk management. Companies of all sizes, both public and private, face a considerable amount of change and transformation to create actionable steps that will elevate both the governance and performance of their organizations. I do not have a crystal ball that tells me exactly what will happen to alleviate the issues with excessive retesting when control deficiencies occur. However, I do feel that we will move toward greater application of reason and judgment as everyone becomes more familiar with the compliance process.

The greatest remaining challenges are for companies to execute and communicate their strategic vision and select appropriate measures and indicators at all levels of the organization. Much of the simplification of financial reporting and business performance management will develop as management and auditors gain better insight into and understanding of how to deploy and use the new tools and concepts offered for profitable compliance. We have to be in it for the long haul, as it will take time for the Financial Accounting Standards Board to adopt appropriate principle-based standards that can be accommodated by all sizes of both public and private companies. Sarbanes-Oxley has provided a new standard for business practice, internal control, and financial reporting. The secret to attaining new heights of performance is to utilize the concepts and tools for managing business processes that go beyond compliance to achieve greater profitability.

REFERENCES

Chapter 1

Ackerman, Dan, For years HealthSouth could do no wrong, Forbes.com, March 31, 2003.

Ackman, Dan, Causey may put GAAP on trial, *Top of the News,* January 23, 2004.

American Institute of Certified Public Accountants, *AICPA Code of Professional Conduct,* December 1, 1994.

Anderson, J. Michael, *Enron: A Select Chronology of Congressional, Corporate, and Government Activities,* Congressional Research Service, April 9, 2002.

Associated Press, Auditor Duncan Saved Some Records on Enron, May 17, 2002.

Baltimoresun.com, WorldCom Accounting Fraud, August 9, 2002.

BBC News, June 28, 2002.

Chicago Tribune, January 18, 2004.

Citizens Works, *CEO Pay in the 1990s,* May 2003.

Clerk, U.S. District Court, United States of America Against Arthur Andersen, LLP, March 7, 2002.

CNN Money, April 11, 2002.

CNN Money, February 19, 2004.

CNN Money, Skilling Indicted for Fraud, February 19, 2004.

Collins, James C., *Good to Great,* HarperCollins, 2001.

Ethics Business Resource Center, *2003 National Ethics Survey,* May 21, 2004.

Gutman, Huck, The Statesman, Dishonesty, *Greed and Hypocrisy in Corporate America,* July 14, 2002.

Johnson, Carrie, The Freedom of Information Center, *Washington Post,* May 14, 2002.

Johnson, Carrie, Lea Fastow sentenced to 1-year term, *Washington Post,* May 7, 2004.

KPMG, *Fraud Survey 2003.*

McRitichie, James, Editor, *Corporate Governance,* December 14, 2003.

Northrup, C. Lynn, *Dynamics of Profit-Focused Accounting,* J. Ross Publishing, July 2004.

Russo, Michael S., *Deontology and Its Discontents: A Brief Overview of Kant's Ethics*, Department of Philosophy, Molloy College.

Saporito, Bill, How Fastow helped Enron fall, *Time Business and Technology*, February 10, 2002.

SecuritiesFraudFYI.com, WorldCom Fraud.

U.S. Securities and Exchange Commission, News Release 2003-70.

U.S. Securities and Exchange Commission, Sarbanes-Oxley Act of 2002 (Public Law 107-204), July 2002.

Wong, Paul T. P., Lessons from the Enron debacle: Corporate culture matters! www.meaning.ca, February 22, 2002.

Chapter 2

Armstrong Laing, Inc., *The Sarbanes-Oxley Act Section 409—Real Time Issuer Disclosure*, 2003.

Baue, William, *GAO Report Says Financial Restatements Cost Investors Billions*, www.socialfunds.com, November 2, 2002.

Collins, Pete, Senior executives divided on cost of complying with Sarbanes-Oxley Act, *PriceWaterhouseCoopers Management Barometer*, July 2, 2003.

Financial Executives Institute, FEI Survey on Sarbanes-Oxley Section 404 Implementation, January 2004.

Goeizer, Daniel L., *The Work of the PCAOB—Why Should Public Companies Care?* PCAOB, October 31, 2003.

Hartman, Thomas E., *The Cost of Being Public in the Era of Sarbanes-Oxley*, Foley & Lardner LLP, May 19, 2004.

Huron Consulting Group, *Study Reveals Leading Causes of Financial Restatements in 2003*, American Institute of Certified Public Accountants, January 19, 2004.

Jones, Del, Sarbanes-Oxley: Dragon or white knight? *USA Today,* October 19, 2003.

Journal of Accountancy, One on one: The PCAOB chairman and JofA, December 2003.

Katz, David M., *The Reality of Real-Time Reporting*, www.CFO.com, June 10, 2004.

Logan, Debra, *You'll Have to Spend to Attain Sarbanes-Oxley Compliance*, Gartner Research, October 3, 2003.

McClenahen, John S., Pro forma's bottom line, *Industry Week*, February 1, 2002.

Morris, Tom, *If Aristotle Ran General Motors*, Henry Holt and Company, 1997.

PriceWaterhouseCoopers, *The CEO in an Integrating Uncertain World*, 5th Annual Global CEO Survey, April 2002.

Schiff Hardin & Waite, *Sarbanes-Oxley Act of 2002*, August 2, 2002.

Taub, Stephen, *Independence Bowl?* www.CFO.com, May 21, 2002.

Taub, Stephen, SEC toughening up on noncooperation, *CFO.com*, June 7, 2004.

Taub, Stephen, Company size and 404 compliance, *CFO.com*, June 8, 2004.

Teach, Edward and Reason, Tim, Lies, damn lies, and pro forma, *CFO.Com*, April 1, 2002.

Travers, Frank J., How to Put the "Count" Back in Accounting, CIC Group, Inc., February 25, 2002.

USINFO.STATE.GOV, Bush Administration Actions Against Corporate Fraud, September 26, 2002.

U.S. Securities and Exchange Commission, ACTION: Cautionary Advice Regarding the Use of "Pro Forma" Financial Information in Earnings Releases, Release Nos. 33-8039, December 4, 2001.

U.S. Securities and Exchange Commission, Conditions for Use of Non-GAAP Financial Information, Release 2003, January 15, 2003.

Whirlpool Corp., *4th Quarter and Full-Year Results for 2002*, February 25, 2003.

Chapter 3

Collins, James C., *Good to Great*, HarperCollins, 2001.

Deloitte IAS Plus (Deloitte Touche Tohmatsu), Status of Some of Key Differences Between IFRSs and U.S. GAAP as of June 30, 2004, 2004.

Financial Accounting Standards Board, Proposal—Principles-Based Approach to U.S. Standard Setting, File Reference 1125-001, October 21, 2002.

Gazzaway, Trent, *Tone from the top: Walk the talk, walk the walk*, Corporate Governor, Grant Thornton, June 2003.

Goodyear Tire & Rubber Company, Form 8-K filed with SEC, November 20, 2003.

Hymowitz, Carol, Experiments in corporate governance, *Wall Street Journal,* June 21, 2004.

Lubin, Joann S., Back to school, *Wall Street Journal,* 21, 2004.

Morris, Tom, *If Aristotle Ran General Motors,* Henry Holt and Company, 1997.

PCAOB, *Ethics Code for Board Members, Staff and Designated Contractors and Consultants*, PCAOB Release No. 2003-008, June 30, 2003.

Plitch, Phyllis, Blowing the whistle, *Wall Street Journal,* June 21, 2004.

Reason, Tim, On the same page, *CFO Magazine,* May 1, 2002.

Schroeck, Michael, *Evolution of the CFO*, Hyperion and IBM, 2004.

U.S. Securities and Exchange Commission, Disclosure Required by Sections 406 and 407 of the Sarbanes-Oxley Act of 2002.

U.S. Securities and Exchange Commission, Management's Reports on Internal Control over Financial Reporting and Certification of Disclosure in Exchange Act Periodic Reports, Section 404, August 14, 2003.

Chapter 4

Chapman, Christy, *Bringing ERM into Focus*, Institute of Internal Auditors, June 2003.

Committee of Sponsoring Organizations of the Treadway Commission, *Enterprise Risk Management—Integrated Framework,* American Institute of Certified Public Accountants, 2004.

Committee of Sponsoring Organizations of the Treadway Commission, *Internal Control—Integrated Framework*, American Institute of Certified Public Accountants, 1992.
Institute of Internal Auditors, Managing risk from the mailroom to the boardroom, *Tone at the Top,* June 2003.
Martens, Frank and Nottingham, Lucy, *Enterprise Risk Management: A Framework for Success*, PriceWaterhouseCoopers, 2004.
Northrup, C. Lynn, *Dynamics of Profit-Focused Accounting*, J. Ross Publishing, 2004.

Chapter 5

Committee of Sponsoring Organizations of the Treadway Commission, *Internal Control—Integrated Framework*, American Institute of Certified Public Accountants, 1992.
Committee of Sponsoring Organizations of the Treadway Commission, *Enterprise Risk Management—Integrated Framework,* American Institute of Certified Public Accountants, 2004.
Financial Accounting Standards Board, *Statement No. 5: Accounting for Contingencies.*
Protiviti, *Guide to the Sarbanes-Oxley Act: Internal Control Reporting Requirements*, 2003.

Chapter 6

Committee of Sponsoring Organizations of the Treadway Commission, *Internal Control—Integrated Framework*, American Institute of Certified Public Accountants, 1992.

Chapter 7

Barton, M. Frank, *Management Accounting*, Institute of Management Accountants, 1991.
Bell, Timothy B. and Ponemon, Lawrence A., *Directors Monthly,* National Association of Corporate Directors, November 1996.
Committee of Sponsoring Organizations of the Treadway Commission, *Internal Control—Integrated Framework*, American Institute of Certified Public Accountants, 1992.
Doctor, Jonathan R., *Knowledge Management Best Practices for Service and Support*, ServiceWare Technologies, October 2003.
Generation 21 Learning Systems, *Improved Profitability Through Generation 21 Enterprise*, 2004.

Chapter 8

Gile, Keith, *Grading BI Reporting and Analysis Solutions*, Forester Research, Inc., August 23, 2004.

Hyperion, *Business Performance Management, Gaining Insight and Driving Performance*, 2003.

IT Governance Institute, *IT Governance Implementation Guide*, September 2003.

Kahn, Randolph and Blair, Barclay T., *The Sarbanes-Oxley Act, Understanding the Implications for Information and Records Management*, Kahn Consulting, Inc., 2004.

Lindseth, Steven, The stick and the carrot—charting the rapid rise of enterprise, governance, risk and compliance management, *DM Review*, September 2004.

Taub, Stephen, Sarbanes-Oxley and information management, *CFO.com*, July 15, 2004.

Van Decker, John, *The Need for Continuous Controls Monitoring*, Meta Group, June 9, 2004.

Wilhide, Kathleen and Morris, Henry D., *Policy Hub for Compliance: Fuego's Process Management Addresses Sarbanes-Oxley*, IDC, June 2003.

Chapter 9

Business Software Alliance, *Information Security Governance: Toward a Framework for Action*, 2003.

Entrust, *Information Security Governance (ISG): An Essential Element of Corporate Governance*, 2003–2004.

Horton, R. Thomas, Information Security: What Directors Are Doing About It, National Association of Corporate Directors, 2001.

Institute of Internal Auditors, *Building, Managing, and Auditing Information Security*, 2001.

Institute of Internal Auditors, *Information Security Governance: What Directors Need to Know*, 2001.

IT Governance Institute, *IT Governance Implementation Guide*, September 2003.

National Association of Corporate Directors, Board Leadership Series, Information Security Oversight: Essential Board Practices, December 2001.

www.internetindicators.com, *The Internet Economy Indicators*, October 14, 2004.

Chapter 10

Lindseth, Steven, The stick and the carrot—charting the rapid rise of enterprise, governance, risk and compliance management, *DM Review*, September 2004.

www.pwc.com/governance, *Integrity-Driven Performance*, 2004.

Chapter 11

Clark, Yvonne R., Schettl, Lynda, and Shattuck, Dian, *Control Self-Assessment: Threats, Tips, and Techniques*, Institute of Internal Auditors, 2000.

Hubbard, Larry, *Control Self-Assessment: A Practical Guide*, Institute of Internal Auditors, 2000.

Taub, Scott A., U.S. Securities and Exchange Commission, The SEC's Internal Control Report Rules and Thoughts on the Sarbanes-Oxley Act, speech to University of Southern California Leventhal School of Accounting SEC and Financial Reporting Conference, May 29, 2003.

Chapter 12

ACL Services Ltd., *U.S. Corporations Struggling to Meet First Sarbanes-Oxley Filing Deadline*, July 13, 2004.

Leone, Marie, Where material weaknesses really matter, *CFO Magazine*, November 18, 2004.

Rubenstein, Herb and O'Flynn, Paul E., The role of training for boards of directors, *The CEO Refresher*, 2004.

Shumukler, Evelina, *Wall Street Journal Online*, December 1, 2004.

Chapter 13

American Institute of Certified Public Accountants, *The State Cascade—An Overview of the State Issues Related to the Sarbanes-Oxley Act*, 2004.

Blenkhorn, Kristine, Copycat Rules, www.insight-mag.com 2004.

Capelle, A. Ann and Topinka, James E., Corporate governance for private companies: Paying the price of compliance now—or later, *California Business Law Review*, March 2004.

Hartman, Thomas E., The Impact of Sarbanes-Oxley on Private Companies, presented at the 2004 National Directors Institute, Chicago, May 19, 2004.

Liberman, Larry D., Sarbanes-Oxley affects your private company clients, *Wisconsin Lawyer*, 77(6), June 2004.

Molin, Michelle and Adams, Jay, Ice Miller, *Sarbanes-Oxley and Private Companies*.

Perkins Cole, *The Impact of Sarbanes-Oxley on Private Companies*, 2004.

Robert Half International, Inc., The Impact of Sarbanes-Oxley on Private Business, July 2003.

Sachdev, Ameet, More rules, transition, turnover and competition, *Chicago Tribune*, December 24, 2002.

Chapter 14

AICPA, Auditing Standard No. 2: A Framework for Evaluating Process/Transaction-Level and Information Technology, General Control Exceptions and Deficiencies, Version 2, November 29, 2004.

AICPA, Center for Public Company Audit Firms, *Results of the Quick CPCAF Survey— Section 404 Compliance for Smaller Companies*, December 1, 2004.

American Assembly, Columbia University, The Future of the Accounting Profession, New York, November 13–15, 2003.

Bunting, Robert, Remarks at the AICPA, SEC-PCAOB Conference, AICPA, New York, December 6, 2004.

FASB, Proposal, Principles-Based Approach to U.S. Standards Setting, October 21, 2002.

FASB, Facts about FASB, 2003–2004.

FASB, *Private Company Financial Reporting, Discussion Paper*, May, 2004.

Herz, Robert H., Remarks at 2004 AICPA National Conference on Current SEC and PCAOB Reporting Developments, FASB, December 7, 2004.

Public Company Accounting Oversight Board, Audit Standard No. 1: References in Auditors' Reports to the Standards of the Public Company Accounting Oversight Board, approved May 14, 2004.

Public Company Accounting Oversight Board, Audit Standard No. 2: An Audit of Internal Control over Financial Reporting Conducted in Conjunction with an Audit of Financial Statements, approved June 17, 2004.

Public Company Accounting Oversight Board, Audit Standard No. 3: Audit Documentation, approved August 25, 2004.

Public Company Accounting Oversight Board, Staff Questions and Answers, Auditing Internal Control over Financial Reporting, November 22, 2004.

U.S. Securities and Exchange Commission, Study Pursuant to Section 108(d) of the Sarbanes-Oxley Act of 2002 on Adoption by the United States Financial Reporting System of a Principles-Based Accounting System, submitted to Committee on Banking, Housing, and Urban Affairs of the United States and Committee on Financial Services of the U.S. House of Representatives by the Office of the Chief Accountant, Office of Economic Analysis, and U.S. Securities and Exchange Commission, 2003.

Chapter 15

Howson, Cindy, BI scorecard: The best BI tool, *Intelligent Enterprise,* June 2004.

ITtoolbox, BI tools Sarbanes-Oxley compliant? *Get Real,* July 16, 2004.

Langseth, Justin and Reilly, Greg, When time is money, *Intelligent Enterprise,* April 2003.

Smith, Mark, The performance decade, *Intelligent Enterprise,* January 2001.

Smith, Mark, *Performance Management: 2005*, Intelligent Enterprise, December 2004.
Songini, Marc L., ETL quickstudy, *Computerworld*, February 2, 2004.
Winters, Bruce I., Choose the right tools for internal control reporting, *Journal of Accountancy*, February 2004.
www.getty.edu, *Introduction to Metadata*, July 5, 2000.
www.sunguard.com, *Basle II and the Role of Technology*, June 2003.

Chapter 16

Eckerson, Wayne, *Best Practices in Business Performance Management: Business and Technical Strategies*, The Data Warehousing Institute, 101Communications LLC, March 2004.
Informatica Corporation, *The Real-Time Enterprise: The Case for Building a Real-Time Analytics Infrastructure*, 2002.
Kahn, Rashid and Little, Thomas A., *Understanding Business Process Modeling & Analysis*, Ultimus, 2003.
Moncla, Brenda, *Corporate Performance Management, Part 1—Fundamentals and Part 3—What Lies Beneath*, ThinkFast Consulting, 2004.
Sellers, Gordon, *Manage by Process Enable with Technology*, Fuego, June 2004.
Sinur, Jim, Magic Quadrant for Pure-Play BPM, Gartner, Inc., 2004.
Skea, Martin, *Business Process Management: The Foundation for Six Sigma Success in Financial Services*, Filenet Corporation, November 2003.
Smith, Howard and Fingar, Peter, *Outoperate Your Competition Using BPM*, www.bptrends.com, May 2004.
Ultimus, *A Closer Look at BPM*, January 2005.
Ultimus, *Adaptive Discovery™: Accelerating the Deployment and Adaptation of Automated Business Processes*, September 2004.

INDEX